WISDOM

WISDOM
A World History

TREVOR CURNOW

SPEAKING
TIGER

For Martin, Andrew, Brian, Janie, Lucy and Stephen

SPEAKING TIGER PUBLISHING PVT. LTD
4381/4 Ansari Road, Daryaganj,
New Delhi–110002, India

Wisdom: A History by Trevor Curnow was first published
by Reaktion Books, London, UK 2015

First published in India as *Wisdom: A World History* in paperback
by Speaking Tiger 2016

ISBN: 978-93-86050-28-1

10 9 8 7 6 5 4 3 2 1

Printed at Manipal Technologies Ltd, Manipal

Contents

Sapience. This engraving by the French artist Etienne Delaune depicts the personification of Wisdom, 1569. Although such personifications existed in classical art, this work was inspired by a very different tradition. The figure here, shown holding a book and gazing up to the heavens, has her origins in the biblical books of Proverbs and Sirach.

Introduction

Wisdom has fascinated the human race for thousands of years. Ancient authors sought to capture it in collections of proverbs and fables, while modern researchers seek to uncover its essence. It has been thought about in many different ways and looked for in many different places. It has been prized for its rarity, and its value has been proverbially compared to that of precious stones. Some have been reluctant to believe that it is within the grasp of humanity at all and have treated it as something essentially divine in nature. Even when it is accorded a lowlier status, there is still a considerable kudos attached to it. Historically, wisdom has been closely associated with the roles of counsellor, judge, healer, magician, diviner, poet, inventor and many others. While they might not necessarily be found in the ranks of a society's most powerful, most privileged or most wealthy, the wise may nevertheless be considered a kind of social elite. If they are not themselves to be found amongst the ranks of a society's shakers and movers, those who seek them out often are. While there may be some very arcane areas within the world of wisdom, many of them are surprisingly close to the world of everyday life. While some sages may seek a life of seclusion and contemplation in order to escape from material concerns, the same can scarcely be said about the person frequently referred to today as 'the sage of Omaha', the billionaire businessman Warren Buffett.

The aim of this book is to provide an introduction to the world of wisdom in its many different forms as it has manifested itself over the course of human history. In attempting this task I am confronted by two fundamental problems. First, the volume of materials from which I have had to make my selection is vast. Second, there is no single agreed definition as to what wisdom is. It may be helpful for me to say something here about how I have tried to address these problems in the chapters that follow. With regards to selection, my aim has been to try and present as wide a variety of materials as possible, and variety is better illustrated than explained. My selection is inevitably limited by my own knowledge and guided by my own interests, but within those limits I have sought to represent as many periods, cultures and places as possible. Different chapters also seek to look at wisdom from different perspectives.

In any subject of significant size, the problem of selection is perhaps inevitable, but the problem of definition is not. However, anything that can be attributed to counsellors, judges, healers, magicians, diviners, poets, inventors and others is likely to be multifaceted or elusive or both. Whichever is the case, a single agreed definition of wisdom does not exist. A small selection of some of the options available may help to convey something of the nature of the problem. For example, Aristotle regarded wisdom as the knowledge of first principles.[1] A knowledge of these principles gives us a deep and fundamental understanding of how the world works. The idea that wisdom is connected with knowledge, especially knowledge of a special breadth or depth, is often encountered. On the other hand, Cicero took the view that wisdom was a healthy condition of the soul.[2] The idea that wisdom is related to psychological or spiritual health is also by no means uncommon. For St Augustine, wisdom was neither of these. Instead he identified it with piety, which involves the worship of and devotion to God.[3] Again, the idea that there is a religious dimension to wisdom is not unusual. It is important to note that the differences between Aristotle, Cicero and St Augustine are not about matters of detail; they are absolutely fundamental. And there are many other definitions of wisdom that could have been presented as examples.

Without an agreed definition, there is no agreed standard against which to judge what does or does not count as wisdom. There are two obvious ways of responding to this predicament. The first is to pick a particular definition of wisdom and stick to it, even though it is not favoured by all. The second is simply to accept at face value the claims of others that something is an example of wisdom. I have tried to take an approach that combines elements of both. In order to present as wide a variety of materials as possible, I have taken the view that if someone or something was widely thought to be wise somewhere sometime, then that fact has to be taken seriously. On the other hand, I have also used my own views of wisdom to shape the way in which those materials are selected and presented. What I have tried to do is achieve a balance between what wisdom means to me, and what it has meant to millions of people for thousands of years. Because I have not yet said what wisdom *does* mean to me, that is the next issue to be addressed.

My own view of wisdom is that it is principally about *people*. By this I mean that wisdom is above all manifested in and derives its source from wise people. Although this is not a universally held view, it is certainly not unique to me either. I believe this view lay behind a common practice in the ancient world of attributing wise sayings to people with a reputation for wisdom, whether or not there was any evidence that they actually said them. King Solomon was credited with being the author of 3,000 proverbs. While this is not wholly impossible, there is no particular reason to believe it. It *is*, however, wholly *im*possible that he wrote the deuterocanonical book of the Bible known as the Book of Wisdom or the Wisdom of Solomon, which did not see the light of day until hundreds of years after his death. The work was not attributed to him by accident: its author planted massive clues in the text in order to encourage readers to come to that conclusion. By hiding behind the figure of Solomon, the later author hoped to secure greater credibility for the work. Throughout human history the wise saying seems to seek a wise person to which to attach itself. This was not a new practice even in the time of Solomon. An ancient Mesopotamian text known as 'The Instructions of Shuruppak to his son Ziusudra' attributes many wise sayings to the legendary King Shuruppak.[4] It is dated to around 2500 BC, more than a thousand years before Solomon was born.

But what is it that makes wise people wise? One of the themes that have emerged from recent research is a connection between wisdom and the ability to cope with whatever life throws at us. But what is it that *prevents* us from coping with life? In his classic study, *The Hero with a Thousand Faces* (1956), Joseph Campbell wrote: 'every failure to cope with a life situation must be laid, in the end, to a restriction of consciousness.'[5] The idea that most of us are as good as sleepwalking most of the time can be found in many different spiritual traditions. A typical outcome of the heroic quest is some kind of awakening, as a result of which the hero sees the world in a new light. This new light is not only a *different* one, it is also a *better* one. The mystic, the shaman, the hero achieves a more profound understanding of the world and is therefore better able to deal with the world. In his *Republic*, Plato tells the famous story of the cave to illustrate this idea.[6] He imagines people chained up inside a cave in such a way that all they can see are shadows on its wall. These are cast by things that are outside the cave, but only those who manage to leave the cave and emerge into the light may discover that. What those in the cave think are real those outside know to be only shadows. Whether we take the connection between wisdom and perception in a metaphorical or a literal sense, it is a theme that is encountered at many different times in many different cultures. The wise are those who can see the bigger picture, whose horizons are broadest, whose vision is clearest, who live in the light. Because of this, throughout history people with a reputation for wisdom have been sought out for their advice.

Advice comes in all shapes and sizes, and a wise person is not necessarily the best one to go to for advice on how to build a boat, how to paint a fence or how to mend a shoe. The kind of advice that is associated with wisdom is less specialized, less technical. The skill possessed by the wise person is the ability to live well, to make good decisions in life. This could mean an ability to 'cope', but that seems to me to be a minimal understanding of wisdom. Aristotle talked about the life that is lived well in terms of 'flourishing', which is a rather more elevated concept, while at the absolute top end of the spectrum we might encounter what Buddhists call 'enlightenment'. Unfortunately, in everyday life someone who gives me 'good advice' too often turns out to be someone who simply tells me what I want to hear. It is often difficult to decide who is and who is not a purveyor of sound advice, and this is a problem that pervades the study of wisdom. The pages of history are littered with stories of false prophets, heroes with feet of clay and supposed visionaries who turned out to have been looking in the wrong direction. The passage of time may help to separate the wheat from the chaff, and contemporary research is seeking to root the identification of wisdom in objective criteria, but we are a long way from arriving at a universally shared and scientifically based understanding of what wisdom is and how it can be recognized.

Because I believe that wisdom is principally about people, a lot of them will be found in the pages that follow. However, the study of wisdom is not only about people. In the case of the Wisdom of Solomon, we simply do not know who wrote it, but the association of this and many other pseudonymous or anonymous works with wisdom is too strong to be ignored. For those who believe that wisdom lies with the divine, the problem lies in gaining access to it. Here, people are largely secondary to practices such as divination in its many forms. Again there is a long-standing association of divination with wisdom that has to be respected. Consequently, while some chapters focus on some selected individuals, some are more thematic in their treatment, and others combine the two approaches.

The approach taken to the history of wisdom in this book is a kaleidoscopic one. Many facets of wisdom are explored and examined from a number of different thematic and historical angles. The arrangement of chapters is mainly meant to make the materials manageable, and the assignment of materials to one chapter or another is as much pragmatic as it is based on principle. The materials selected are wide-ranging, but not exhaustive. Inevitably, areas and periods with which I am more familiar have had an advantage in the selection process, and matters about which I have little or no knowledge have been at an obvious disadvantage.

Finally, a lot of words, especially names, from languages other than English appear in this book, bringing with them problems of transliteration. While I have tried to be consistent, I have not always succeeded. The correct has sometimes been sacrificed in favour of the familiar. For Chinese words and names, I have used Pinyin as a default position from which there have been occasional deviations. All biblical translations are from the *New English Bible* unless otherwise indicated.

Fukurokuju. Ink sketch by the Japanese artist Kensai. Fukurokuju is one of the Seven Gods of Happiness of Japan, although his origins may be Chinese. He is associated with happiness, wealth and wisdom; he is also linked with longevity and always appears as an old man.

1
Wisdom, Gods and Goddesses

I shall begin this exploration of the world of wisdom with a visit to its highest realm, that of the divine. Many societies, cultures and religions have had their wise gods and goddesses. While some may belong to cults and religions that have long since disappeared from the face of the earth, others belong to religions that continue to attract millions of followers. These deities have come in many different shapes and sizes, and while they have all had *some* association with wisdom they have not necessarily all had the *same* association with it. They may be seen as exemplifying different aspects and different understandings of wisdom. Moreover, because of the durability of many cults and religions, associations may change over time. This may explain some of the apparent confusions and contradictions we see when we look back at the distant past. In the case of some cults and religions the distant past is very distant indeed. But I shall begin this survey in the much more recent past.

Hinduism

In the spring of 1982 I was walking along a road in northern India when I met a procession of young people coming in the opposite direction. As they went past me I was hit by a consignment of red powder. A passer-by helpfully explained that I had unwittingly become caught up in celebrations connected with the feast of the goddess Sarasvati. Sarasvati is a very ancient Indian deity who may have originated as a river goddess. Later she became recognized as the consort of Brahma, the creator god. While some consorts are little more than pale reflections of their partners, however, Sarasvati has a strong identity of her own. Among her many accomplishments, she is above all associated with wisdom and learning. This makes her particularly popular among students, who were the people who had covered me in powder. While the connection between students and wisdom is often a tenuous one, in India it is provided by Sarasvati.

Being associated with learning is not in itself enough to support a reputation for wisdom, and the knowledgeable person is sometimes pointedly contrasted with the possessor of wisdom. Sarasvati, however, is credited with far more than just a wealth of knowledge; she is also regarded as the inventor of the Sanskrit language and the Devanagari script in which it is usually written. Language and literacy are generally regarded as two of the foundation stones of human civilization. Many societies attribute wisdom to those beings (whether divine, legendary or human) who are regarded as responsible for the basic inventions that make civilization possible, and Sarasvati is only the first illustration of this important fact.

It may be noted that as a species we label ourselves *Homo sapiens* (i.e. 'wise'), to distinguish ourselves from other similar species that historically failed to attain what we regard as civilization. If we are wise as a species because we are civilized, then the founders of civilization must possess a special wisdom. Although it may not be explicitly framed or articulated in this particular way, this basic thought seems to run throughout a lot of human history. The scope of civilization extends far beyond mere language and literacy, and so do the accomplishments of Sarasvati. Literature as well as literacy fall within her domain, especially poetry. She is also associated with music and is often depicted holding a lute.

Hinduism has many different gods, but undoubtedly one of the most popular of them is Ganesh, who is also associated with wisdom. He is very distinctive in appearance, having the head of an elephant atop a human body. His popularity derives in large part from the fact that he is believed to be a remover of obstacles and a bringer of success, so he is frequently invoked in everyday life. His connection with wisdom comes through his reputation as a patron of literature and learning. In this respect his domain overlaps that of Sarasvati. He is sometimes regarded as the scribe who wrote down the *Mahabharata*, the great

Indian epic, and in cultures where relatively few people are able to write, the position of the scribe is often associated with wisdom. The scribe is often a member of a social elite (distinguished by its education) and sometimes close to, or part of, the political elite. Is it too fanciful to see in Ganesh's ability to remove obstacles a semblance to the powerful official's ability to 'fix' things? Or, in his ability to put obstacles in the way of those who do not show him enough respect, a semblance of the lowly official angling for a bribe?

Ancient Egypt

A connection between the figure of the scribe and wisdom can also be found among the gods of ancient Egypt. Here the invention of writing was attributed to Thoth, who was regarded as the scribe of the gods. As such, one of his duties was to be the world's historian, the divine recorder of events. Because he was divine, his knowledge of history extended into the future as well as into the past. As a recorder, he was believed to play a role in the judgement of the dead, and he is often depicted in representations of this process. This led to him being closely associated with the kind of life that people should live, a life that was characterized by honesty and integrity. People would declare that they had conducted their lives in a way that was 'straight and true like Thoth'.[1] He was credited with many kinds of different knowledge, and was privy to secrets shared by only a few. When required, he might serve the other gods as a counsellor or mediator. The Greeks came to identify him with their own god Hermes.

The goddess Isis was also associated with wisdom. The origins of her cult lie at least as far back in time as 2300 BC, and for centuries it remained very much an Egyptian affair. From around the third century BC onwards, however, her cult began to establish itself further afield and it became one of the most widespread and popular in the whole of the Roman Empire. The goddess came to be identified with many others in Europe and Asia, and various cults were absorbed into her own before it was driven out, or in some cases absorbed, by Christianity.

Of the goddesses who came to be identified with Isis in antiquity, some, such as the Roman Minerva, had some established connection with wisdom, but several others, such as the Greek Aphrodite, had a tenuous link, if any. Apart from all being female, they appear to have had little in common. The original link between Isis and wisdom seems to have been through her magical powers. As the cult developed and expanded it became increasingly associated with healing and oracular activities, both of which also often go hand in hand with wisdom. In due course, she was even credited with the invention of writing. Although Thoth had long been regarded as the creator of hieroglyphics, it seems that the association of writing with wisdom was so strong in the Egyptian outlook on the world that the wisest of goddesses had to have some connection with writing too.

The story of Isis continues to the present day. As one of the great goddesses of antiquity she has proven to be an inspiration to some working in the field of feminist spirituality. The ability of her cult to provide a home for others makes her an obvious goddess to represent the idea of the more generalized and greater 'Goddess'. As recently as 1976 a new 'Fellowship of Isis' was established in Ireland and it is not a coincidence that H. P. Blavatsky's first book on theosophy, published in 1877, was entitled *Isis Unveiled.*

Ancient Greece

The massive growth of the cult of Isis outside Egypt is remarkable because of the opposition it must have faced. The Graeco-Roman world into which it expanded was certainly not lacking in deities, and some of these were directly associated with wisdom. Perhaps the most important of these was Apollo. His reputation for wisdom rests in large measure on the many oracles attached to his cult, including the most celebrated of them all at Delphi. However, he was also a healer, a function and profession that also has associations with wisdom in many cultures. Apollo was certainly not the only Greek god with oracular shrines, but he had a significant number of them, including some of the most important ones. Delphi became a kind of cult centre for wisdom in general as well as for Apollo in particular. The Seven Sages of Ancient Greece were said to have all met together there, although it is by no means certain that they ever did. Nevertheless, maxims attributed to them were inscribed on the walls of the temple, making it something of a shrine to wisdom as well as to Apollo.

Even philosophers like Socrates deferred to Delphi. When the oracle declared that no living person was wiser than him, Socrates did not dismiss this as nonsense but sought to understand what it meant. Doubting his own wisdom, he came to the conclusion that if he was the wisest person alive then human wisdom could not be worth much, and compared with divine wisdom it was worth nothing. Socrates was by no means the only person to think this. The idea that wisdom is somehow or ultimately divine in nature can be encountered in a number of different traditions. If it becomes an item of faith that *only* gods or goddesses can possess wisdom, then it follows that the only way for humans to approach wisdom is through some form of contact with the divine, whether direct or indirect. Turned around, the same item of faith would attribute to gods and goddesses anything regarded as embodying or closely associated with wisdom. This may be why Thoth was credited with the invention of hieroglyphics and Sarasvati with the invention of Devanagari.

Less well known than Apollo, but also associated with wisdom, was the goddess Metis. Indeed, 'wisdom' is one of the possible translations of her name. 'Counsel' is another one, reflecting the fact that the wise tend to be sought out for their advice. However, it is also possible to interpret it to mean something more akin to 'cunning', a term that carries rather more ambivalence with it. Where the wisdom of Thoth was associated with the morally exemplary life, cunningness can sometimes express itself in ways that are amoral if not actually immoral. If we think of wisdom as a purely positive thing, then we will naturally reject any attempts to portray it in a negative way, but wisdom and cunning are sometimes found together in ways that are difficult to disentangle.

As to Metis herself, not many stories are told about her, and she seems to be more of a personification than a person. Her principal claim to fame is that in some stories she appears as the mother of Athena, for whom she provides a suitable genealogy to associate her with wisdom. Like Thoth, Athena was recognized as a counsellor and mediator, although she was also a goddess of war when occasion arose. Although she seems to have had no oracles to channel it through, she passed on good advice directly to her favourites such as Achilles and Odysseus. She was credited with either inventing or giving to the human race (or both) a number of skills and artefacts. The flute, the plough and the chariot were among her inventions, while weaving and spinning were some of the skills she taught to a grateful humanity. As such, she laid a number of the foundation stones of civilization.

Northern Europe

The old gods of northern Europe also had a variety of associations with wisdom. One of the best known of them was the Scandinavian god Odin. Like Athena, he definitely had a martial side. When he gave advice it was usually on military matters, and he was regarded as a master tactician. His reputation for wisdom may stem, at least in part, from the fact that attributes of an older Germanic god, Tiwaz, found their way into his cult. Tiwaz was very clearly associated with wisdom, along with law and justice. But Tiwaz too had a bellicose side to his nature, which was why the Romans identified him with their god Mars.

Two particular stories forge a strong link between Odin and wisdom. The first pits Odin against Vafthrudnir, a giant with a reputation for wisdom and knowledge. Odin visits him in disguise and a battle of wits ensues, which Odin wins. The notion of a 'wisdom contest' is far from unique to Norse legend. A famous example is provided by the story of the Sphinx, a creature that took up residence outside the Greek city of Thebes. The Sphinx asked passers-by a riddle, and ate those who failed to solve it. It was finally solved by Oedipus, whereupon (according to one version of the story) the Sphinx committed suicide. In folklore, a wisdom contest is often fought to the death, suggesting that these things could be taken very seriously. Because the answer to a riddle is not obvious, and requires more than just *knowledge*, riddles and wisdom are often found associated with each other. Finding the solution to a riddle of any difficulty typically requires an act of the imagination, an ability to think outside established or conventional patterns. The solution may not always require a lot of working out, but if the solution is obvious, it is not a riddle. Metaphorically speaking, solving a riddle is like cutting the Gordian knot. When Alexander the Great was presented with a knot no one could untie, he simply cut it in two with his sword.

The English word 'riddle' has the same origin as the old word 'rede', which means counsel or advice. Alternatively spelt as 'read', it is most often encountered now in the epithet attached to King Ethelred II of England, who was known as 'the Unready'. He was not lacking in preparation, but what he did lack was good advice. It may also be noted that the advice offered by the oracle of Apollo at Delphi was sometimes expressed in something akin to the form of a riddle. However it is to be explained and articulated, a connection between riddles and advice has clearly existed in some cultures.

The second story linking Odin and wisdom involves Mimir, the guardian of a well whose waters brought wisdom to those who drank from them. Naturally he took advantage of this himself and so acquired a considerable reputation for wisdom. Odin was so desperate to drink from the well that he was prepared to sacrifice one of his eyes in order to do so. He got his wish. Later, after Mimir's death and decapitation, Odin kept his head and consulted it when he needed advice. There is a curious parallel to this in the story of Orpheus; it is said that after his killers threw his head into the sea, it washed up on the shores of the island of Lesbos. Those who found it put it in a cave where it functioned as an oracle.

Perhaps because of his general connection with the bloody battlefield, and with the halls of Valhalla where the fortunate slain were received, Odin was associated with the dead. In some stories told about him he takes on a positively shamanistic character, gaining access to knowledge that others are denied. He was also sometimes credited with the invention of runic writing, although this does not seem to have been a particularly strong tradition. As with Isis, it may be that Odin was given credit for inventing writing because of an already established reputation for wisdom. He also had a reputation for treachery, which might be regarded as an aspect of the darker side of cunning.

In Ireland, the invention of writing was attributed to Ogma, after whom the Ogham alphabet is named. Although scholars disagree as to where the alphabet actually originated, most of the surviving inscriptions do come from Ireland. Like Sarasvati, he was also a god of literature. His sister was Brigit, a goddess of divination, prophecy and healing (and blacksmiths). Between them they manifest a number of connections with wisdom that are plentifully evidenced elsewhere. Over the centuries elements of her cult became combined and confused with that of the Christian St Brigid, who is also known as St Bride. Like Brigit, St Brigid is also associated with healing (and blacksmiths). In some respects and places, the old gods are still with us.

Buddhism and Taoism

We have already seen several examples of gods and goddesses being credited with providing the foundations for civilization. The case of Manjusri is a little different. He may perhaps best be thought of as a divine personification of wisdom within Buddhism. The full picture, however, is far more complicated than that, and only some of the complications may be addressed here. It has already been seen that religions can be very adaptable, responding and adjusting to external influences in a variety of ways. As further evidence of this, according to one tradition, Manjusri was the consort of none other than Sarasvati. Other traditions have him taking on human form in a variety of guises. If he is a personification, then he is certainly no abstraction. He is regarded as a protector of those who worship him, and may sometimes appear to them in dreams. Dreams are regarded as a vehicle for the transmission of divine wisdom in many cultures. Manjusri was also regarded as the patron of grammar, reflecting another way in which divine wisdom may be associated with language and literacy.

In China he is known as Wen Shu, and is usually depicted holding a sword, which is one of his weapons against ignorance. The other is the Buddhist text he carries with him, which contains teachings on wisdom. Tradition has it that he spent many years in China, although there is evidence that his cult had its origins in India. Where the story of Manjusri gets particularly interesting is in Nepal. Local legend has it that the Kathmandu valley was a lake until he used his sword to cut what is now known as the Chhobar Gorge in order to drain it. This made the occupation of the valley possible. A great stupa, known as Swayambhunath, commemorates this feat. Because the Kathmandu valley became the centre of Nepal, many Nepalese regard Manjusri as the effective founder of their nation. Such traditions make it clear that Manjusri is regarded as far more than a simple personification of wisdom. There is a biography as well as an iconography. The story of Chhobar Gorge marks an interesting and rare association of wisdom with what might be regarded as a work of civil engineering, however miraculous it might be.

In Japan, Manjusri is known as Monju, where he finds himself alongside different gods of wisdom such as Fukurokuju. Fukurokuju was probably originally a Chinese Taoist god, although he is also sometimes regarded as a Buddhist one. In one capacity or another he was clearly admitted to the Japanese pantheon. He is usually depicted as an old man with an elongated bald head and carrying a book. He is often accompanied by a crane, which is a symbol of long life in Japan. His name literally means 'happiness-wealth-longevity', reflecting what might be regarded as three very common human aspirations. He is frequently to be found in the company of six other deities, and together they are known as the *Shichi Fukojin*, a term usually translated as 'Seven Gods of Happiness' or 'Seven Bringers of Good Fortune'. The deities themselves have a variety of origins and the stories told about them are confusing and contradictory. What is important is that they are seen to represent different dimensions of happiness and good fortune, such as prosperity and health, love and laughter. If we are known by the company we keep, then Fukurokuju's choice of companions brings out an aspect of wisdom that has so far been little in evidence. In the example of Fukurokuju we can read the clear message that wisdom brings benefits. Far from being something abstract or esoteric or remote, wisdom is something that can improve the quality (and the duration) of our everyday lives. In the figure of Fukurokuju, divine wisdom puts on a very human face. And although Manjusri may in one sense be seen as a pure personification of wisdom, in another he represents something that is in principle attainable by all. Few may actually get there, but ultimately wisdom within Buddhism is human in scale.

Zoroastrianism

In Zoroastrianism wisdom takes on more of a cosmic nature. The Zoroastrian world is a mighty battleground between the forces of good and evil. The forces of good are led by the great god Ohrmazd. He was known in earlier times as Ahura Mazda, which literally means 'Lord of Wisdom'. Ohrmazd is also the creator of the world, which means that the world itself is the product of wisdom. Some Zoroastrian texts also mention a 'Spirit of Wisdom' who is given a major role in the creation of the world, emphasizing the association of wisdom with the creative process. The Spirit of Wisdom may have evolved out of one or other of a group of beings known as the Holy Immortals. These are not quite independent beings, but neither are they mere aspects of Ohrmazd. They are both his helpers and himself at the same time.

Opposing Ohrmazd is Ahriman. He was once known as Angra Mainyu or 'Hostile Spirit', making it clear that the relationship between Ohrmazd and Ahriman is an essentially antagonistic one. It is the belief of Zoroastrians that Ohrmazd will win the cosmic battle, but victory will be neither easy not quick. He brought human beings into existence in order that they might help him in his great struggle, so humanity will play a role in the ultimate triumph of wisdom.

The great prophet of Ohrmazd was Zarathustra, and among the writings of Zoroastrianism are some very old hymns that may have been written by him. In one sense they are simply hymns of praise in which the greatness and, in particular, the wisdom of Ohrmazd are extolled. However, some of them incorporate elements that seem to be looking for a response in one way or another. When Zarathustra asks 'Who, among those whom I address, is just and who is wicked?',[2] it does not appear to be a rhetorical question. On the contrary, what is sought seems to be some kind of guidance. Because the question asked is about the just and the wicked, it is specifically moral guidance that is sought. Because the Lord of Wisdom is leading the troops of good against those of evil, Zoroastrianism takes a very moral view of wisdom. Whereas Odin, for all his wisdom, can appear to be a morally ambiguous character, in the Zoroastrianism world wisdom and immorality are simply incompatible.

Judaism and Christianity

In moving from Zoroastrianism to Judaism and Christianity we enter what for most readers will be more familiar territory. Although they are two different religions, they will be dealt with together here because in their treatment of wisdom there is a considerable overlap between the two. With Judaism and Christianity we are clearly dealing with monotheistic religions. In a polytheistic context, wisdom and creation are often the domains of very different deities, but in a monotheistic religion everything has to come together. Most of what is written in the Bible about wisdom appears in either the Old Testament or the deuterocanonical books (the Protestant Apocrypha), which are both collections of texts from the Judaic tradition. In the Old Testament book of Proverbs, the figure of Wisdom says: 'The Lord created me at the beginning of his work' and 'When he established the heavens I was there' (Proverbs 8:22 and 27).[3] Scholars have long pored over these and other texts, in which 'Wisdom' is clearly intended to be a personification, in order to understand their meaning and significance. What is her nature, what is her status? (Because the Hebrew word for 'wisdom', *hokma*, is feminine, wisdom personified is always *female* in Judaic texts.) That the treatment of wisdom to be found in Proverbs is not simply an anomaly to be dismissed can be seen in the later books of Sirach and the Wisdom of Solomon (both in the Apocrypha), which take this line of personification significantly further. In the Wisdom of Solomon can be found the startling claim that 'She is initiated into the knowledge that belongs to God, and she decides for him what to do' (8:4). Here Wisdom clearly takes on an active role, although it is not clear what the precise remit of that role is.

Clearly, the one thing Judaic monotheism could not admit was the presence of a second deity, of whatever gender. However, it is not difficult to see Wisdom as in some ways resembling goddesses from other neighbouring traditions. The Egyptian Isis has already been encountered, but there were many more, such as the Syrian Astarte and the Babylonian Ishtar. In the event, Judaism managed to resist the temptations of the goddesses of wisdom and remain true to monotheism. Nevertheless, the position Wisdom held within that monotheism, at least for a time, was distinctly ambiguous. Like the Spirit of Wisdom of Zoroastrianism, Wisdom was both part of the deity but also the deity's assistant. Some of this ambiguity carried over into Christianity. The doctrine of the Trinity, whereby the divine is simultaneously both three and one by virtue of being 'three in one', might be seen as a vehicle for managing it.

The ambiguity surrounding wisdom in Christianity can be seen in how wisdom has been treated in its iconography. Wisdom is often identified with Christ, the second person of the Trinity. Christ is represented iconographically in many ways, but when wisdom is being emphasized, the image known as the Pantocrator is often used. This depicts an enthroned and austere figure, the wise ruler and judge of the universe. However, there is another iconographic format that clearly depicts wisdom as an angel, and as an entirely separate figure from Christ. Still other representations of wisdom show a figure who is neither Christ nor an angel, but clearly female. Sometimes this figure wears a crown. It is widely accepted that the St Sophia who supposedly lived in the second century and had three saintly daughters called Faith, Hope and Charity is an invention, but all inventions have a purpose and hers seems to have been to play the role of Wisdom personified. Just like *hokma* in Hebrew, *sophia* is feminine in Greek. The only unambiguously female character in the immediate vicinity of the Christian trinity of Father, Son and Holy Spirit is the Virgin Mary, the mother of Jesus, and some theologians have sought to bring her and Wisdom closer together, although this is to say the least pushing the bounds of orthodoxy.

It is difficult to avoid the conclusion that the Hebrew language of the Old Testament and the Greek of the New create a kind of linguistic pressure for an explicitly female figure of wisdom that is theologically problematic. But if wisdom were theologically unimportant, the simple solution would be to dispense with it, and this is not done. Indeed, some modern Russian theologians have been prepared to move wisdom even closer to the centre of the theological stage and risk the unorthodox consequences.

The Argument from Design

Before bringing this chapter to an end, I want to take a short detour away from particular gods and goddesses to consider the general question of whether we can prove that any god exists. The idea that the world bears the imprint of a wise creator has been frequently drawn upon in theology. There is a type of philosophical argument that works along the lines that the world is an incredibly impressive, complex thing, and it stretches credibility to believe that such a thing could just have happened by accident. This is known as the argument from design. There is a variation on it known as the argument from analogy. This says that just as something complex like a clock could not exist without a clockmaker, so something far more complex like the world could not exist without a creator. If someone presented us with, for example, an amazingly complex and perfectly executed piece of embroidery, we would simply not believe it if they told us that it just somehow happened to come into existence without anyone actually designing it or making it. The argument does not actually prove anything, but it invites us to consider the possibility that the existence of a creator is the least unlikely explanation of the world's existence.

However, this kind of approach can be taken a step further. If the *fact* of the world's existence is evidence for the *fact* of a creator's existence, then is the *nature* of the world evidence of the *nature* of its creator? And if *wisdom* can be found in the world does that mean that its creator was *wise*? The title of a book by John Ray, first published in 1691, clearly reveals his position on this particular point: *The Wisdom of God Manifested in the Works of the Creation*. Ray summarizes his basic argument in this way:

> There is no greater, at least no more palpable and convincing Argument of the Existence of a Deity, than the admirable Art and Wisdom that discovers itself in the Make and Constitution, the Order and Disposition, the Ends and Uses of all the parts and Members of this stately Fabrick of Heaven and Earth . . .[4]

It may be noted that Ray's particular interest was in scientific classification and it was the *order* of the world that especially interested him. The order that scientists discovered in the world was a reflection and product of the wisdom of its creator.

This chapter has looked at a selection of deities associated in one way or another with wisdom. They have been taken from many different cultures and many different periods. Some belong to religions and cults that belong only to the distant past, some are very much part of the contemporary world. It is tempting to think that all cultures have had their gods or goddesses of wisdom, but there is not enough evidence to support such a claim. Of the cultures that do have gods or goddesses of wisdom, the evidence clearly demonstrates that they are not all the same. No one could plausibly claim that Ohrmazd and Odin came from the same mould. Even among those that might reasonably be regarded as simple personifications of wisdom, there is a significant difference between Metis and Manjusri. The differences are even more obvious in the cases of complex characters like Athena and Fukurokuju.

On the other hand, there cannot be *only* differences since all those discussed are *in some way* associated with wisdom, and when we look at the materials from this point of view it is possible to pick out significant similarities. A recurrent theme is the crucial contribution a particular deity made to civilization and culture. Sarasvati invented the Devanagari script, Thoth invented hieroglyphics, Ogma invented the Ogham alphabet and Odin invented runes. It is easy to see why a literate society would attach such importance to writing, given how much cultural currency tends to be based on it. Some of these were also more broadly associated with one or more genres of literature. Athena was recognized as the inventor of the plough and flute, among other things, making a distinct contribution to both agriculture and the arts.

All these inventions can be seen as examples of creativity. Ohrmazd, the Spirit of Wisdom, and the Judaic figure of Wisdom had more fundamental creative roles since they were involved in the creation of the world itself. Creativity is also involved in the kind of battle of wits that Odin won against Vafthrudnir, where an ability to think outside obvious or established patterns is invaluable. And because of the connection in some languages between riddles and advice, it may be worth pointing out that advice is most needed where the best way forward is the least obvious. Thoth and Athena were both valued as advisers and mediators, while Ganesh was adept at removing obstacles that blocked the way ahead. I would not want to labour these points or make too much of them, but I think it can be seen that some patterns can be discerned in the variety, and that some materials can be linked together in ways that are not immediately obvious.

If some differences may be more apparent than real, however, I think at least one genuine problem can also be identified. To put it at its simplest, can Odin be both wise and treacherous? Zoroastrianism clearly pulls wisdom and morality together, but the stories about Apollo abound with incidents in which he behaved in ways that seem to fall somewhat short of propriety. The more we think of wisdom as akin to some body of *knowledge* or set of *skills*, the easier it is to accommodate apparent incompatibilities. There is absolutely nothing to stop me from being both an excellent musician and a mass murderer. But the more we think of wisdom in terms of the whole *person*, or a person's *character*, the harder it becomes to make allowances. However, it is only fair to point out that stories told about Odin and Apollo are just that, *stories*, not theories. Mythology does not play by the same rules as theology, even if they can be found in the same ballpark from time to time. And the stories we have been looking at here were told over *centuries*, giving them plenty of time to change and merge. Alternatively, it may be that the Zoroastrians are wrong and that wisdom is nothing to do with morality at all.

The Ascension of Enoch. Flemish print from the late 16th century based on a design by Maarten de Vos. It was believed that Enoch did not die but physically ascended to heaven, and this scene shows him taking leave of his friends and family.

2
Wisdom, Myth and Legend

The world of myth and legend is populated by a vast array of characters displaying a wide range of strengths and weaknesses. Some are brave, some are foolhardy, some are knowledgeable, some are foolish, some we might wish to emulate, some we might not. Some may have a basis in fact, some may be pure invention. Among all these there are a number who have been regarded as wise.

Ancient Mesopotamia

Some of the earliest myths we know about come from ancient Mesopotamia, and some of the earliest of them concern wisdom. Among the most fascinating are those that relate to a group of beings known as the *apkallu*. They were somewhat bizarre creatures, at least in appearance, but they fulfilled a very clear explanatory role. There were traditionally seven *apkallu*, and the oldest known written account of them dates to around 2000 BC. Sumerian tradition locates them in the period between the creation of the world and the great flood that nearly destroyed humanity. During this time kings reigned in the cities of Mesopotamia for thousands of years each, and the *apkallu* served as advisers to some of them. Since the word *apkallu* means 'wisest' or 'sage', it is entirely appropriate that they should be consulted by those who ruled. However, the *apkallu* were far more than mere advisers. As is often the case in mythology, stories are difficult to reconcile with each other, but there is a strong tradition that the *apkallu* also brought all of the elements of civilization to humanity. These included a knowledge of the arts, architecture, agriculture, geometry and lawmaking.

The *apkallu* were not the actual inventors of these things, but they were intermediaries between humanity and Ea, a Mesopotamian god of wisdom who was himself an adviser to the other gods. Perhaps because there was a close association between Ea and water, the *apkallu*, his messengers, were sometimes thought of as creatures with human heads and feet, but the bodies of fish. Sometimes they were depicted with wings and their heads were those of birds. This was another and more conventional way of representing messengers from the gods, because the gods were often thought to reside in the heavens. Sometimes they were conceived in human form, and become altogether more mundane

Most of the *apkallu* are little more than names, and different versions of these exist. One name stands out from the rest, however: that of Adapa (who is also sometimes known as Uan). He is always regarded as the first of them, and in some accounts he is credited with single-handedly bringing to the human race all the foundations of civilization. In some myths he appears as a human being created by Ea who is endowed with great wisdom and becomes his priest in Eridu, traditionally the first city to be established in Mesopotamia. The city was an important symbol of Mesopotamian civilization, and both Adapa in particular and the *apkallu* in general were associated with its invention. Eventually the age of the *apkallu* was brought to an end by a great flood. One myth says that this happened because the *apkallu* angered the gods in some way, although it is not clear what offence they committed.

The flood did not mark the end of the Mesopotamian mythology of wisdom. Ea made sure that the destruction of the world was not total by warning a man called Atrahasis of what was going to happen. Atrahasis (whose name literally means 'extra-wise') is also known as Ziusudra and Utnapishtim. As a result of the warning from Ea he built a large boat, which makes him an obvious Mesopotamian equivalent of Noah. Ziusudra was also said to be the son of Shuruppak, a legendary king of the Mesopotamian city of the same name with a reputation for wisdom in his own right. As such, many wise sayings and stories were attributed to him.[1]

Ancient China

Many 'immortals' populate the pages of Chinese legend. These are a special group of people who are thought to have achieved a state of human perfection. Sometimes these people are thought to have achieved immortality in the literal sense and found a way of eluding death altogether. Sometimes immortality is understood in a more mystical way and suggests a particularly high level of spiritual attainment. Sometimes the two are blended together, with a little magic occasionally added to the mixture. The important thing about all the immortals is that they all began as ordinary human beings, and so can be held up as exemplars to others. Because the immortals are regarded as the most illustrious of sages, they can be taken as exemplars of wisdom. Stories are told about many hundreds of immortals, but over the centuries a handful of them have been singled out for special attention and reverence. These are known as the Eight Immortals.

No one knows when the idea of a special group of eight immortals was first conceived, or why this particular eight were chosen for it. Whether historical or legendary, they are assigned to different periods and there is never any suggestion that they were ever all in the same place at the same time. Perhaps all that can be said is that in the popular imagination, at least, they represented the various aspects of wisdom in a tangible and memorable way, just as the Japanese Seven Gods of Happiness represented different kinds of good fortune. Their names sometimes appear slightly differently in different sources, but they are most commonly encountered as Li Tieguai, Zhang Guolao, Cao Guojiu, Han Xiangzi, Lü Dongbin, He Xiangu, Lan Caihe and Zhong Liquan. So many stories are told about them that only a flavour of them can be given here. Because Lü Dongbin is sometimes seen as the most important of the eight, and the one most often encountered as an individual rather than as a member of the group, I shall focus principally on him.

As with many special people in legend, the birth of Lü Dongbin was attended by strange phenomena, in his case a wonderful perfume and heavenly music. Again like many legendary figures, he was a prodigy and as a child was able to memorize vast amounts of poetry every day. This makes it unsurprising that he embarked upon a literary career, which occupied him for many years. Two themes dominate the transition to the next stage of his life. First, he is subjected to a number of ordeals, and secondly he meets two immortals. The stories reveal the kind of character he needs to develop in order to become worthy of immortality. He must be indifferent to material possessions, lacking in fear, immune to the temptations of the flesh, without personal ambition, and accepting of what life brings. Having passed all the tests and acquired from his teachers the secrets of invisibility and immortality, he spends hundreds of years wandering through China and performing beneficial deeds.

Lü Dongbin possessed a magic sword and accomplished some amazing feats. Other members of the eight also had impressive powers. Zhang Guolao had a magic donkey that could carry him vast distances in a day. When he had no use of the donkey he would fold it up and put it in his pocket. He Xiangu could fly and did not need to eat. Cao Guojiu could also go without food for long periods. More prosaically, Han Xiangzi and Zhong Liquan were both regarded as philosophers, Lan Caihe was a beggar who liked a drink, and Li Tieguai walked with the assistance of an iron crutch. Most of them lived as hermits at one time or another.

Many supernatural feats are scattered across the stories about the Eight Immortals, and clearly this is one way in which they can be identified as exceptional beings. Yet in other ways they are also very human. The tests to which Lü Dongbin was submitted, such as a death in the family or burglary, are ones that people without any supernatural powers have to deal with in everyday life. Even if it brought him immortality, his wisdom also helped to get him through the day.

The Eight Immortals were also associated with prosperity, good luck and a long life, and are often depicted in popular art for this reason. They continue to appear on vases, in paintings, as statues and even in films. While their origins are in the distant past, they continue to play a role in the present.

The Five Emperors also belong to the distant Chinese past, but they play a very different role from that of the Eight Immortals. They are collectively regarded as the founders of Chinese civilization and are credited with all the basic inventions that make civilization possible: 'To them were attributed the inventions of fire, fishing, hunting, agriculture, housebuilding, medicine, calendars and writing.'[2] The

Five Emperors (or Five Model Rulers, or Five Sages, as they are also sometimes known) played the same role in China as the *apkallu* played in Mesopotamia. Many of these inventions were credited personally to the first of the five, Huangdi (which is not a name but a title meaning 'the Yellow Emperor'). He is said to have lived around 2600 BC and according to some legends even brought mankind itself into existence. The potter's wheel and the compass were also said to be of his design.

Huangdi was followed by Zhuan Xiu and Gu, both of whom are extremely shadowy figures. After them came Yao and Shun. Yao is said to have introduced the calendar and established some kind of administrative structure for the state. He abdicated and chose Shun as his successor, thus making the point that rulers should be selected on the basis of merit, not on the basis of birth. Shun followed suit, and the two are seen as pioneers and exemplars of good governance. The Eight Immortals and the Five Emperors represent two distinct strands in Chinese legendary wisdom. The emperors represent the founders of civilization while the immortals represent those who achieve human perfection. There is a connection between the two in that, of the emperors, Huangdi, at least, was thought to have become an immortal. The emperors are there to admire, the immortals are there to emulate.

The Seven Sages of Rome

I turn now to a very different group of figures. The Seven Sages of Rome are characters in a famous story, of which there are many different versions. They are not always named, and when they are the names are not always the same. The story is thought to have originated far from Rome, perhaps as far away as India, and sometime during the first millennium BC. It seems to have started life as a work called *The Book of Sindbad*, and in some versions of it Sindbad (or Sindibad) is the name of one of the sages. In one particular case, the other six are implausibly listed as Hippocrates, Aristotle, Pindar, Homer, Apuleius and Lucian! If this were true, it would mean that the action of the story would have to be implausibly spread over the many centuries that separated their lives. In another version even a pretence at realism is abandoned and the characters are given names that are purely fictitious.

The basic shape of the story is simple enough, although it takes on a variety of guises. A king has a son who is sent away to be educated by seven sages. In the son's absence, the king remarries. On the prince's return, his stepmother tries to seduce him. When she fails, she conspires against him and makes false accusations. For his protection, the sages insist that the prince takes a temporary vow of silence while they try to rescue him from his plight. Each day for the next seven days the stepmother tells the king a tale calculated to set him against his son. Her stories contain many examples of children's disloyalty. Each day a different sage tells the king a tale designed to save the prince. Their stories make regular reference to the wickedness of women. At the end of the seven days, the son breaks his silence and reveals the truth. He is forgiven, and it is the stepmother, not the prince, who meets an untimely end. The king soon dies and the prince goes on to rule wisely in his stead. In a version of the story known as *Dolopathos*, the story is given a Christian ending when the prince converts to Christianity after becoming king.

It is not clear whether any particular significance is to be attached to the fact that there are precisely seven sages, but lists of seven sages can also be found in Mesopotamia (the *apkallu*), Greece and India (the *Saptarishi*). There were also seven wonders of the world, seven pillars of wisdom, and so on. Many more examples can be given, but so can lists and sets based around other numbers.[3] Without knowing exactly where and when the story first saw light of day, it is impossible to tell the significance of the number in its composition. For narrative purposes, having seven sages conveniently spreads the action over a week, and in a medieval European context the seven sages neatly corresponded to the seven liberal arts (grammar, rhetoric, logic, arithmetic, geometry, astronomy and music) that would make up the prince's education. In the end, however, the plot is an excuse for telling different tales, and the number of the sages is an excuse for telling seven of them. The fact that they are specifically identified as sages seems to be tied to a desire to identify the tales they tell as being about more than simple entertainment. They are also moral tales and, as befits tales told by sages, they are intended to educate. As such the story of the Seven Sages of Rome may be seen as a piece of wisdom literature. In various versions and languages, it was widely known and enjoyed for centuries.

The Three Wise Men

Christian tradition tells of mysterious wise men, sometimes called kings, who travelled from the east to Bethlehem to pay homage to the infant Jesus. Their names are often given as Balthasar, Caspar and Melchior, and the relics of the three kings have lain in Cologne Cathedral since the twelfth century. It can therefore come as a surprise to find out that the Bible nowhere says that there were three of them, or that they were kings. The names are pure invention, and the number three seems to have been arrived at on the basis that St Matthew's Gospel (the only place in the Bible where they are mentioned) tells of them bringing three gifts: gold, frankincense and myrrh. They are sometimes represented as the kings of Arabia, India and Persia respectively. There is also an alternative tradition in which there are twelve of them rather than three.

The term used in the Gospel to refer to them is 'magi', which some translators of the Bible have rendered as 'astrologers'. Clearly astrology comes into their story because they claim to have seen something in the stars that they interpreted to mean that a new king had been born. Whatever the term 'magi' means, however, it definitely does not mean 'king'. Nevertheless, the idea that they were either kings or in some way similar to kings appears to have developed as early as the second century in the writings of the theologian Tertullian, perhaps because they were depicted as sufficiently important to meet King Herod himself. The idea that there were three of them goes back at least as far as the writings of the third-century theologian Origen. The earliest known depiction of what has come to be known as the Adoration of the Magi dates from the second century and can be found in a fresco on the wall of the Catacombs of Priscilla in Rome.

Had there been a tradition that three *priests* visited Bethlehem, this would have been more understandable. The magi may have originated as a tribe or clan or caste (scholars are deeply divided as to which) of the Medes, a people who settled around what is now the border between Iran and Azerbaijan. They seem to have provided all the religious functionaries for their own people, and subsequently for the Persian Empire of which Media became a part. Some believe they may have acquired their priestly arts from the Brahmins of India. Although this is not impossible, there is little actual evidence to support it. Because of the problems involved in tracing the history of Zoroastrianism it is difficult to know whether the magi originated from within that religion or from outside it, but what is clear is that at some point they became identifiable as its priests. As such they became the custodians of the cult in all its practical aspects. They were clearly identifiable as a people apart: 'The magi are said to have worn white robes and lived a life of privation, and they had a curious habit of killing with their own hands birds, snakes, ants, and other undomesticated creatures save dogs and their kin.'[4] Given the spread of the Persian Empire westwards, at the time when Jesus was born magi could be encountered in what is now Turkey, where the historian and geographer Strabo (*c.* 64 BC–*c.* AD 22) says he saw several of them in Cappadocia. So if three Zoroastrian priests turned up in Bethlehem, there is more than one direction they could have come from because Cappadocia lies to the north of Bethlehem, not to the east of it.

The magi were clearly more than simply priests, although exactly what they were is not always easy to ascertain. Herodotus (*c.* 485–425 BC) says they interpreted dreams, and it can reasonably be assumed that they practised other forms of divination as well. The term 'magi' is clearly closely related to the term 'magic', but exactly what occult powers they possessed or professed to possess is unclear. Dio Chrysostom (*c.* AD 40–*c.* 112) says that they were responsible for the education of the Persian king, giving them considerable influence. This also gave them a role similar to that of the fictional Seven Sages of Rome, and it may therefore not be a coincidence that some think *The Book of Sindbad* originated in Persia. It might also explain why they were thought of as in some way associated with kings even if they were not kings themselves.

Although the wise men of the Bible are ill-defined and mysterious, they are certainly recognizable in general terms. Such characters did exist at that time and in that part of the world. While they could justly be called wise because of the accomplishments they could boast and the roles they fulfilled, they were certainly not kings. However, they *were* human and I want now to turn to a group of characters who mainly appear in animal form.

The Culture Hero and the Trickster

The term 'culture hero' frequently appears in the literature on both folklore and anthropology to denote a particular kind of character or being. Sometimes he (it is usually a 'he') is credited with bringing the world itself into existence, and so stands on a par with a creator god. Often, however, his achievements are more modest in scale but no less important in practice. It is the culture hero who brings, or invents, or teaches the basics of everyday life. The particular foods, the particular technology, the particular practices, the particular beliefs and values of a culture are all regarded as in some way the gift of the culture hero. The association of the role of a cultural founder with wisdom is something that has already been observed and illustrated on several occasions. The culture hero also embodies a society's identity, and that identity is inextricably linked with its origins. Stories are told about the culture hero to explain how things came to be as they are and why they should remain as they are. Sometimes the culture hero is believed to be still alive, sometimes to belong to a time that is long gone.

The idea of the culture hero is particularly strong in the folklore of North America, South America and Africa, although it also appears elsewhere. In theory, the culture hero may take any form, but in fact often appears as an animal. In North America he is often Coyote (capitalized here to distinguish the culture hero from the animal) or Rabbit. There is a story told among the Papago people, now mainly found in southern Arizona, that Coyote saved them from extinction long ago because he warned their chief that a great flood was coming, so they built a giant canoe to escape it. The resemblance to the stories told about Atrahasis and Noah is striking, especially given the very different topographies that provide backgrounds to the stories. The story told by the Papago is far from unique. Flood stories were remarkably common in the folklore of the Americas, from Alaska in the north to Tierra del Fuego in the south.

The figure of the Rabbit (or Hare) can be encountered in the folklore of North America, Africa and Asia. In parts of North America he was regarded as the bringer of fire and light. In parts of West Africa, the Spider is the culture hero and is known as Ananse. He is credited with the bringing of light, and sometimes with the creation of the whole world. In the northwest of North America it is sometimes the Raven who is regarded as the creator. Among the Aztec of Mexico, Quetzalcoatl was regarded as the bringer of the arts, the calendar and maize, as well as being the creator of the human race. His name means 'feathered serpent', and he is often depicted as this curious hybrid creature, although he is sometimes given more human form, reflecting the fact that not all culture heroes are animals. Kutoyis is a culture hero of the Blackfoot people who made their land safe for them by hunting out and killing demons and monsters, and he appears in human form. Neither are all culture heroes male. The Acoma people of New Mexico have two sisters, Iatiku and Nautsiti, as culture heroes. One is the bringer of life, the other the bringer of prosperity.

It is impossible to discuss the idea of the culture hero without discussing another idea to which it is strongly and frequently linked. This is the idea of the trickster, who has been characterized as a 'wily amoral hero'.[5] Like culture heroes, many tricksters are animals, but they are also encountered in human form. The trickster is also usually male. Perhaps the most distinctive feature of the trickster is a mischievous nature. If the culture hero is like a stern parent, the trickster is like a naughty child.

Having been introduced to the trickster as almost the opposite of the culture hero, it may come as a surprise to discover that most of the culture heroes who have been mentioned so far are also tricksters. In the case of Coyote and Rabbit/Hare, it is hard not to think of the cartoon characters Wile E. Coyote (always trying, but failing, to catch the Roadrunner) and Bugs Bunny (always trying, and managing, to torment Elmer Fudd). This reflects the fact that the stories told about tricksters are *entertaining*. And that can make them bestselling. It is a matter of conjecture as to whether they originated in North America or Africa, but there can be little doubt that the character of Brer Rabbit who appears in the stories of 'Uncle Remus' collected by Joel Chandler Harris is a typical trickster, and books about his adventures have sold in their millions simply because of their entertainment value.[6] While the stories of Brer Rabbit are often read to children, other trickster stories incorporate more adult themes, and many have a sexual element.

The trickster is cunning, in all senses of the word. He is the 'little man' who wins against all the odds, but he does not seem to care how he wins as long as he wins, hence the judgement that he is amoral. A creature who sometimes appears as a trickster in African folklore, particularly in Nigeria, is the Tortoise. The rivalry between the Tortoise and the Hare is the subject of a number of tales: 'In a Western version of a trickster tale, Tortoise wins against Hare by slow persistence rather than complacency; in the African version the trickster wins by a brilliant deceit.'[7] The trickster deserves to win not in a moral sense, but because he outsmarts his opponents. He succeeds by neither might nor right but by his wits.

If the culture hero can be seen as the embodiment and guarantor of a society's values, then the trickster can be seen as the one who challenges them, who pushes them to their limits, if not beyond. Combining both roles in one character on the face of it creates a contradiction. There are two obvious ways to respond to this apparent problem. First, like mythology, folklore does not seem to abhor a contradiction. Stories accumulate over time, and in an oral tradition they soon become timeless. To measure folklore by the standards applicable to a philosophical tract is to miss the point.

Another way of looking at the problem is to accept that as the bringer and guarantor of a society's values, the culture hero is also in a sense above them. The position of the trickster is obviously different, but he also seems to be granted a kind of immunity from established cultural norms. It is his role to test them, and in order to do so he must be given a degree of leeway that is not granted to others. The combined figure of the culture hero and trickster is therefore at the same time both a champion and a challenger of a society's conventions. The culture hero establishes a society's conventions, but the trickster keeps reminding people that they are *only* conventions. The interaction of culture hero and trickster produces a creative tension between on the one hand keeping conventions intact and enforced, and on the other keeping them under critical review. When both roles are found within the same character, what emerges is a recognizable semblance of the kind of sage who transcends conventional values, who is 'beyond good and evil'.[8]

The Rishis of India

'Rishi' is the term used in India for a sage and, like the immortals of China, there have been lots of them. As with the immortals, many tales are told about the rishis, and a number of these have found their way into the great Indian epic the *Mahabharata*. It tells the story of the rivalry between two families, a basic plot line that has proved very appealing through the ages. Across its 100,000 verses wander a baffling variety of characters who have become familiar figures in Indian legend and folklore. There is doubtless some authentic history woven into the narrative from time to time, but it is impossible to say where it begins or ends. It is not remotely possible to talk about all the sages to be found in it, but a sample should help to convey something of the flavour they contribute to this mammoth tale.

One particular theme that crops up from time to time is the connection between sages and curses. On a number of occasions sages are either putting curses on people, or threatening to. Clearly some of the sages were credited with magical powers. For example, the sage Parasara seduces a girl on a ferry. She is frightened that he may curse her, and he conjures up a thick fog so that none can see them. Although the seduction leads to pregnancy and the birth of another sage, Dvaipayana, the girl magically remains a virgin and acquires a special fragrance as a result of the encounter. On another occasion, a king who is hunting in a forest spots two deer in the act of mating and fires several arrows at them. He is naturally surprised to discover that they are in fact the sage Kindama and his wife who have decided to take on animal form for their lovemaking! A curse follows, although this seems a bit harsh under the circumstances.

Sex features in one way or another in several stories about the sages. Bharadvaja is so aroused at the sight of a beautiful woman whose dress is caught by the wind that he ejaculates into a bucket. The result is a son called Drona (meaning 'bucket'). Sages are also revealed to have some unexpected skills. Brihadasva, for example, is an expert on gambling. Another, Lomasa, is able to travel to heaven and converse with the dead. Some, such as Sarika, clearly live a more conventional ascetic life. This can lead to trouble. When a king is angered by Sarika's refusal to answer his questions, the reason is that like many ascetics the sage has taken a vow of silence.

Of all the sages of India, a handful of them became identified as a special group, the *Saptarishi*, or the seven sages. I shall refer to them here as the *Saptarishi* to minimize confusion with other groups of seven sages. Some of the *Saptarishi* appear in the *Mahabharata* but some do not, and different versions of the list exist. One of the earliest versions is found in the 'Brihadaranyaka Upanishad', which may have been written before 500 BC. In it the seven are linked with the two eyes, the two ears, the two nostrils and the single tongue to be found in a human head. The *Saptarishi* were also linked with the seven stars to be found in the constellation of Ursa Major. Clearly the number seven was thought to be significant even if there was more then one explanation of that significance available.

Taking the list found in the 'Brihadaranyaka Upanishad', a little can be said about each of the sages who appears on it. Atri wrote hymns and a work on law. Vasistha is credited with a similar output, but also with the possession of a magic cow that was able to fulfil wishes. Visvamitra was a great rival of Vasistha's and many stories were told about the bad feeling between them. Bharadvaja (already mentioned) was a composer of hymns, as was Jamadagni. Gautama wrote on law. Finally Kasyapa was the father of serpents, demons, birds and reptiles. It will be noted that overwhelmingly what most of them have in common is an attributed authorship of hymns or other works. These seven, and many others, stand behind the sacred texts of Hinduism known collectively as the *Vedas*. Their wisdom and the wisdom of the texts are inextricably intertwined: the first guarantees the second, and the second is the fruit of the first.

The other obvious recurrent theme is that of magical powers of some kind, and this was also a feature of many of the Chinese immortals. The possession of wisdom is clearly seen as something out of the ordinary, and it is a fairly short step from the extraordinary to the supernatural. Finally, it should be noted that the Indian rishi is far from being some kind of fossil. The title of rishi or of maharishi ('great sage') is still accorded to or claimed by people today, and stories of magic powers are not unknown.

The Wisdom of Enoch

Enoch is an obscure figure from the biblical book of Genesis who somehow acquired a reputation for inordinate wisdom. Over the centuries more and more accomplishments were credited to him, and books were written in his name or about him. If we regard Enoch's curriculum vitae as a kind of survey of the different kinds of wisdom that could be attributed to legendary characters, it will form a useful focus for pulling together a number of threads that have already emerged, along with some new ones.

According to Genesis, Enoch was the son of Jared and father of Methuselah. After the birth of Methuselah, 'he walked with God for three hundred years'. At the end of this time, at the age of 365, 'Enoch was seen no more, because God had taken him away' (Genesis 5:22–4). Out of these few pithy statements a whole mythology of Enoch was created. Some interpreted the statement that 'he walked with God' to mean that he was particularly close to God, perhaps visited heaven, perhaps conversed with angels, perhaps followed God around like a pupil. From this it was but a short step to believing that Enoch was privy to a divine wisdom that had been revealed to him. The statement that he was 'taken away' was interpreted to mean that he did not die, further evidence of his highly elevated status. The name of Enoch came to carry an enormous authority.

A whole genre and body of literature grew up around what was supposedly revealed to Enoch (and others), which has come to be called apocalyptic (from *apokalypsis*, the Greek word meaning 'revelation'). In principle, God might permit any number of things to be revealed, but in practice apocalyptic literature had one very dominant theme: the end of the world. The angels taught Enoch about how and when the world would end. They revealed that there was a moral dimension to history, and that the wicked would be punished for their sins at the final judgement. For the virtuous, there was the promise of a new heaven and a new earth.

The angelic education was not limited to history. The angels tell Enoch something about themselves, about their names, how they are organized and what they do. They tell him all about the world he lives in, as well as about the sun, moon and stars. There is particular emphasis on the calendar. Some writings attributed to Enoch seem to have played a part in a campaign to reform the calendar of the Jewish world during the late first millennium BC. The angels reveal to Enoch that a year has 364 days, a position apparently held by some sects at that time but not others. The invocation of Enoch's name in support of this position was clearly intended to enhance its authority.

Enoch is said to have produced 366 books at an angel's dictation. He seems to have been taught how to write by the angels too, and is credited with bringing the written word back to earth. Clearly the knowledge attributed to him was meant to be encyclopaedic. According to an ancient historian, Enoch 'learned all things through angels of God, and thus we gained our knowledge'.[9] Enoch became regarded not only as an authority on many matters, but also as the founder of whole disciplines such as astronomy and astrology.

Although the reputation of Enoch arose within the specific context of Judaism, it spread far beyond it. Christians came to believe that he played a role in the end of the world. Both Manicheans and Gnostics held him in high esteem. Because they were both regarded as revealers of divine wisdom, some identified Enoch with Hermes Trismegistus, while some Muslims identified him with the mysterious Idris who briefly appears twice in the Qur'an.

The case study of Enoch brings together a number of different themes connected with wisdom that have appeared in other contexts. He has an encyclopaedic knowledge. He has a special relationship with the divine. He is credited with the invention, or at least transmission, of writing and other gifts to humanity. Because the angels have shown him the future, he has the gift of prophecy.[10]

Tiresias, Manto and Mopsus

If Enoch was an individual with the gift of prophecy, Tiresias was the head of a whole family that possessed it. He was perhaps the greatest of the seers of ancient Greece and had a unique career. As a young man he came across two snakes mating. For some reason he decided to intervene, and for some even more obscure reason he became a woman as a result. A few years later, he was passing the same way, saw the same thing, intervened again, and changed back into a man. This gave him a very special outlook on life, so when the god Zeus and his consort Hera were arguing about sex, they decided to consult Tiresias, who had experience of the matter from both sides of the equation. Hera disliked what he said and blinded him, but Zeus liked it and gave him the gifts of prophecy and long life. An alternative version of events says that it was Athena who bestowed these gifts on him, thus making the link between his prophecy and his wisdom more explicit. His gift of prophecy is also sometimes explained in terms of an ability to understand the language of birds. He went on to become the most celebrated seer of his time, for a long time. After his death he had an oracle at Orchomenos, but he also continued to function as a seer in the underworld and was visited there by Odysseus. It is clear that his reputation for wisdom was specifically tied to his gift of prophecy.

Tiresias had a daughter called Manto. Since 'Manto' is extremely similar to the Greek word for 'prophesy', she appears to be little more than a cipher, although a few stories are told about her. Like her father she was said to have the gift of prophecy and spent time at Delphi developing her skills at its oracle of Apollo. The god then sent her to Claros with her son Mopsus and they set up an oracle there. Mopsus then went on to have his own oracle at Mallus (or Mallos; both Claros and Mallos lie in what is now Turkey). Another oracle at Mallus belonged to Amphilochus, and the two are said to have fallen out. Given that they were both seers, it is tempting to see this as a kind of 'wisdom contest', especially since Mopsus is said to have had an earlier divination contest with another seer, Calchas. As with Tiresias, the connection of both Manto and Mopsus with wisdom is clearly their ability to see into the future, but whereas there is little more to be said about Manto than has been said here, Mopsus presents a much more rounded and complex figure. He is said to have ruled in Colophon (near Claros) and been instrumental in founding the cities of Aspendos and Perge. And some scholars think that an individual called Mukshush, whose name appears in some materials unearthed at the ancient Hittite capital of Hattusha, may be one and the same person as Mopsus, meaning that he may have lived in the ninth century BC.[11] And arriving, however tenuously, at real names of real people with real dates takes us from legend into history, which is the subject of the next chapter.

Although all the characters assembled in this chapter had, and in some cases still have, a reputation for wisdom, due to the very sketchy nature of some of the available materials, few of them emerge as anything resembling real people. Enoch is a receptacle for knowledge of all kinds, but little more than that. Manto is not even that. Bugs Bunny and Wile E. Coyote are, literally, cartoon characters, but many of the others mentioned also fail to get beyond two dimensions. It is not difficult to see why the Eight Immortals remain remembered and revered because they at least have a recognizably human side to them, their attainments notwithstanding. The culture hero/trickster combination has been shown to be problematic, but not without hope of resolution. The trickster is like a child who keeps pushing the boundaries, who keeps asking 'Why?' and keeps getting an inadequate answer. Perhaps the culture hero/trickster combination is there partly to remind us that, however much we may want to be like the culture hero, there is always going to be something getting in the way, and that the obstacles are as real as the aspirations.

It is difficult to tell how many of the characters and stories brought together in this chapter have their basis in history. It is likely that many of the names mentioned here belonged to real people who lived real lives, but that reality has long been buried under the accretions of legend. Although the boundary between history and legend is very indistinct in places, in the next chapter the emphasis will shift firmly to the historical side of it.

The Seven Sages of the Bamboo Grove. Japanese print by Isoda Koryusai, 18th century. It shows the Seven Sages, accompanied by a small boy, perusing a scroll. They were renowned for, among other things, enjoying the art of conversation, which seems to be the principal theme here.

3

Wisdom in History

To select a handful of wise individuals from the whole of human history is clearly a challenging task. My main criterion for selection in this chapter is whether or not people were called, or clearly regarded as, wise by those who lived when they did, or at least not too long afterwards. While this may omit many who might have a greater claim to wisdom, it at least provides some kind of objective yardstick for selection. It also throws up an interesting group of individuals. With these selection criteria in place, there are a number of exclusions from this chapter that require some explanation. Many philosophers would qualify for inclusion, but I have given them their own chapter later. I have also omitted Zarathustra, the Buddha and Jesus. In their case the problem lies in disentangling what is historical about them from everything else. For example, a book on the history of Buddhism states: 'The Buddha can be considered from three points of view: *As a human being; As a spiritual principle; As something in between the two.*'[1] While this may be an accurate account of Buddhist doctrine, it is unhelpful as history. The same problem arises with Jesus, who in the person of Christ is both human and divine, both historical and eternal. With regards to Zarathustra, even scholarly estimates of when he lived can vary by up to a thousand years. In the face of such problems, it has seemed simplest not to tackle them at all. Fortunately there remains more than enough material to try to get to grips with.

Imhotep and Solomon

While both are legendary figures in their own ways, the stories told about Imhotep and Solomon nevertheless have a definite historical core. It is true that Imhotep became regarded as a god after his death, but so too did many Roman emperors whose names nevertheless continue to appear in works of history, and quite rightly so. Solomon's posthumous reputation developed in interesting directions, but that does not discredit his life.

Imhotep belongs to a very early period of Egyptian history. His greatest monument is the so-called step pyramid at Saqqara, which he designed for the pharaoh Djoser, who probably ruled Egypt from 2668 to 2649 BC. It was one of the first monumental stone structures in the world, and it still stands. It is evident that Djoser relied on Imhotep in a number of ways, and he was appointed to several high offices. He was a scribe, an administrator, a treasurer, a priest, an adviser and doubtless more. He is said to have written a number of works, but none of them now survives. It is possible that he was also a physician, because a healing cult grew up around the site of his tomb after he died. The Greeks came to identify him with Asclepius, their pre-eminent healing god. The identification was facilitated by the fact that the cults of both practised incubation, whereby the sick would be helped or healed through the medium of dreams.

Because his achievements were so exceptional, later generations decided that Imhotep must have been more than merely human, so the god Ptah (whom he had served as a priest) became recognized as his father. Imhotep himself was deified, but not until centuries after his death. Imhotep was clearly the possessor of a considerable body of knowledge that in his own time could pass as encyclopaedic. Being a scribe in itself would have given him a credible connection with wisdom in ancient Egypt. Although never identified with him, he came to be closely associated with Thoth. A mastery of other arts and skills would only have added to his sapiential curriculum vitae.

Imhotep seems to have had a reasonably good start in life because his father held an official post. Solomon had a very good start in life because his father was the king. Born around 1000 BC, he was not, however, the eldest son of King David and had to do some manoeuvring to get himself onto his father's throne. After a reign of 40 affluent years, during which he spent lavishly, he left his son a kingdom that was disunited, and after his death it split into two. On the face of it, this is not such a great record of achievement for any monarch, let alone for a wise one. However, the name of Solomon is indisputably and indissolubly linked with wisdom to the extent that books written hundreds of years after his death were attributed to him in order to benefit from the kudos of his name. Thousands of proverbs are attributed to him. Although he may not be the author of them all, and indeed may not be the author of any, it is possible that he is the author of some. A proverb is frequently attributed to an individual with a reputation for wisdom, and Solomon was clearly a popular choice for this honour.

According to the Bible, after he had obtained the throne, God appeared to Solomon in a dream and asked him what he wished for. What he asked for was 'an understanding mind' so that he might 'discern between good and evil' (1 Kings 3:9).[2] In return God gives him 'a wise and discerning mind' (1 Kings 3:12).[3] It is also made clear that the request for wisdom was particularly well received, when Solomon might have asked for anything else (such as wealth, longevity or success) instead.

In the Bible this story leads directly into the most famous anecdote told about Solomon. This concerns his judgement in a dispute involving two women, both of whom claim to be the mother of a particular child. Unable to decide between them, Solomon commands that the child be cut in two with a sword so that the women can have half each. One woman agrees to this solution while the other begs the king not to kill the child. Solomon sees that she is the real mother and the child is given back to her.

This is the only story actually told to illustrate the wisdom of Solomon, yet it is said that as a result of this everyone was amazed. Although it is a simple story, it still has the ability to impress. A king was often called upon to dispense justice and exercise judgement, and in the face of the irreconcilable claims of the two women, Solomon has to find a solution. His approach may be seen as something of a creative leap of the imagination designed to get at the truth. This seems to be what made such a strong impression on his contemporaries.

What would have happened had both women begged the king not to kill the child is another matter. There is a curious parallel to this in a Zen story:

> When Nansen saw monks of two sections of his monastery quarrel over the ownership of a cat, he held up the animal before them and declared, 'If you say a word I will not cut it in two.' Nobody uttered a word and the poor creature was sacrificed for their not being able to solve the dilemma of 'to be' and 'not to be'.[4]

There is another, somewhat darker, side to Solomon's reputation, which may relate to his biblical reputation for great knowledge. The Qur'an tells of Solomon commanding an army of men, spirits and birds. He also has power over the wind.[5] However all this is to be understood, it reflects a tradition associating Solomon with the realm of the supernatural. Writing in the first century AD, Josephus says that Solomon was also able to perform exorcisms and effect cures through the use of spells.[6] This puts him firmly in the realm of the magical, and a famous book on magic is called the *Key of Solomon* (fourteenth or fifteenth century). Quite when and why Solomon became associated with magic is unclear, but the association clearly goes back a long way. Whether this association grew up *because of* his reputation for wisdom or for a different reason is hard to say. What can be said is that, for century after century, Solomon was seen as a kind of 'brand name' in the world of wisdom.

Seven Sages of Ancient Greece

The idea that there are seven, and precisely seven, sages has already been encountered more than once. Exactly why this number of sages has been so irresistible is a mystery. Perhaps the *apkallu* have something to answer for, or perhaps the tradition is older than them. In any event, with the Seven Sages of ancient Greece we are at least on firm historical ground, even if we know considerably more about some of them than others. Furthermore, although it was always agreed that there were seven of them, it was not always agreed who the seven were. More than twenty names appear on one list or another. The oldest surviving list is found in Plato's *Protagoras*, a work written around 400 BC. All the names on it (and almost all of the names on every list), however, are of people who lived in the seventh and/or sixth century BC. It is possible that all the people on Plato's list could have met at Delphi as he says they did, and the year 582 BC has been suggested as when this could and might have happened.[7] The names given by Plato are Thales of Miletus, Pittacus of Mitylene, Bias of Priene, Solon of Athens, Cleobulus of Lindus, Myson of Chen and Chilon of Sparta.

Since the names of Thales, Pittacus, Bias and Solon appear on every surviving list it makes most sense to start with them. Thales is often regarded as the first 'Western' philosopher, and because he seems to have predicted an eclipse of the sun in 585 BC, this is the first reasonably reliable date in the history of Western philosophy. To modern eyes, Thales may appear as much scientist as philosopher because he interested himself mainly in questions about what the world was made of and how it worked. Pittacus was regarded as a wise ruler and legislator. Bias was a gifted orator and defender of those who had been wronged. Solon reformed the laws of Athens and was also a gifted poet. Of the other names on Plato's list, that of Cleobulus is the most obscure. He had a reputation for composing poems, epigrams and riddles. Myson was identified in his time by the oracle of Apollo at Delphi as the wisest man alive and seems to have lived a very simple life. Finally, Chilon was highly regarded for his personal integrity and sound advice.

It is not entirely easy to see why all these people should have been regarded as wise, or wise in the same way, or wiser than everyone else. An exception might perhaps be made of Myson who clearly received Delphi's endorsement, just as Socrates would in Plato's own time. This question clearly bothered Plato, so he looks for an explanation and comes up with an interesting one: they all admired Spartan culture, 'and their wisdom may be recognized as belonging to the same category, consisting of pithy and memorable dicta uttered by each'.[8] (One of the ancient names for Sparta was Laconia, and the Spartans' habit of expressing themselves in few words is the origin of the word 'laconic'.) I used to regard this explanation as pure fantasy on Plato's part, but now I am inclined to take it a little more seriously.

Something wise that is said in a succinct and memorable way might otherwise be described as a proverb. As has been seen with Solomon (and as will be seen in other cases too), the tendency to attribute a proverb to someone with a reputation for wisdom can be difficult to resist. This phenomenon is not restricted to proverbs: wisdom literature in general tends to be associated with wise people. The role of the Indian sages in underpinning the sacred texts of Hinduism has already been observed, and other examples will emerge in due course. Given that Plato was writing his *Protagoras* nearly 200 years after the seven are meant to have met in Delphi, it is quite possible that he was simply reflecting what was regarded as common knowledge in his own time.

In his account of the life of Solon, Plutarch comes up with a different explanation. He says that, with the exception of Thales, they were all successful as statesmen. And in fact it is possible to show that Thales also contributed to the well-being of his home city of Miletus. No one ever claimed that all the seven *governed*, but through their advice, leadership, advocacy or legal reform, they all made a difference to the places where they lived. And at the time they lived, the roles of adviser and legislator/reformer in particular were strongly associated with wisdom.

Both Plato and Plutarch try to advance an explanation of the selection of this particular group of seven on the basis of something they all shared, but they both seem to interpret this 'something' in relatively restricted terms. It may be that each of the seven was wise in some way or another, but that does not necessarily mean that they were all wise in the same way.

The Seven Sages of the Bamboo Grove

I turn now to the last set of seven sages to appear in these pages. The Seven Sages of the Bamboo Grove were a group of Taoists who lived in China in the third century AD. At the heart of the group was Xi Kang, a poet and musician. The bamboo grove where they would reputedly meet was near his house. Although historical fact is not easy to sift from later embellishment, the seven are said to have turned their backs on the court and political intrigue and retired to the country to lead a simpler and more aesthetic life, engaging in 'philosophical discussion, writing poetry and drinking'.[9] All were either scholars or artists of some description or both.

Xi Kang had spent several years travelling and studying Taoism before settling with his wife at the house by the grove. Liu Ling was in many ways the most colourful of the group. It is said that he went about accompanied by a servant who carried a bottle of wine and a spade. The wine was for when he wanted a drink, and the spade was to dig his grave as soon as he died. To him are attributed the words that 'the affairs of this world appear as so much duckweed in a river' to one who is drunk.[10] At home he normally dispensed with clothes, which tended to shock some of his visitors. By way of explanation he would declare that 'he considered the whole universe his home, and his room his trousers'.[11] Two of the others, Ruan Ji and Ruan Xian, were also fond of drinking, and used a large bowl that they would sometimes share with a local pig. The remaining three were Xiang Xiu, Wang Rong and Shan Tao.

It is known that some of the seven, such as Wang Rong, eventually returned to public life, while others, such as Xi Kang, refused to do so. While they were together they collectively exemplified a kind of playful life that contrasted sharply with the expectations of the world they had left behind. Where public life required and valued conformity, they embraced spontaneity. Where public life insisted on sobriety, they took delight in drunkenness and revelry. Their bucolic lifestyle became a popular theme in Chinese art, and a model for other rebellious natures to emulate. As with the Cynics of ancient Greece, the natural home of the Taoist was outside, or on the edge of, society: 'The Taoists could not imagine that a man of true wisdom and holiness would involve himself in the mundane affairs with which politicians and servants have to deal.'[12]

I think it is possible to push this point a little further. The sage is almost by definition an outsider. If the wise are those who can see 'the bigger picture', and if partisanship stems from seeing only part of the picture, then the wise person is one who transcends partisanship. But if most people are partisans and are 'inside' particular limited perspectives, then the wise person is an outsider. It might seem strange to say that Solomon was an outsider, since monarchs are reasonably seen as at the heart of 'the establishment'. Politically, Solomon was clearly an insider, as were the other rulers who will be looked at shortly, but mentally he was able to step outside the perspectives of others, and in that lay his wisdom. The Seven Sages of the Bamboo Grove were outsiders in a more radical, or more thoroughgoing, way. Like the trickster, they took delight in pushing against boundaries.

Ten Wise Rulers

It is relatively easy to guess why kings Charles I and II of France might have been called respectively 'the Bald' and 'the Fat'. It is rather harder to guess why some rulers have been called 'the Wise'. I want here to look at some rulers (whether emperors, kings, princes, dukes and so on) who were called 'the Wise', either during the period they ruled or soon after. In order to simplify the exercise, I have limited myself to the course of European history and have compiled a list of ten names, although obviously there may be more that I have overlooked. It is also possible that some might have been called 'the Wise' had they not instead been called 'the Great'.

Although our knowledge of some of the names on the list is extremely sketchy, it is immediately apparent that there are significant differences between them. If they were all regarded as wise, they do not all seem to have been wise in the same way. Because of that fact, it may be easiest to deal with them in a thematic way, and I shall begin with those who had a reputation for learning.

Leo VI was the Byzantine emperor from 886 to 912, acceding to the throne at the early age of twenty. Before he reached the age of 30, he had already become known as 'the wise' or even 'the wisest'.[13] Long after his death he acquired a reputation as an astrologer and soothsayer, and a book of prophecies was attributed to him. In this respect, his posthumous fate somewhat resembles that of Solomon. During his lifetime, however, he was regarded primarily as a man of formidable intellect and learning who was also a constitutional and legal reformer. He was a prolific author, writing many poems and hymns, along with sermons he would deliver personally in Hagia

Sophia, the great church dedicated to the 'Holy Wisdom' that still stands in what is now Istanbul. Leo was perhaps less than wise in certain areas of his private life: he married four times, although even a third marriage was technically illegal at that time.

Alfonso x was the king of Castile from 1252 to 1284. A man of great learning and intellectual tolerance, he was the driving force behind the Toledo School of Translators, which brought together Christian, Jewish and Muslim scholars. On the battlefield he was rather less tolerant towards Muslims, and he played a role in the reconquest of Spain for its Christian kingdoms. Like Leo, he was also a legal reformer, although his vision in this area went further than his achievement. And although he kept the title of king until his death, Alfonso lost all his power in 1282 when his son led a successful rebellion against him. Like Solomon, his political achievements were somewhat modest.

That is more than can be said about the man himself: 'Alfonso is reported to have said that had he been consulted about the creation of the world he would have arranged things very much better.'[14] Although his actual contribution to them is unclear, he is best known for the *Cantigas de Santa Maria*, a collection of more than 400 musical pieces. They are mainly songs bringing together stories from different parts of Spain, although stories from other parts of Europe also appear in them. Many tell of miracles, but some relate to the life of Alfonso himself. What proportion of the words and music can be attributed to the king personally is not known, but his was clearly the project's guiding hand. Finally, it may be noted that he took an interest in astronomy, and in recognition of this a lunar crater was named 'Alphonsus' in his honour in 1935.

Charles v ruled France from 1364 to 1380. He had a reputation for intelligence and piety, and was the proud possessor of a large personal library of more than a thousand volumes. He did not just collect books. Like Alfonso he was also interested in having books translated so that the learning contained in them might reach a wider audience. To this end, the king secured the services of Nicolas Oresme (*c.* 1320–1382) to translate works of Aristotle from Latin into French. Nicolas was himself a philosopher as well as being a mathematician. Later, with the king's help, he also became a bishop. Charles v certainly benefited from comparisons with his father, John II, who was a distinctly poor ruler, and his son, Charles VI, who was nicknamed 'the Mad'. If not quite the intellectual powerhouse that Leo was, Charles was clearly someone whose abilities marked him out. And like Alfonso, his support of translation projects helped to associate him with the learning of others.

Albert II, who was duke of Austria from 1330 to 1358, is perhaps more fortunate to find himself in this select company. At around the time of his accession he seems to have lost the use of his legs, and so was initially known as Albert the Lame. Obviously he made such a strong impression on his contemporaries that at the end of his reign he became known as Albert the Wise. From what we know about his reign it is not easy to identify any specific achievements that might have earned him his later reputation. However, in common with Leo, Alfonso and Charles, it is clear that Albert was a man of well above average learning for his time, and that may have been enough, or at least a good start. It is also possible that he benefited from some other comparisons with many of his contemporaries: 'in an age of persecution and bigotry, [Albert] displayed proofs of tolerance and humanity'.[15] He was an early member of the Habsburg dynasty, which went on to dominate central Europe for centuries, and if Albert himself was never more than a duke, plenty of his descendants were emperors. But none of the Habsburg emperors was ever called 'the Wise'.

A reputation for 'tolerance and humanity' may have been a factor in Elector Frederick III being regarded as wise. He ruled Saxony from 1486 to 1525, and this places him firmly in the middle of the Reformation, in which he played an active role. In 1502 he founded the University of Wittenberg, and then appointed both Martin Luther (1483–1546) and Philip Melanchthon (1497–1560) as professors there. When Luther was threatened by Pope Leo X, Frederick protected him. He was regarded as a just ruler and a pious man. He was also a patron of the arts, and both Albrecht Dürer (1471–1528) and Lucas Cranach the Elder (1472–1553) benefited from his patronage. In 1519 he was offered the chance to become Holy Roman Emperor, but he turned it down, protesting that at 56 he was too old for the job. This was probably a wise move since others clearly wanted the imperial honour more than he did and would probably have made his life difficult had he accepted it.

Apart from the fact that they were also patrons of the arts, it is difficult to see where Sancho VI (king of Navarre from 1150 to 1194) and Robert of Anjou (king of Naples from 1309 to 1343) obtained their reputations for wisdom from. The position of William IV is rather stronger. He was Landgrave of Hesse-Cassel from 1567 to 1592. He was another patron of the arts, and like Frederick III, a supporter of Luther's teachings. However, William also took an active interest in the sciences and was a keen astronomer. Thanks to him, Kassel became a centre for astronomical observation and a catalogue of stars based on these observations was published after his death. A number of discoveries were credited to him personally. As a ruler he achieved a sound economy and kept out of wars. Putting all these factors together, it is not too difficult to see how William earned his reputation.

The remaining two names on the list are more problematic. Albert IV was duke of Bavaria from 1467 to 1503. He became duke when his brother died, having previously sought to live a more spiritual life in Italy. Having chosen to return to the secular world, he fully threw himself into the intrigues and politics of his time. His lasting legacy was a law ensuring that the eldest son inherited all the dukedom's lands, meaning that the death of a duke no longer led to divisions and strife. Finally, Frederick II was Elector of the Palatinate from 1544 to 1556. It has to be said that of all the rulers considered in this section, his claim to the epithet of 'the Wise' seems the thinnest. He had a relatively short reign and was a man of uncertain principle. He had a clear tendency towards toleration, although some of this may simply have been indecision.

Each of these ten ruled a Christian nation (wholly or partly) in Europe during a period of a little less than 700 years. Many of them clearly had a reputation for learning or toleration or both. Another recurrent theme is a patronage of the arts. The fact that they were all apparently wise 'by popular acclaim', as it were, may indicate the importance of these factors in the public eye. Some may have benefited simply from comparison with others who were distinctly unwise. It is certainly not the case that they were all successful as rulers, which is perhaps one of the reasons why, although all were known as 'the Wise', none was known as 'the Great'.

Nezahualcoyotl

Nezahualcoyotl was rather more successful as a ruler than some of his European counterparts, and could boast a number of other accomplishments as well. His name means 'fasting coyote' and he ruled Texcoco, a small state just to the east of what is now Mexico City, from around 1430 to 1472. As a young man he had to go into exile when Texcoco was conquered by the neighbouring city of Azcapotzalco. He spent many years forging alliances, fighting battles and eventually reclaiming his kingdom. This was the prelude to what became recognized as a cultural golden age in which he played the leading role. As a ruler he reorganized the constitution and laws of his state. He built up an impressive library and established a school for the study of music. He promoted the construction of public buildings, and took an active interest in architecture. Some of the ruins of his city can still be seen at the site of Los Melones on the edge of the modern town of Texcoco. He also took an interest in astronomy and astrology.

Nezahualcoyotl is sometimes seen as a religious innovator, and it is claimed that he set up a temple to an unknown but omnipresent god in which living sacrifices were forbidden. He was also known as a poet and orator, and poems attributed to him still survive. Significantly, he was regarded as a *tlamatini*, a Nahuatl word signifying someone who possesses knowledge, but which is frequently translated as 'sage' or 'philosopher'. A number of the poems attributed to him are philosophical in nature: 'In his poems, he asks the great questions that have occupied philosophers in every culture. Where does one come from? Where does one go after death? Is there a life after death? And how should a person act while here on earth?'[16] It has to be said that his own conduct here on earth was not always exemplary. He sent a loyal follower into a battle with the clear hope and intention that he would be killed. Nezahualcoyotl wanted to make his friend's wife a widow so that he could marry her himself.

It seems that during his reign Nezahualcoyotl attracted a number of other *tlamatinime* (the plural of *tlamatini*) to his court, which became a major centre of Mesoamerican culture during this time. When he died he was succeeded by his son Nezahualpilli ('fasting prince'), who continued the good work of his father. Like his father, Nezahualpilli was also a poet. Unlike his father, however, he was credited with magical powers and the ability to take on the form of different animals. It was also said he could see into the future and predicted the destruction that would happen at the hands of the Spanish. Between them, father and son ruled their state effectively and wisely for nearly a hundred years. Not long after the death of Nezahualpilli, the Spanish appeared and Texcoco as a state disappeared. Long after his death it was rumoured that Nezahualpilli still lived on in a far-away cave. Between them, father and son managed to display an impressive number and variety of abilities connected with wisdom.

Five Sufi Sages

Sufism may be characterized as the mystical dimension of Islam. More will be said about it later when mysticism is addressed as a topic in its own right. Here I want to look at a small selection of Sufi sages from across the centuries, beginning with Rabia (717–801), sometimes called Rabia al-Adawiyya, Rabia al-Qaysiyya or Rabia al-Basriyya. It may fairly be said that the individuals looked at in this chapter (and in the book so far as a whole) have been predominantly male. Rabia, one of the first important figures in the history of Sufism, is one of the exceptions. Little is known about her life. Tradition has it that she was born into poverty near Basra, in what is now Iraq. She was sold into slavery while very young, but set free when her owner became impressed by her piety. Although she received many offers of marriage, she rejected them all on the basis that she had gone beyond such worldly matters. Although the historical record tends to suggest otherwise (he died in 728 when she was only eleven), she was said to have had a close relationship with Hasan of Basra, the leading religious authority of his time and an ascetic. Many anecdotes are told of their exchanges: 'The anecdotes are built upon the medieval Sufi convention of the spiritual joust in which two sages compete verbally with one another, one of them coming out the wiser or more sincere.'[17] This is another variation on the 'wisdom contest' theme that has already been encountered more than once. In these exchanges, Rabia consistently comes out on top, emphasizing and authenticating her spiritual accomplishments. But this duelling is only a sideshow. What is important is the life she led, not the words she spoke. For Rabia, it was the total, utter, selfless love of God that counted, and nothing else.

Ahmed Yesevi (1093–1166) was born and died in what is now Kazakhstan. When he was young, his family moved to Yasi (now known as Turkistan), from which the epithet 'Yesevi' (which sometimes appears as 'Yasawi' or 'Yasavi') is derived, and where he later died. At the end of the fourteenth century no less a person than Timur the Lame (Tamerlane or Tamburlaine) built a mausoleum over his grave, and to this day it is the city's main architectural attraction. He is said to have spent some years in Bukhara studying under the mystics there. Because he wrote in a Turkic language (as opposed to Persian or Arabic), Ahmed Yesevi is particularly revered in Turkey. He is notable for two things in particular. First, he founded his own order of Sufis. Second, he is credited with writing the *Divan-i-hikmet* ('Book of Wisdom'), which contains many poems on mystical themes, although there is some doubt as to whether he actually wrote any of them. Both the order and the poetry had a popular dimension, making him a sage of the people.

Muhyiddin Ibn al-Arabi (1165–1240) came from an Arab family living in Spain. He travelled extensively, living several years in Mecca and eventually died in Damascus. As a young man he is said to have met with the ageing philosopher Ibn Rushd (also known as Averroës) on a visit to Cordoba, but it was the old man who came away the more impressed from the encounter. He was a prolific writer, compiling encyclopaedic works as well as composing shorter works of poetry. He influenced not only the development of Muslim mysticism, but that of Christian mysticism too. He was particularly influential in the development of what is sometimes known as negative theology or apophatic thought. Here the emphasis is on what *cannot* be said, and the limits of language when it comes to dealing with the divine. Like many Sufis, he danced on the edge of orthodoxy, and sometimes beyond it. Some of his interpretations of the Qur'an in his best-known work, *The Bezels of Wisdom*, have been described as 'at best, reckless, and, at worst, flagrantly heretical'.[18] Despite this, he was known in his day as 'the supreme master'.

Jalaluddin Rumi (1207–1273) came from what is now Afghanistan, but his family moved to the town known today as Konya in Turkey, where he has a magnificent tomb. His followers became colloquially known as the 'whirling dervishes' after their distinctive dance ceremony. They are more correctly called Mevlevi dervishes, from the title *mevlana* (meaning 'our master') that Rumi's followers gave him. The word 'dervish' itself is a commonly used synonym for 'Sufi'. I suggested earlier that the sage could be thought of as an outsider, and this seems to have been true of Rumi. He had little respect for social conventions and even his own followers tried to kill him on one occasion. His lasting fame derives in large part from the poems he wrote, especially the work known as *Mathnawi*.

Nur al-Din Abd al-Rahman Jami (1414–1492) also came from what is now Afghanistan, and spent most of his life in Herat. His tomb, a very modest affair, can still be seen there. He achieved a considerable reputation as a scholar and wrote works on philosophy, mysticism and music. He also produced volumes of poetry, including a collection known as 'The Seven Thrones', a reference to the stars of Ursa Major. One of his most famous works was called *Lawaih*, meaning 'flashes of light'. In it he concisely sums up the Sufi's aspiration: 'O God, deliver us from preoccupation with worldly vanities and show us the nature of things "as they really are." Remove from our eyes the veil of ignorance, and show us things as they really are.'[19]

This is just a very small sample of Sufi sages, but they serve to illustrate broader themes. The anecdotes told about Rabia resemble the wisdom contests that are a feature of various cultures. Both Ibn al-Arabi and Jami were clearly people of considerable learning, and all except Rabia were associated with poetry. The idea that the poet is a purveyor of wisdom is encountered in many cultures, in part, perhaps, because in oral cultures the pattern of poetry is an aid to memorization and so to the transmission of learning. It is also possible to see poets as capturing in their works and words the traditions and values of their cultures, thus making them in some ways akin to culture heroes. But in their dalliances with heterodoxy they are perhaps also akin to tricksters?

Two Wizards

Magic is often associated with wisdom, and wisdom is often thought to bring with it magical powers. Here I want to look at two very different individuals who were both recognized as 'wizards' by their contemporaries. The first is Sæmundur the Wise or Sæmundur fróði, originally known as Sæmundur Sigfússon (1056–1133). Although he is most definitely a historical figure, a great deal of legend has also grown up around him. Many stories are told of how he outwitted the devil on numerous occasions. It is said that he studied at a mysterious place called the Black School in Wittenberg. The school acquired its name from the fact that it had no windows and was always dark inside. 'There were no teachers, either, the students learned from books written with fiery red letters that could be read in the dark.'[20] Those who studied there were not allowed outside again until they had finished their course, which took at least three years. The truth is a little more prosaic, in that Sæmundur left his native Iceland for France in order to study for the Church. When he returned to Iceland he became the priest at Oddi. He was evidently a man of some learning and wrote a book in Latin about the kings of Norway. Later legend, however, turned Sæmundur into something of a folk hero, and an Icelandic symbol of resistance to Danish rule. His magical exploits sometimes resemble those of a trickster.

The identity of my second 'wizard' may come as something of a surprise because it is Thomas Edison (1847–1931). His initial research work was in the area of telegraphy, where he was responsible for making many improvements. However, it was the invention of the phonograph in 1877 that sealed his reputation. It seemed so magical that it earned him the nickname 'The Wizard of Menlo Park' (Menlo Park being the town in New Jersey where he had his laboratory and workshops). Some initially found this new invention so unbelievable that they were convinced there must be some kind of trickery involved! Edison went on to register more than a thousand patents in the USA, but this was the one that had the greatest impact on the public imagination. The idea that there was something magical, almost supernatural, about an invention was nothing new. Many different cultures have attributed the invention of writing to gods or mythical beings, and the same has been true for other inventions such as the potter's wheel. Certain things just seem beyond the powers of human invention, and so must be attributed to some other cause. Edison's 'magic' was based on hard science and hard work (sometimes the hard work of others) but that did not diminish its power to astonish. The life and career of Edison is rather better and more reliably documented than that of Sæmundur, and it is therefore rather harder to understand quite where the latter's reputation for magic came from. But the wizardry of Edison, at least, can be seen to fit into a very old tradition concerning the nature and fruits of wisdom.

Two Great Sages

We have already seen some of the legends concerning ancient Indian sages. However, the Indian sage or *rishi* is far from extinct and here I want to look at two relatively recent examples. Debendranath Tagore (1817–1905) was the famous father of a famous son (Rabindranath Tagore, who won the Nobel Prize for Literature in 1913), and the wealthy son of an extremely wealthy father. Of Debendranath Tagore it was said that 'His great and noble character and his lofty spiritual nature so impressed his fellow-citizens that he was universally known as *Maharshi*, the great Rishi or Seer.'[21] His life was for many years bound up with the movement known as the 'Brahmo Samaj' ('Society of Brahma'), which sought to reform and modernize Hinduism. When the movement split in 1864, he became the undisputed leader of one of its factions. His approach to the reform of Hinduism was radical, to say the least. He came to reject the authority of the *Vedas*, the most sacred scriptures of Hinduism, along with such fundamental doctrines as that of *karma*. His 'reform' practically involved cutting Hinduism loose from its moorings, although Debendranath Tagore never ceased to regard himself as a devout Hindu. In 1863 he founded a small religious retreat called Shantiniketan ('peaceful haven') about 100 miles north of Calcutta. It attracted a number of like-minded souls, and his son later developed it into a university, which still exists.

Far to the south of Calcutta, on the edge of Tiruvannamalai, Ramana Maharshi (1879–1950) also attracted a group of followers around him. Originally called Venkataraman, he had a profound religious experience at the age of seventeen and felt a compulsion to leave his native village near Madurai and go to Tiruvannamalai, a modest town with a great temple that sits at the foot of a holy hill known as Arunachala. In his early years there he lived in temples, groves and caves before moving to what is now the site of an ashram bearing his name. He was a charismatic figure who naturally charmed people and animals alike. Ramana Maharshi was also a teacher, and all his teachings revolved around one idea: self-enquiry. In the experience that changed his life, he thought he had died. Then he thought: 'Well, this body is now dead. It will be carried to the funeral pyre and there reduced to ashes. But do I die with the death of this body? Is the body I?'[22] Self-enquiry persistently asks the question 'Who am I?' The end of self-enquiry is self-knowledge, and the idea that wisdom is connected with self-knowledge is a very old one. 'Know thyself!' was one of the inscriptions set up on the temple of Apollo at Delphi. Apollo dispensed his wisdom beneath Mount Parnassus, whereas Ramana Maharshi became known as the sage of Arunachala.

Debendranath Tagore and Ramana Maharshi were clearly very different characters, but in each one people recognized a certain something, a greatness of spirit, a depth of understanding, a special wisdom that set them apart and made them great sages.

The House of Wisdom

This chapter has mainly been about individuals, but I want now to look at an institution. The Abbasid caliph Abu Jafar al-Mansur, who reigned from 754 to 775, founded the city of Baghdad in 762. He was determined that his new city should be a seat of learning as well as a seat of power, and one of his first acts was to invite Hindu scholars to visit Baghdad, which they did, bringing many important texts with them. The caliph was an avid collector of texts of all kinds and founded a library to house them. Because many were in Persian or Sanskrit or Greek, translators had to be collected as well so that they could all be rendered into Arabic. Once translated, they would become available to Arab scholars to assimilate, develop and use. The institution that took on, performed and coordinated all these tasks became known as the *Bayt al-Hikma*, the House of Wisdom. 'Over time, the House of Wisdom came to comprise a translation bureau, a library and book repository and an academy of scholars and intellectuals from across the empire. Its overriding function, however, was the safeguarding of invaluable knowledge.'[23] The output and achievements of this institution were astonishing. Every Greek book on science or philosophy that could be tracked down was brought to Baghdad and translated into Arabic. But these translations were only the launching pad for further discoveries and debates.

One of Abu Jafar al-Mansur's successors was the caliph al-Mamun, who reigned from 813 to 833. It was he who formally established the House of Wisdom on the foundations of what had gone before. He initiated a major project that involved the mapping of the whole known world and the heavens. The project delivered the best maps of the world there had ever been. It was he who set his researchers the task of measuring the circumference of the earth. It was also during his reign that the great scholar Muhammad Ibn Musa al-Khwarizmi (*c.* 780–*c.* 850) was active at the House of Wisdom. His principal genius was in the area of mathematics, and he wrote the first book in Arabic on the system of numbers that we use today, which had been developed in India. It is largely because of him that we call them Arabic numerals. His own name has since metamorphosed into the word 'algorithm', while the title of one of his books gives us 'algebra' (from *al-jabr*, which means 'completing' or 'balancing').

It is clear that the House of Wisdom was principally a house of knowledge, a place where existing knowledge was collated and processed, and new areas of knowledge developed. The translation activities of the House of Wisdom played a crucial role in the transmission of knowledge from Asia to Europe, and the School of Translators established in Toledo by Alfonso X would have much to thank it for. The House of Wisdom also played a key role in the preservation and return of knowledge that had once been in circulation in Europe but which had been largely forgotten. For example, Latin scholars knew little or nothing of the geometry of Euclid, which had been seized upon with enthusiasm by Muslim mathematicians. Caliph Abu Ja'far al-Mansur was sufficiently inspired by Euclid to have his new city of Baghdad designed along geometrical lines, and those who followed him ensured that Euclid's *Elements* was one of the first texts to be translated from Greek into Arabic.

Over the centuries the importance of Baghdad and the House of Wisdom declined. The last of the Abbasid caliphate was executed when the Mongols sacked the city in 1258. Fortunately, by that time the labours of the House of Wisdom were already bearing fruit in other centres of Muslim learning such as Cairo, Damascus and Isfahan.

As in previous chapters, one of the aims of this chapter has been to display the variety of understandings of wisdom available. As far as possible, I have also tried to allow the sources to speak for themselves, selecting individuals who have been called wise by their contemporaries or posterity. At least three types of individual seem to emerge. There is an obvious spiritual dimension to the Seven Sages of the Bamboo Grove, Debendranath Tagore, Ramana Maharshi and the Sufi sages I have mentioned. Many of the wise rulers, along with such stately figures as Imhotep and some of the Sufi sages, were clearly people of great learning. Solomon, some of the Seven Sages of Ancient Greece, Nezahualcoyotl and several of the wise rulers had qualities that were valuable in public life: they were good legislators, or good judges, or good advisers. Spirituality, learning and statesmanship may be regarded as three widely recognized forms or manifestations of wisdom. Many of those discussed in this chapter were also poets, and poetry is often linked with wisdom. The talents of Sæmundur and Edison are of a different kind, but wizardry and invention also have authentic historical links with wisdom. We may, perhaps, be more impressed by some of these abilities and individuals than by others, but what is clear is that the wise stand out from the crowd in a variety of ways. Some of these ways may have a cultural background: different cultures are impressed by different things, and all of those discussed here stood out in culturally positive ways.

The House of Wisdom's importance partly derives from the fact that it stood at a cultural crossroads where it could help the learning of one culture to become the learning of many.

Prajnaparamita. Bronze figure of Prajnaparamita, Kashmir, 9th or 10th century. The goddess is depicted as the personification of the perfection of wisdom. She is generally shown accompanied by symbols that emphasize her role as a great teacher; the most important of these is a book holding *Prajnaparamita* writings.

4
Wisdom and Literature

The term 'wisdom literature' is often used to denote a small group of books in the Bible, and other works like them. I have called this chapter 'Wisdom *and* Literature' to make it clear that I am taking a much broader view of things. The extent to which wisdom can be captured or transmitted in the written word is an interesting question in its own right. Socrates was called the wisest man in Greece, but he never wrote anything, and he was far from alone in making that choice. Everything we know, or think we know, about what Jesus or the Buddha said is due to the writings of others. Whatever its value, the written word remains frozen in time, becoming ever more remote from where and when it was authored. More than that, we cannot assume that language is able to capture and transmit all we would wish to capture and transmit. Perhaps words are inadequate to the task of communicating what is really important? As Zhuangzi said, 'If it could be talked about, everybody would have told their brother.'[1] Nevertheless, enough have had sufficient faith in the power of language and the written word to create an impressive body of literature related to wisdom.

The *Upanishads* and Vedanta

The Sanskrit word *upanishad* is usually understood to derive from three words meaning 'sitting down near', suggesting something that is handed down from a teacher to pupils gathered around him or her. The works usually referred to as the *Upanishads* are a collection of texts (traditionally numbered at 108, but there are many more) from the earliest centuries of Indian philosophy. Some are long, some are short, some are in poetic form, some in prose, and all were probably composed between around 800 BC and 200 BC by a variety of anonymous individuals. 'They are the utterances of the sages who speak out of the fullness of their illumined experience . . . and the records of their experiences are the facts to be considered by any philosophy of religion.'[2] According to the 'Mundaka Upanishad', these sages experience: 'That which is ungraspable . . . eternal, all-pervading, omnipresent, exceedingly subtle, that is the Undecaying, which the wise perceive as the source of beings.'[3] Although translations of this passage vary, they all agree that it concerns what the wise somehow *see* or *perceive*. The clear implication is that the wise are distinguished by their ability to see more deeply into the nature of reality than others.

If the *Upanishads* are regarded as accounts given by the sages of how things really are, then it is reasonable to expect their accounts to tally, and orthodox Hindus assume that they do. However, extracting a single coherent system from such a variety of texts is no easy task. Those who claim to be able to do so rely on either an extremely selective approach to the texts or imaginative interpretations of certain passages, or both. The general term for any philosophy extracted from the *Upanishads* is Vedanta. Given how many different ways the *Upanishads* can be interpreted and understood, there are many different Vedanta philosophies.

The different texts found in the *Upanishads* do not simply repeat and recapitulate each other. On the contrary, collectively they are wide-ranging and address many different issues. This is one of the reasons why it is so difficult to extract a single system from them. For many people, however, the heart of the *Upanishads*, the very core of their teaching, relates to matters of metaphysics, the fundamental problem of what the world is really like. The position taken by the *Upanishads* is at once simple, profound and yet somehow obvious. *If* there is a spirit that pervades or underlies everything in the universe, *then* it must be present in us, because we are part of that universe. *And*, say the sages, that is exactly how it is. The *Upanishads* use the terms *Brahman* to refer to the universal spirit underlying all reality and *atman* for the spirit that underlies individual reality. So what the sages experience is *Brahman* as known through, or as, *atman*. This basic belief underpins a great deal of Indian philosophy, or, to put it another way, a great deal of

Indian philosophy addresses itself to working out the implications of this belief.

The knowledge of the sages comes from their experiences, and although the *Upanishads* (along with the many commentaries written on them) attempt to convey that knowledge *as far as words are able*, it is never assumed that the words can be an adequate substitute for the experience. So while the *Upanishads* sought to articulate the experiences of the sages, techniques were also derived to enable others to replicate them. Loosely speaking, these techniques can be summed up in one word, yoga. The Sanskrit word *yoga* has the same remote ancestor as the English word 'yoke', and both refer to a joining or union of two (or more) things. The idea behind the practice of any kind of yoga is very simple: we acquire knowledge of something by entering into a relationship with it, and ultimately by becoming it. In the context of the *Upanishads*, yoga is the means or method whereby the identity of *atman* with *Brahman* may be experienced.

Yoga takes many forms, some of which can be regarded as simply types of meditation. The point of all of them is to remove the obstacles that prevent us from seeing things as they really are. The aim is, as the 'Brihadaranyaka Upanishad' puts it, to become 'calm, self-controlled, withdrawn, patient and collected'.[4] In everyday life our perceptions are routinely distorted by our desires, our interests, our ambitions. We are constantly perceiving the world in terms of what it can do for us. The *Upanishads* can therefore be understood as exhorting us to live more unselfish and less self-centred lives. The reason for this is not a moralistic one, but a pragmatic one. Selfishness is one of the obstacles that prevent us from seeing things as they really are. If I am looking *for* something, I see far less than I do if I am just looking. Yoga aims at stripping our perception bare until we end up with pure awareness of ourselves as we really are.

It may be a little surprising that since I have been discussing the *Upanishads* in a chapter on wisdom literature, I have used very few quotations from the *Upanishads* themselves. It has to be said that even for those who purport to understand them, the texts are far from easy, and many of them assume a knowledge of Hinduism and Indian philosophy that is far above that of the average reader (or author). Consequently, although many more direct quotations might be given, paraphrases, interpretations and explanations have probably served the purpose of communication better. But to conclude this section I shall give one last quotation from the 'Mundaka Upanishad' (3.2.5):

> The seers, sated with knowledge,
> when they have attained him [i.e. *Brahman*],
> become free from passion and tranquil,
> and their selves are made perfect.
> The wise, their selves controlled,
> when they attain him altogether,
> he who is present in All,
> they enter into that very All.[5]

Prajnaparamita and *Madhyamika*

Although there are many opinions, there is no agreement as to exactly where or exactly when the Buddhist writings known as *Prajnaparamita* originated. However, somewhere in India, and sometime in the first century BC is a reasonably good bet. That means that the beginnings of *Prajnaparamita* probably follow hot on the heels of the end of the *Upanishads*. The word *Prajnaparamita* is usually translated as 'perfection of wisdom', with the *paramita* element signifying 'perfection', although it can also be translated as 'ultimate'. The meaning of *prajna* is less straightforward. Although it *can* refer to forms of understanding that are far from perfect, in the context of *Prajnaparamita* literature it is better understood as an insight into the true nature of things. The perfection of *prajna*, *Prajnaparamita*, may therefore be described as 'the cultivation of such wisdom that enables a person to see things as they are'.[6] It will already be seen that there is not only a chronological and geographical connection between *Prajnaparamita* and the *Upanishads*, but a philosophical one as well.

Although the earliest *Prajnaparamita* writings may date to the first century BC, as a genre it continued in existence for at least 1,000 years, roaming far and wide in the process. Two of the best known Buddhist texts, known as 'The Heart Sutra' and 'The Diamond Sutra', belong to this genre. As with the *Upanishads*, it is not entirely clear what the texts mean, and this is partly intentional: 'Indian tradition assumes that without a *commentary*, a holy book is incomplete. In the case of the *Diamond Sutra* it is quite obvious that a bare translation cannot possibly convey its full meaning.'[7] A whole body of commentaries grew up around texts like 'The Diamond Sutra', but even the best written commentary may itself require some explanation. We should not underestimate the importance of a living teacher in the transmission of any tradition. Without the living teacher we are likely to become too attached to the dead word, whether it be in an original text or a subsequent commentary.

Not all *Prajnaparamita* writings are totally impenetrable. A work known as 'The Ashtasahasrika [i.e. 8,000-verse] Prajnaparamita Sutra' contains the following helpful description of *Prajnaparamita*:

> The perfection of wisdom is the state of all-knowledge . . . She brings light to the blind so that all fear and distress may be forsaken . . . She disperses the gloom and darkness of delusion. She guides to the Path those who have strayed on to a bad road . . . She protects the unprotected . . .[8]

It may be noted that Prajnaparamita is here personified as a deity, hence the references to 'she'. Such a personification is far from unique to Buddhism. As a personification, Prajnaparamita is a helper and protector, but what, in hard philosophical terms, is the perfection of wisdom that she personifies?

Like the *Upanishads*, the *Prajnaparamita* writings are not philosophical tracts. Their aim is not to prove or persuade. Like the *Upanishads*, the *Prajnaparamita* writings aim to set out, as far as is possible, the experiences of their authors. They tell us how they see things. Ultimately, what they see is that things are 'empty of self-existence and inseparable from the mind that conjures them into existence'.[9] 'Self-existence' here is a translation of the word *svabhava*, which can also be translated as 'essence' or 'independent real existence.' Something that has self-existence exists totally independently of the existence of anything else. But what kinds of things can be said to possess this self-existence? Anything that is created clearly lacks self-existence because its existence depends on whatever or whoever created it. And anything that is a compound made up of two or more things coming together also lacks self-existence because its existence depends on its constituent parts. And so on.

The term 'emptiness' is frequently encountered in *Prajnaparamita* writings, as well as in those of the philosophical movement that takes its inspiration from them, the *Madhyamika* ('Middle Way'). The whole point of the *Madhyamika* system of philosophy is to demonstrate that nothing whatsoever has 'self-existence'. To put the same point another way, the world is 'empty' of self-existence. However, that does not mean that the world is empty of 'existence', only that it is empty of 'essence'.

The fact that the world is empty of 'essence' is important, because we use language to name things, to distinguish between 'this' and 'that', or, more fundamentally, between 'this' and 'not this'. A horse is not a cow because the 'essence' of a horse is different from the 'essence' of a cow, and we use two different words to refer to them. But if there are no essences, then ultimately our words have nothing to fasten on to. If we try to do things with language that it is not equipped for, then we can expect it to misbehave. Similarly, the logic we use is also based on the idea that if something is 'this' then it cannot also be 'not this'. This is called the principle of non-contradiction. Some *Madhyamika* texts push language and logic to their limits:

> Everything is real and is not real,
> Both real and not real,
> Neither real nor not real.
> This is Lord Buddha's teaching.[10]

This is a fairly typical verse from the second-century work known as the *Mulamadhyamakakarika* ('Root Verses on the Middle Way') by Nagarjuna, one of the greatest of Buddhist philosophers. On the face of it, it seems completely meaningless, let alone true. So how, if at all, is it to be understood? The first point to note is that this verse is what is known as a tetralemma: it sets out four options to choose from. The options are 1) Everything is real, 2) Everything is not real, 3) Everything is both real and not real, and 4) Everything is neither real nor not-real. But which option (if any) is correct? Sometimes a tetralemma is used to introduce 'proofs' of all four options, sometimes it is used to introduce 'disproofs' of all the options. But if all four can be 'proven', they cannot all be correct because they contradict each other. On the other hand, if all four can be disproven, what is left, since all the options available seem to be exhausted? Whichever of these two ways the tetralemma is used, the aim is the same: to shake us out of our complacency and make us realize that if this is the outcome of the way we are looking at things, *we must be looking at things the wrong way*.

There is also a third option. It could be said that everything is real *in one sense*, because even if there is no 'self-existence' to be found anywhere there is still existence. But everything is not real *in another sense*, because nothing has 'self-existence'. Similarly everything is real in one sense *and* not real in the other, while nothing is real in one sense *or* not real in the other. This approach resolves the contradiction and makes it only an apparent one: the contradiction disappears when two different senses of 'real' are identified and separated out. This solution is more philosophically satisfying, because a contradiction is philosophically problematic. However, if we think of the *Madhyamika* philosophy as the offshoot of, or inspired by *Prajnaparamita* literature, then the basic point that that literature makes is that we must come to *see* things differently. Only if we regard the tetralemma as *insoluble* are we likely to take a radically different view of things and move on. Resolving the contradiction leaves us where we are. By resolving the contradiction we are giving in to logic when we need to be going beyond it.

The wisdom of both the *Upanishads* and the *Prajnaparamita* writings (along with that of the Vedanta and Madhyamika philosophical systems that grew out of them) has a primarily metaphysical focus and concern. They set out accounts of how, ultimately, the world really is and challenge us to verify those accounts through our own experiences. I want to move on now to a very different kind of wisdom literature, which is concerned not so much with how the world *is* as how to live in it.

Instruction Literature

'The instruction of the superintendent of the capital, the vizier, Ptahhotep, under the majesty of King Isesi, who lives forever and ever.'[11] So begins one of the earliest works of ancient Egyptian literature known to us, which goes by the name of 'The Instruction of Ptahhotep'. King Isesi, more often known as Djedkare-Isesi, was the ruler of Egypt from 2414 to 2375 BC. Although he might have been, it is not known whether Ptahhotep actually was the author of this work. As has been noted with regard to Solomon and others, people with reputations for wisdom might have works attributed to them even though they were not, or could not have been, their authors. The word 'instruction' in this quotation is a translation of the Egyptian word *seboyet*, and simply points to a work that seeks to teach its reader something. However, it came to be particularly associated with a kind of literature that set out to teach its readers how to live well. This might be done in a variety of ways, and some works of instruction literature include fables and proverbs as well as what might be regarded as sermons or lectures on what to do and what not to do.

Whether or not it was actually the case, instruction works were often written as if a father were passing on his accumulated wisdom to his son. In the work named after him, Ptahhotep says that he is getting old and wants to prepare his son to succeed him in his high office. Consequently, a large part of the advice on offer might be regarded as professional in nature: 'If you are one to whom a petition is made, be kindly when you hearken to the speech of a petitioner . . . A petitioner likes it well if one nods to his addresses, until he has made an end of that about which he came.'[12] The same father/son convention can be found in a work sometimes known as the 'Proverbs of Amenemope', although it is more properly referred to as 'The Instruction of Amenemope' because its opening words are: 'The beginning of instruction for living and precepts for well-being'.[13] The reason for calling it the 'Proverbs of Amenemope' is very simple: as soon as it was translated, scholars realized that the work attributed to Amenemope bears a striking resemblance to part of the biblical book of Proverbs, far more than can be attributed to coincidence. Because of the problems involved in dating both works, it is impossible to say what the exact relation between the two is. What we can say with some confidence is that this kind of literature was evidently widely distributed across Egypt and West Asia in antiquity.

The work attributed to Amenemope may be over a thousand years later than the one attributed to Ptahhotep, and there is a significant difference in content between them. While Amenemope is clearly an official of some ranking (because he tells us so), he gives considerably less professional advice than his predecessor and considerably more advice about life in general. Indeed, his aim is 'to set one right on the ways of life, and to cause him to prosper in the world . . . to guide him away from evil'.[14] Some of his advice tells us that dubious business practices have been going on for thousands of years: 'Do not make heavy the scales, nor falsify the weights, nor diminish the fractions of the measure.'[15] Honesty in all dealings is important. In the end, the general message that underlies the whole text is a simple one: the virtuous life leads to good fortune and wickedness will be punished.

About a thousand years after Amenemope, a work appeared known as 'The Instruction of Ankhsheshonqy'. Ankhsheshonqy appears in it as a wise physician who has been condemned to death. Before his execution he asks to be given writing materials so that he can compose a work of instruction to be passed on to his son. Some of the advice is timelessly pragmatic: 'Do not borrow money at interest in order to live high on it.'[16] Some of it appears distinctly puzzling: 'Do not laugh at a cat.'[17] This is presumably a piece of superstition connected with Bastet, a goddess who was often portrayed with the head of a cat. The Greeks identified her with their own Artemis, who could be distinctly prickly. Perhaps Bastet had the same reputation and did not take kindly to ridicule. Some effort has gone into arranging the different sayings collected in 'The Instruction of Ankhsheshonqy' under different themes. For example, there is a group of sayings about wealth, including: 'The wealth of a temple is its sanctity . . . The wealth of a storehouse is its stock . . . The wealth of a wise man is his speech.'[18] While this thematic treatment is not enough to make the text a systematic one, there was clearly a sense that certain sayings belong together. Whatever the differences between them, the general purpose of all works of instruction literature was to convey, whether directly or indirectly, what the good life looks like, whether as a whole or in part. And to help the reader to achieve that life.

Many more examples of wisdom writings from Egypt and its ancient neighbours could be discussed, but I shall look at only one. A work variously known as 'The Words of Ahikar' or 'The Story of Ahikar' or 'The Wisdom of Ahikar' achieved a wide circulation in antiquity.

Its hero Ahikar (or Ahiqar) was reputedly an official serving Sennacherib and/or Esarhaddon, who between them ruled Assyria from 704 to 669 BC. He is mentioned in the biblical book of Tobit, where he is said to be Tobit's nephew. In the work named after him he is an old man, and is pressed by the king to suggest a successor. Being childless, Ahikar proposes his nephew, Nadan. This is agreed to, and the next part of the text is a traditional piece of instruction literature. The narrative then takes an unexpected turn: Nadan takes over his uncle's duties, but then conspires against him and manages to get him condemned to death. Fortunately, Ahikar manages to escape his fate. In some versions of the story, Ahikar then goes to Egypt. There he is put to the test by the pharaoh, who confronts him with a number of problems and riddles. Ahikar succeeds every time, and returns to Assyria. He gives his nephew a long sermon on the error of his ways, and Nadan dies. As with 'The Instruction of Ankhsheshonqy', the narrative element of 'The Story of Ahikar' is to some extent little more than an excuse for the teaching that lies within it. Indeed, it is entirely possible that the author of 'The Instruction of Ankhsheshonqy' was familiar with 'The Story of Ahikar'. So widely known was 'The Story of Ahikar', and so many versions of it existed, that no one was certain where it originated, although the fact that it has an Assyrian setting speaks strongly for an Assyrian origin. On the other hand, the narrative contained in 'The Story of Ahikar' has some entertainment value in its own right, which doubtless contributed to its popularity.

There are many different versions of 'The Story of Ahikar'. The oldest surviving text, dated to the fifth century BC, was found in Egypt but is written in Aramaic. Some of the sayings found in it have a familiar ring to them. There is a very early version of the familiar proverb 'Spare the rod and spoil the child', while 'Keep watch over your mouth lest it bring you to grief' has probably always been good advice.[19] More strikingly expressed is: 'I have tasted even the bitter medlar, and have eaten endives, but there is nothing more bitter than poverty', which sounds like the voice of personal experience.[20] There are also imagined discussions between a leopard and a goat and between a bramble and a pomegranate, a common kind of fable found in wisdom literature.

Instruction literature has had a long and geographically dispersed history. It seems reasonable to suppose that the desire to pass on the benefits of one's experience to others, especially one's children, is a fairly common phenomenon in human history. Consequently there is no reason to suppose that the ancient instruction literature of Egypt has directly influenced the instruction literature of other cultures. On the other hand, as has been seen in the case of 'The Story of Ahikar', instruction literature seems to have been circulated quite widely, so it is certainly possible that it, or works like it, could have travelled to some very distant places.

A relatively recent example dates from 1925. Maharaja Madhav Rao Scindia of Gwalior in northern India had very clear views on how those destined to be rulers should be prepared for the elevated position that awaited them and set them out in his 'Notes on the Education and Upbringing of the Ruler'. Some of these notes could have come straight from an ancient work of instruction literature: 'Be neither miserly nor extravagant. Speak out the truth and fear not . . . Accept what is just and be always polite . . . Respect your parents and elders.'[21] There is nothing in this that specifically relates to royalty or India, and most people would probably regard it as good advice. The Maharaja's views on marriage were that 'The selection of a bride or bridegroom for their children or for the Ruler of a State is, as a rule, made by their parents or guardians', which is common practice in many cultures.[22] In one particular area of life, however, the Maharaja had what many might regard as unusual views: 'Children of both sexes should be taken out shooting once a week without fail, and when they have advanced in years they should, as a rule, be made to spend not less than a couple of weeks annually on tiger-shooting.'[23] However, in the Maharaja's world, hunting played an important role, and his observations on this matter serve as a timely reminder that instruction literature was designed to help people live *the lives they were expected to lead*. Consequently, a degree of cultural relativism should come as no surprise.

Moving further east, and some distance north, we come to a rather different work. Sakya Pandita (1182–1251) was a Tibetan scholar, states - man, teacher and author. He is most famous as the author of a work known as *A Jewel Treasury of Good Advice*, a work that is still used for educational purposes in Tibet, India and Bhutan. As a scholar, he was familiar with works in languages other than his own, and *A Jewel*

Treasury of Good Advice is something of a compendium drawing on many different sources. On the other hand, as a Buddhist he subscribed to a particular philosophy of life and this shaped all his writings. The book is arranged into 457 verses, each of which offers a self-contained piece of advice or wisdom. Many of them are memorably expressed. For example, in verse 331 we read:

> One should not vacate one's original residence
> Without properly investigating other places first.
> If one's leg is not properly positioned,
> When the second leg is raised, one falls down![24]

And in verse 203:

> When many are of the same opinion,
> Even the weak can achieve great things.
> Through the united force of many ants
> A lion cub was slain, it is said.[25]

This very brief selection barely does credit to Sakya Pandita, but the basic approach of his book can be discerned from it. He is generally not so much concerned with giving advice as with making shrewd observations about how the world works and allowing people to draw their own conclusions. If people *want* to fall down, they may happily ignore verse 331, but the presumption is that they do not, and that this observation will help them.

Moving further east again, we come to the work of a so-called 'scholar-bum' who lived a reclusive life in China about 400 years ago. Hong Yingming wrote a book with the engaging title of *Vegetable Root Discourses* (*Caigentan* in Chinese). The title was apparently inspired by a quotation from the philosopher Wang Xinmin: 'If one is able to chew the vegetable greens and roots well, he should be able to do all things.'[26] The work had little impact in China, but was taken up and achieved some fame in Japan, which is why it is usually known by its Japanese name, *Saikontan*. Hong clearly possessed an eclectic mind and he drew on Confucianism, Taoism and Buddhism for his materials. Like Sakya Pandita, he was a shrewd observer of the world, and his 357 verses are full of advice on how to live in it. Here is a sample of some of the more transparent ones:

> Though one should tolerate the mistakes and faults of others,
> He should not tolerate those that reside within himself.[27]
> He who detests conversations about fame and profit
> Has not yet forgotten such themes.[28]
>
> A tendency for deliberation and composure
> Is not obtained while drinking strong wines,
> But rather when sipping simple bean soup and drinking
> plain water.[29]

It is not always easy to discern a common theme or thread linking the individual verses. However, if the apparent inspiration for the book's title is taken seriously, then the person who absorbs all its teachings 'should be able to do all things'. Certainly within the Taoist tradition such an achievement would mark an individual out as a sage. So perhaps it is possible to see *Saikontan* as a book that provides instruction on how to become a sage.

For the final topic in this long section we head further east again, and arrive in the Americas. Mention has already been made of Nezahualcoyotl and the *tlamatinime*, or sages, of the Aztec. Although much of their literature was destroyed by the conquistadors and their followers, not all was lost. A number of documents known as *Huehuetlatolli* ('Discourses of the Elders') have survived and these shed significant light on the kind of instruction that took place in their world. Just as in Egypt, many of these were written as if a father were passing on advice to his son.

One such document describes the harsh regime imposed on young princes. They stayed in a temple and at midnight were woken and set to work sweeping the place. Then they were sent off to the forest to bring back branches and ferns to decorate the temple with. When they had completed their tasks they received a meagre breakfast of a couple of tortillas each. After that, their daily classes began. They were taught: 'how to live, how to obey, and how to honor people, to give themselves to the good and to relinquish and shun evil, bad behavior, and excess'.[30]

Respect for others and self-control were highly prized in Aztec society. What comprised 'the good' was understood 'in terms of appropriateness to the human being'.[31] What was 'appropriate' was compared to what was edible, what it was natural for a human being to assimilate, what would not do internal damage, what would help an individual to grow.

Another word for 'instruction' is 'education', and the reason why so many works of Egyptian instruction literature survive is precisely because they were copied, generation after generation, century after century, by Egyptian children as part of their education. They copied them as part of the process of learning how to write, but *what* they copied shaped their values. And since few Egyptian children learned how to write, the values that instruction literature embodies are often the values of the social elite. The educational system of the Aztec seems to have been less elitist, so the values that were inculcated through it appear to have been those of the wider community. What was 'appropriate' helped a child to grow into being a full member of that community.

Greed appears to have been a cardinal sin in the Aztec world. And as in most known worlds, the relationships between males and females were definitely matters of concern. A father advises his son: 'Do not throw yourself upon women', comparing the person who does so to 'the dog which throws itself upon food'.[32] Learn to wait, learn that there is a right and a wrong time for things, these are the lessons that are being taught here and that might resonate in many different cultures and many different centuries. Much of what can be found in instruction literature of all kinds transcends both history and geography. On the other hand, as the notes of Maharaja Madhav Rao Scindia remind us, what appears to be good advice in one society can appear to be extremely odd advice in another. The point of instruction literature may be seen as the transformation of human raw material into a human finished product, and different societies (as well as different classes within the same society) may value different finished products differently. What is more interesting, perhaps, is how much we can relate to the instruction literature of different cultures. Perhaps in those shared values and ideas we can see at least the outlines of a wisdom that is genuinely human and universal?

Wisdom Literature and the Bible

While the wisdom writings of Mesopotamia and Egypt lay unknown and untranslated for centuries, a very different fate lay in store for those of ancient Israel. Three works, usually known as the books of Job, Proverbs and Ecclesiastes, became recognized as authoritative within Judaism, and went on to become part of the Old Testament of the Bible. Two more works, the Wisdom of Solomon and Sirach (also known as Ecclesiasticus) are accepted as authoritative by some, but not by all. At an unknown time (but thought by some to be during the second century BC), Job, Ecclesiastes and Proverbs became regarded as a distinctive group of writings within the canon of Judaism because of their association with wisdom. They became the core wisdom writings of both Judaism and Christianity, with the Wisdom of Solomon and Sirach being added to them later. The Wisdom of Solomon was the last of these to be written, and dates to the first century BC. All these texts have therefore been continuously read and debated for more than 2,000 years.

The first thing that may be said about Job, Ecclesiastes and Proverbs is that they have virtually nothing in common, although they do have plenty in common with other works from outside the Judaic and Christian traditions. The story of Job is about human suffering. He is introduced to the reader as a man full of virtue and piety, but God permits Satan to test Job's faith in any way he wishes, as long as his life is spared. He loses his wealth, his children and his health, but bears all his sufferings with acceptance. Four friends visit him, and they discuss the meaning and management of suffering. The general line they take is that in some way or other Job *must* have brought it all upon himself. But Job, God and the reader know that this is not true. Finally God appears to Job, proclaims his power and justice, and makes Job even more prosperous than he was before.

The story of Job is not unique to the Judaic tradition, and may even have originated as a folk tale. Other writings on the theme of suffering and its meaning have survived from Mesopotamia, bearing various degrees of similarity to Job. What makes Job an engaging text is the eternal relevance of its theme and the way in which the different speakers contribute to the debate. But the book's obvious conclusion, that suffering is not always deserved, brings little comfort.

Ecclesiastes is a very different kind of text, and takes the form of an essay or sermon, but its concerns are not too far away from those of Job. If the theme of Job is why people suffer, the theme of Ecclesiastes is 'What does man gain from all his labour and his toil here under the sun?' (Ecclesiastes 1:3). Both books are therefore concerned with the law of cause and effect, with what does or does not follow from what. The answer provided by Ecclesiastes is a pessimistic one: experience shows that everyone is subject to the same fate however they live their lives. The good may suffer and the wicked may prosper. The only logical response appears to be a form of fatalism: 'Go to it then, eat your food, and drink your wine with a cheerful heart; for already God has accepted what you have done' (Ecclesiastes 9:7). In the end, there is nothing to be done except to trust in God's providence and enjoy what it brings.

The book of Proverbs is more than just a collection, or collection of collections, of proverbs, although it certainly has proverbs in it. Proverbs as a topic will be looked at separately in a later chapter. Proverbs as a book of the Bible is a piece of instruction literature that closely parallels an Egyptian work. That is not the only similarity. The first nine chapters of the book comprise another piece of instruction literature. The sayings that follow in the next thirteen chapters constantly contrast the wise person and the fool, in a way that echoes another Egyptian work known as 'Papyrus Insinger'. For example, in Proverbs we find 'A wise son brings joy to his father; a foolish son is his mother's bane' (Proverbs 10:1); and in 'Papyrus Insinger', 'The wise one among the children is worthy of life. Better the son of another than a son who is an accursed fool.'[33] It is impossible to say which influenced which, but what is abundantly plain is that there was what might be termed a traffic in instruction literature that clearly crossed cultural and geographical boundaries. Sitting on routes linking the cultures of Anatolia to the north, Mesopotamia to the east and Egypt to the south, it is scarcely surprising that the writings of ancient Israel displayed some characteristics of the literature of its neighbours.

Another feature of Proverbs is the way in which Wisdom appears in personified form. This feature is taken further in both Sirach and the Wisdom of Solomon. In Sirach there is a close connection, almost an identification of wisdom with law. If someone masters the law, then, 'She will come out to meet him like a mother; she will receive him like a young bride' (Ecclesiasticus 15:2). This imagery can be found in the Wisdom of Solomon: 'Wisdom I loved; I sought her out when I was young and longed to win her for my bride, and I fell in love with her beauty' (Wisdom of Solomon 8:2). However, Wisdom of Solomon can also be seen as a work emerging from another tradition altogether, for the author was clearly subject to Greek influences. We read: 'If virtue is the object of a man's affections, the fruits of wisdom's labour are the virtues; temperance and prudence, justice and fortitude, these are her teaching' (Wisdom of Solomon 8:7), and this list of virtues is the same as the one given by Plato in *Phaedo*. His strong emphasis on the law (meaning the law of Moses) keeps the author of Sirach firmly within the Judaic tradition, whereas the author of the Wisdom of Solomon is far more cosmopolitan in his outlook.

The author of Sirach, known both as Sirach and Ben Sira, is thought to have written the book around 200 BC. Proverbs, Ecclesiastes and Wisdom of Solomon are all attributed to Solomon. Some parts of Proverbs may be his, but nothing else is. The author of Job is totally unknown. Scholars have pondered over the reason why these books were written, their authors and their intended audiences. What is perhaps a more interesting question is why these and only these seem to have been accepted as authoritative, since it would be stretching credulity to believe that they were the only five books of their kind produced over a period that lasted hundreds of years. The fact of the matter is that, even if these texts sit somewhat uncomfortably within the theological context of Judaism, they sit entirely comfortably within the context of the ancient world and its literature. It is difficult to see them as constituting a specific literary genre because their differences are as great as their similarities. It is not difficult to see them as examples of different kinds of literature that were in circulation for hundreds of years in the world of which ancient Israel was a part.

Fables, Fairy Tales and Parables

I know of no human culture that does not take pleasure in the telling of stories. India had its *Mahabharata* and *Ramayana*, the Greeks had their *Iliad* and *Odyssey*, the Mesopotamians had their *Epic of Gilgamesh*, and so on. But the great epics are the exceptions in storytelling, not the rule. Here I am concerned with the other end of the storytelling scale, with the modest fable, fairy tale or parable. The exact differences between these three (as well as folklore, jokes, allegories and other related genres) is not important here. I am simply concerned with short, and sometimes incredibly short, stories that seek to make a point. In a story, *something happens*, and this is enough to distinguish the fable from the proverb; and a point is being made, which takes the fable beyond pure entertainment. Some fairy tales make a point, some do not, but parables always do. It may be noted that fables generally have animals as protagonists, which perhaps enhances their entertainment value.

Some of the earliest literary works known to us are collections of fables from ancient Sumer. But they contain more than *just* fables: they also contain quotations, jokes, proverbs, poems and so on. At least one of the reasons for making such compilations seems to have been so that they might be used for educational purposes. There was also the genre known as 'contest literature', where different animals, plants or other natural phenomena would enter into a debate as to which was most valuable. A god would then judge between them. 'The Tamarisk and the Palm', in which the two plants argue their relative merits, is a very early surviving example, with both emphasizing their strengths and playing down their weaknesses.

Many collections of fables are known from all over the world. In India there was the work known as the *Panchatantra* ('Five Chapters'), said to have been compiled perhaps as early as the third century BC. Whether or not this is the case, many of the materials within the collection are thought to be far older. Some of the stories can also be found in the *Book of the Buddha's Previous Existences*, usually known as the *Jataka*. This tells of the historical Buddha's 550 earlier incarnations, some of which were as animals, including an elephant, an antelope, a lion, a vulture, a rat and a quail. The *Panchatantra* spread far and wide, picking up some alternative names in the process. In some places it is known as *The Fables of Bidpai* (or Pilpai), and it found its way into the Muslim world, where it was reincarnated as *Kalilah and Dimnah*, the names of two jackals that served as advisers to the lion king. The book named after them was full of lessons in political cunning. It was translated into various languages, and in its Latin form later became the *Directorium vitae humanae* ('Guide for Human Life') written by John of Capua in the thirteenth century. John of Capua's title for his work was well chosen, because the *Panchatantra* was said to have been composed in order to teach its readers the nature of *niti*. The Sanskrit word *niti* can be translated as 'ethics' or as 'the art of living' or as 'wise conduct'. The *Panchatantra* might therefore be regarded as a piece of instruction literature that takes the form of a collection of fables. However, it is a matter of opinion as to how *ethical* some of the teachings actually are. Many of the characters who parade across the pages of fables bear a strong resemblance to the character of the trickster. The *Jataka* too can be understood as instruction literature, and there are certainly some moral tales among its stories.

Some *Panchatantra* stories have close parallels in the collection of fables attributed to Aesop. He is said to have lived in the sixth century BC, although some doubt whether such a person ever existed. If he did he would have lived centuries before the *Panchatantra* was supposedly compiled. Many of the stories attributed to him only came into existence centuries after he is supposed to have lived. Demetrius of Phalerum produced the first known book of Aesop's fables in the fourth century BC, and the extent of his contribution can only be guessed at. One of the stories with a strong resemblance to a *Panchatantra* tale tells of the ass who put on a lion's skin: 'both men and women took him for a lion and fled from him. But when a puff of wind stripped off the skin and left him bare, everyone ran up and began to beat him with sticks and cudgels.'[34] While this tale may be said to have a moral, it is not a particularly moral tale. The actions of the animal may have been ill-advised, and possibly stupid, but it would be difficult to accuse him of immorality. On the other hand, in some of the fables it is possible to accuse Aesop himself of immorality, by modern standards if not his own. His story about the cart driven by Hermes that was 'stuffed with falsehoods, wickedness and deceit' being plundered by Arabs is simply racist.[35] Some fables resemble Rudyard Kipling's famous *Just So Stories*, for example, when an explanation is given as to why kites do not sing. Most, however, are simply wry observations about life and human nature:

> A tortoise asked an eagle to teach it to fly. The eagle pointed out that it was ill-adapted by nature for flight, but the tortoise only importuned him the more. So the eagle, taking it up in his talons, bore it to a great height and let it go. It fell at the foot of some rocks and was dashed to pieces.[36]

Another famous collection of fables was assembled by the Roman writer Phaedrus (*c.* 15 BC–*c.* AD 50) and both his work and that of Aesop were later drawn on by Jean de La Fontaine (1621–1695) for his own collection of fables. One of his more entertaining efforts deals with people's inability to keep secrets. In order to test her, a man convinces his wife that he has just laid an egg, but insists that she must tell no one. Of course, she tells a neighbour, who tells a friend, and so on. And the story gains so much in the retelling that by the next day it is being said that the man had laid not one egg but a hundred! Although the wife's behaviour might be open to criticism, the moral of the tale is clearly that if you want a secret kept you should keep it to yourself. This is the wisdom born of experience.

In the Italian Renaissance, many collections of fables were assembled. However, the term then used to describe such a fable, *facetia*, indicates a shift of emphasis, because a *facetia* (pleasantry) is essentially something designed to amuse rather than instruct, although it may do both. Collections contained anything from highly moral tales to the bawdiest of jokes. Here is one of the more edifying examples from the *Book of Pleasantries* compiled by Gian Francesco Poggio Bracciolini (1380–1459):

> A conceited Milanese soldier, born of a noble line, came as an ambassador to Florence; and every day, out of ostentation, he wore various types of chains around his neck. Niccolò Niccoli, a most learned and caustic man, noticed his stupid vanity and said: 'Other madmen bear to be tied with one chain, but he is such a madman that he is not satisfied with one.'[37]

Like fables, fairy tales come in many different shapes and sizes, and many seek to make a point in one way or another. An interesting example can be found in the story of 'The Clever Farmer's Daughter', which is to be found in the collection assembled during the nineteenth century by Jacob and Wilhelm Grimm. Part-way through this short story the daughter is given a challenge by the king: 'Come to me, not dressed, not naked, not on horse, not by carriage, not on the road, not off the road, and if you do, I'll marry you.'[38] This kind of test resembles a riddle. The daughter went home and undressed, but then wrapped herself in a fishing net so that she was neither dressed nor naked.

> Then she took some money, leased a donkey, and tied the fishnet to its tail. The donkey had to drag her along so that she neither rode nor drove. And since the donkey had to drag her along the wagon tracks, only her big toes touched the ground so that she was neither on the road nor off it.[39]

The daughter succeeds because she sees that 'not dressed' and 'not naked' do not exhaust all the possibilities. Instead of being trapped by the apparent logic of the problem, she approaches the problem creatively and sees the way out. By doing so, she proves herself wiser than the king who set what he thought was an inescapable trap.

Finally, a Buddhist parable. While a fable or a fairy tale might be enjoyed purely for its entertainment value, whatever lesson it might be trying to get across, the point of a parable is purely to teach, and it teaches through making comparisons.

> Suppose . . . a man were to carry a blazing torch of grass against the wind . . . In case that man did not very quickly let go of that blazing torch of grass, would not that blazing torch of grass burn his hand or burn his arm or burn some other major or minor member of his body? and would he not, because of it, incur death or mortal pain?[40]

So what actually is the point being made here? This is one of many Buddhist parables relating to the passions. If we can see that the passions are *in some ways like* a blazing torch that is going to burn us, then we can also see that we should 'drop the torch'. If we cannot make or see the connection, then the parable is ineffective.

I have obviously looked at only a minute sample of the fables, fairy tales and parables of the world. Many of them can reasonably claim to belong to the wisdom literature of the world, although as has been seen some seem to have considerably more to offer in terms of wisdom than others. Some bear a close resemblance to works of instruction literature, and offer pithy insights dressed up in narrative form. Some, such as the less edifying observations of Aesop, are reminders of how much of what passes for wisdom is culturally based. Stories like 'The Clever Farmer's Daughter' carry within them evidence of some very old themes and traditions indeed, and continue to be read by parents to their children.

This chapter has ranged far and wide, but one certain conclusion can be reached that applies to all the world's wisdom literature: nothing we read can actually make us wise. The different works and genres examined here may encapsulate in different ways the wisdom of their authors but they are not identical with that wisdom. If all we needed to do to become wise were to read enough of the right books, wisdom would be rather more plentiful on our planet than it is. Certain kinds of writing may help to point us in the right direction, but we must always be careful not to confuse the signpost with the destination.

Even this short survey has revealed something of the variety of types of literature that tend to be associated with wisdom, and texts like the *Upanishads* are very different from Aesop's fables. The sheer *volume* of materials to draw on is itself testimony to the popularity of these types of literature, and some stories seem to have travelled around large parts of the globe for centuries, perhaps for the simple reason that so many people can make connections between them and their everyday lives.

Although most of the materials I have drawn upon in this chapter are from the distant past, not all of them are. It should not be thought that the connection between wisdom and literature is a purely historical phenomenon that died out centuries ago. Obviously opinions are going to vary, but I think a case could be made that some twentieth-century novels such as *Zen and the Art of Motorcycle Maintenance* are concerned with wisdom in their own way. Clearly the novel *as such* is not a variety of wisdom literature, but it can serve as a vehicle for wisdom in the same way that other genres can. Indeed, it has been argued that a number of Victorian novelists were specifically working within a wisdom tradition because they sought 'to express notions about the world, man's situation in it, and how he should live'.[41] Authors such as George Eliot, Benjamin Disraeli and Thomas Hardy are cited as examples of those who sought to change the ways their readers saw things. The 'wisdom novelist' does not try to argue with the reader, but to show the reader a different way of looking at things. In that fact, at least, it may be said that they share something with the sages of the *Upanishads*.

Astrology. German engraving by Virgil Solis, 17th century. The personification of astrology is shown holding a globe in her hand, and there is a crown of stars around her head. Her wings derive from an ancient association between astrology and angels.

5
Wisdom and Divination

What is divination, and what is its connection with wisdom? Dictionary definitions of divination tend to emphasize the supernatural element of the phenomenon, but while some forms of divination may involve the supernatural, not all of them do. In order to understand why this is the case, it is important to understand that there are two fundamentally different kinds of divination. The first kind is based on the idea that specific messages are sometimes sent by supernatural beings of one kind or another, either spontaneously or in response to some kind of prompt. It is this kind of divination that takes place at oracles. Someone asks a question, and a response is given, usually by or on behalf of a god or goddess. Divinities have been associated with wisdom in many ways, so the connection between this kind of divination and wisdom is not difficult to see.

However, there is a quite different kind of divination that does not rely on the supernatural at all. Palmistry is a good example. Palmists believe that there is a connection between the lines on people's hands and (at the very least) the general patterns and directions of their lives. Palmists want nothing to do with the supernatural, but believe they are practising an ancient science based on observation and experience. By way of analogy, a classic defence of palmistry argues: 'Almost all medical men admit now that the different formations of nails indicate different diseases.'[1] Palmistry may be good science or bad science, but it makes no appeal to the supernatural.

Whether you believe in it or not, there is at least a plausibility to palmistry that is harder to find in divinatory techniques such as lecanomancy. This was practised in ancient Mesopotamia, and a painting in the Villa dei Misteri in Pompeii seems to depict it. It involved a container full of water, on the surface of which a film of oil floated. Divination took place by studying the behaviour of the oil when an object was dropped into the container. Like many forms of divination, lecanomancy seems to have been based on the idea that there were networks of connections throughout the world such that the study of one part could lead to the knowledge of something else. Whereas a palm is clearly connected to the person whose palm it is, lecanomancy presumes a much broader kind of connection. And unlike palmistry, lecanomancy has to *create* something to study before it studies it. There is clearly no sense that the oil on the water *causes* anything to happen, it just provides a window on the order of the world. The basis of lecanomancy is not supernatural, but a particular way of understanding nature. The connection of this kind of divination with wisdom is perhaps less obvious, but it is there. First, it provides the same kind of insight as the other kind of divination, but by a different means. Second, and this is something I have discussed at length elsewhere, it is possible to argue for a connection between wisdom and insight into the order of the world.[2]

Before moving on to look at some particular kinds of divination in greater depth, two more general points may be made. First, it is a common misconception that divination is about looking into the future. While divination *may* be resorted to for that purpose, it is by no means its only function. Sometimes what is sought is knowledge about the present, sometimes what is sought is advice, sometimes what is sought is a decision. Divination is certainly not just about prediction. Second, even if some kinds of divination like to be thought of as sciences, some people are better scientists than others and we should not underestimate the role of the diviner in the divinatory process. Some clearly had a greater talent for their craft than others.

Astrology

If lecanomancy needs introducing to the modern reader, astrology assuredly does not; it is estimated that there are thousands of people who claim to be astrologers today in the USA alone. Astronomers tend to get very annoyed when their science is confused with astrology, so it is best to be clear at the outset as to the difference between the two.

> Astrology is the interpretation and prognostication of events on earth, and of men's characters and dispositions, from the measurement and plotting of the movements and relative positions of the heavenly bodies, of the stars and planets, including among the latter the sun and the moon. This may or may not imply belief in 'stellar influences'; it certainly implies constant and therefore usable relationships between configurations in the heavens and events on earth. Since astrology proper depends on the charting of the movements and positions of the planets, it could not arise until after the growth of mathematical astronomy.[3]

Three basic points may be made here. First, the idea that heavenly bodies may exert an influence on our planet is scarcely controversial. The tidal movements of the world's oceans provide evidence on a daily basis that they do, while more occasional phenomena like solar flares can produce geomagnetic storms that disrupt radio transmissions. Indeed, modern science is able to detect the effects of the sun on the earth in ways that ancient civilizations never could. There is nothing inherently implausible in the belief that life on earth is susceptible to outside influences. Secondly, astrology is not necessarily based on the belief that celestial bodies *influence* us at all. As with lecanomancy, it is possible to believe that the different parts of our universe are so intimately connected and bound up with each other that the study of one can shed light on another. While the heavens may offer a rather larger and more complex object of study than a bowl of water, the basic principle is the same. A relationship between celestial and terrestrial events does not have to be a causal one. Thirdly, my concern here will *not* be with celestial omens, those unusual heavenly occurrences (for example, the appearance of comets) that are thought to presage special events. The whole subject of omens will be looked at separately.

Celestial omens relate only to special kinds of change that take place in the observable sky, but the observable sky itself is constantly changing. Some changes, such as the passage of the sun, take place over a short period of time and are obvious to everyone. Other changes, such as the movements of the stars, take place over much longer periods and require far more patience to observe. (For observational purposes, the fact that it is the earth that is moving rather than the stars is irrelevant.) These changes are not random but regular, and these regularities form the bases of various calendars and ways of counting time. 'Astrology proper' requires a knowledge of the precise relative positions of heavenly bodies at any given time, which is why it can only follow in the wake of astronomy. It is the calculation of these positions at any given time that produces a horoscope. Bearing in mind that the development of astrology long preceded the invention of the telescope, it is only to be expected that a horoscope contains only a simplified picture of the heavens, emphasizing the importance of some heavenly bodies while ignoring others. Horoscopes are most commonly used to represent the heavens at the moment of an individual's birth, and so to identify the direction that person's life will take. However, they may also be used to ascertain whether a particular day is auspicious or inauspicious for an individual to undertake a particular activity, and this has led to many an astrologer being retained by many a ruler for many a century. While this might seem entirely normal in some times and places, many eyebrows were raised when it was revealed that the services of an astrologer had been retained in the White House when Ronald Reagan was president in the 1980s.

It seems possible to identify at least three different and independent traditions in astrology (although claims of independence have to be treated as carefully as claims of influence). The first is usually, although not very helpfully, referred to as 'Western' astrology. This is of mixed parentage, possibly originating in Egypt in the late first millennium BC through a coming together of Greek ideas and Mesopotamian data. The connection with Mesopotamia is evidenced in the fact that although the term 'Chaldean' technically refers to an inhabitant of southern Babylonia, it came to mean a soothsayer, and more particularly an astrologer. Greek philosophy and science, however, seem to have been the instruments whereby a mass of Mesopotamian material became converted into something far more systematic, and which has become known as 'Western' astrology. From Egypt, it travelled at least as far east as India, where it became the basis of the system of astrology known as *Jyotisha*. It also travelled into Europe, and one of the oldest surviving works on astrology is a long poem called *Astronomica* written by Marcus Manilius in the first century AD.

While the bland and vague generalizations that adorn many a newspaper's astrological column may be a far cry from a detailed personal horoscope, they are ultimately from the same stable. Fundamental to Western astrology is the notion of the zodiac, a way of dividing the sky up into twelve sections through which the sun, moon and planets travel on their various journeys. Each section, or sign, has a name deriving from a constellation within it. In their traditional order they are: Aries (ram), Taurus (bull), Gemini (twins), Cancer (crab), Leo (lion), Virgo (virgin), Libra (scales), Scorpio (scorpion), Sagittarius (archer), Capricorn (goat), Aquarius (water carrier) and Pisces (fish). 'Popular' astrology looks only at the relationship between these constellations and the sun, and assigns a period of roughly a month to each sign, representing the time it takes the sun to move through it. Aries comes first, and the sun enters it at the spring equinox on or around 21 March. 'Serious' astrology looks not only at the sun but at the moon and planets too. Both kinds assume correspondences between different signs and different personality types.

Although it may have been influenced by Western astrology at some time during its long development, Chinese astrology probably had an entirely independent origin. It seems to have had its beginnings, along with Chinese astronomy, during the period of the Zhou dynasty, which extended over the greater part of the first millennium BC. During the rule of the next dynasty, the Han (206 BC–AD 220), it arrived at what may be considered its classical form. The constellations identified and named by Chinese astronomers often differed significantly from those of their counterparts in the west. For example, what was regarded as simply the 'belt' of Orion in the west was regarded as an independent group of stars by the Chinese.

While there are similarities between Western and Chinese astrology, there are also major differences. In popular terms, the most obvious difference is that whereas Western astrology works on a cycle of twelve months, Chinese astrology works on a cycle of twelve years, each of which is given the name of an animal. In their traditional order these are: Rat, Ox, Tiger, Rabbit, Dragon, Snake, Horse, Goat, Monkey,

Rooster, Dog and Pig. The transition from one to the next takes place at Chinese New Year, which is usually in late January or early February. As with Western astrology, each of the signs represents a different kind of personality. As with Western astrology, while there may be a popular form of Chinese astrology that lays overwhelming emphasis on the year of birth, there is also a more serious one that is rather more sophisticated and subtle. Signs are also attached to different months of the year, days of the month and hours of the day. When all these are taken into account, something much more complex and subtle emerges.

The third and last astrological tradition I shall look at here belongs to Central America. As with many traditional societies, those of pre-Columbian Mesoamerica did not make clear distinctions between astronomy and astrology and their calendar was simultaneously both secular and religious. Although there were important differences between the cultures of such different peoples of the region as the Toltecs, the Aztec and the Maya, their attitudes towards astrology were broadly similar. Although they had a calendar based on the 365-day solar year, they also had another calendar based on a period of 260 days. This was broken down into thirteen periods of twenty days, each of which had its own name and character. (Some people in present-day Guatemala still use a 260-day calendar for a variety of purposes.) It seems highly likely that this system had its origin in astronomical observations of some kind, so a calendar based upon them was in a sense an embodiment or representation of the forces at work in the universe. On each of the different 260 days the combined effect of these forces was different.

The Aztec called this 260-day calendar the *Tonalpohualli*, and in it the twenty days were given the following names: Crocodile, Wind, House, Lizard, Serpent, Death, Deer, Rabbit, Water, Dog, Monkey, Grass, Reed, Jaguar, Eagle, Vulture, Motion, Flint, Rain and Flower. Alongside it they possessed a work known as the *Tonalamatl*. This gave the astrological significance for each of the 260 days, making it a kind of astrologer's ready-reckoner. However, the *Tonalamatl* in itself was not enough. Looking at the bigger picture, each cycle of 260 days took place within a bigger cycle of 52 years that had its own rhythms. Looking at the smaller picture, within each single day there was a certain ebb and flow of influences to be taken into account. The astrologers of Central America had much to think about.

Astrology, in whatever culture it appears, is often thought of as being fatalistic in outlook. What is written in the stars cannot be erased however much we try, but it is clear that the Aztec at least believed that mitigating actions could be taken. For example, if someone was born on an 'unfortunate' day, 'the fortunetellers, in an attempt to improve or even change the fate of the child, would set a favourable date for naming him.'[4] This suggests that 'fate' is something to be worked with rather than simply succumbed to. But that is certainly not the only view, and at the other extreme lies Marcus Manilius, who declared that 'The very fact that I interpret Fate in this way is ordained by Fate.'[5] In that case astrology can tell us what to expect, but cannot help us to avoid it.

Astrology tends to be a very divisive topic. Its critics angrily dismiss it as absurd, while its supporters passionately defend it as profound. Against such a background, intelligent conversation can be difficult. While many may dismiss the possibility of 'stellar influences', these are neither necessary for astrology nor intrinsically nonsensical. And doubtless 'popular' astrology does a lot to give astrology a bad name. On the other hand, just because it could work does not mean that it does.

Oracles

The term 'oracle' tends to be used in a number of different ways. For example, in Mesopotamia a number of Akkadian texts relating to the time of Esarhaddon are often referred to as 'oracles'. Many are attributed to different people from the city of Arbela, a major centre of the cult of Ishtar. Generally speaking, they seem designed to give the king general reassurance, and some almost read like gushing love letters: 'I am thinking of you. I love you very much.'[6] The assumption is that the different people are priests or priestesses of some kind, serving the cult of the goddess in Arbela. But there is no evidence that Esarhaddon had approached them with specific concerns. Consequently, I prefer to label these pronouncements prophecies rather than oracles. Oracles, to my mind, are to do with answers, and in order to get answers there must be questions.

Perhaps the most famous oracle in history was that of the god Apollo at Delphi. So famous was it in its time, and so durable has been its reputation since then, that people are often surprised to discover that it was by no means the only oracle of the ancient Greek world. But Herodotus tells a story about Croesus, the Lydian king of legendary wealth, who wanted to know if any oracles were reliable, and if so which. So he sent his envoys 'to Delphi, to Abae in Phocis, to Dodona, to the oracles of Amphiaraus and Trophonius, and to Branchidae in Milesia. These were the Greek ones he consulted, but not content with them, he sent also to the oracle of Ammon in Libya.'[7] 'Branchidae' is better known as Didyma, and is near Miletus in what is now Turkey, while the oracle of Ammon is in the Siwa Oasis of present-day Egypt. The remains of the others are in Greece, although there is nothing of the oracle of Trophonius to be found. The only one that passed the test Croesus set for them was Delphi.

But if these seven were the main ones, there were many more in Greece alone. Beyond Greece, scattered across the territories that came to make up the Roman Empire, there were literally hundreds of them, and they came in all shapes and sizes. While Apollo presided over many, he had nothing approaching a monopoly. Many were dedicated to Asclepius, the healing god, including the massive complexes at Epidaurus (in Greece) and Pergamon (modern Bergama in Turkey). Popular oracular gods in Egypt were Isis and Serapis, whose cults spread far beyond the lands of the Nile. A temple in Pergamon was thought to have been dedicated to Serapis, and is now known as the Kizil Avlu ('red courtyard'). Beneath what looks to have been a plinth for a statue is a cavity big enough to conceal a person. Similar arrangements have been found in some other temples known to have had oracles. Whether this was for hearing what questions were asked, or delivering responses through a statue, or for other more innocent purposes, is not known.

What is known is that questions were submitted and answers received in a variety of ways. At Dodona, questions were written on thin strips of lead, many of which have been uncovered. This provides useful evidence of the kind of question posed to the oracle of Zeus. Some were made on behalf of communities, including the local one: 'The Dodonaeans ask Zeus and Dione whether it is on account of the impurity of some human being that god sends the storm.'[8] Some were made by individuals seeking advice: 'Cleotas asks Zeus and Dione if it is better and profitable for him to keep sheep.'[9] Some seek information about the future: 'Leontios consults concerning his son Leon whether there will be recovery from the disease on his breast which seizes him.'[10] Some seek information about the present and recent past: 'Did Dorkilos steal the cloth?'[11] If not all human life, then at least much of it is here. Unfortunately, the answers to these and many more questions of a similar nature are not known.

In some cases, the answers are known, but not the questions. Visiting a major oracular centre such as Delphi or Dodona might be a costly and protracted affair, but luckily cheaper alternatives were often closer to hand. One was the dice oracle, where dice were thrown to produce a number or sequence of numbers, each of which had a corresponding pronouncement. This example was found inscribed on a gateway at Termessus (near Antalya in modern Turkey):

> Four sixes and the fifth a one. This is the meaning:
> Just as wolves overcome lambs, and mighty lions subdue
> Horned oxen, so shall you overcome all.
> And with the help of Hermes son of Zeus shall have all
> your desire.[12]

The number of possible responses offered by a dice oracle depended on the number of dice and/or the number of throws. A simplified version of the same idea was the letters oracle. Here there were only 24 responses to choose from (by an unspecified means), one corresponding to each letter of the Greek alphabet. A number of these have been discovered in Turkey, and two of them (those at Olympos and Limyra) have exactly the same texts. For example: 'Z: Flee the very great storm, lest you be disabled in some way.'[13] With only 24 possible ways of responding to any possible question, it is scarcely surprising if the pronouncements of the letters oracles were articulated in very general terms.

Not all the known oracles of the ancient world were in existence at the same time, and what we know about them pales into insignificance compared with what we do not know about them. What is evident, however, is that the belief in and the use of oracles was not confined to any particular place or culture. Although often thought of as an 'ancient' civilization, the Inca only came to dominate South America during the fifteenth century AD, even if their culture and empire both had many predecessors in that region. The heyday of the Inca largely came at roughly the same time as the Italian Renaissance.

Oracles played a highly significant role in the life of the Inca. From the documentary evidence it appears that no major activity, whether public or private, was undertaken without first ascertaining the divine will. Communities of any size all had their own oracles, which might take any of a variety of forms: a standing stone identified with a mythical founder; a mummified ancestor; a natural feature such as a spring and a cave. The term *huaca* was applied to any such place or object that was associated with superhuman beings or powers. The essential feature of a *huaca* was its ability to 'speak'. Those who served as mouthpieces of the divine at *huacas* often prepared for their roles by drinking large quantities of *chicha*, a kind of beer made from maize.

The *huacas* served a variety of functions. The pronouncement of a *huaca* enjoyed an almost scriptural status, and communities regarded their oracles as the authorities on, and custodians of, their particular values. At a social level, the *huacas* helped to maintain cultural norms while also serving to legitimate the political status quo. On a more personal level, the *huacas* functioned as places of pilgrimage where those who felt that their behaviour had fallen below acceptable standards might go and make their confession.

The *huacas* were in existence long before the Inca domination of South America, but just as in other areas of life, the Inca brought with them an organizational sense that their predecessors had often lacked. Representatives from the most important *huacas* were annually invited to the Inca capital at Cuzco. They were then individually questioned about the prospects for the coming year. Those whose prophecies turned out to be correct were rewarded, those whose prophecies turned out to be incorrect could expect to suffer for their mistakes.

The most important of the oracles in the Incan empire was at Pachacamac, near Lima, and its importance long preceded the empire. However, even the most important oracle could be held to account if it failed to perform. When Atahualpa, the great Inca, was being held prisoner in Cajamarca by Francisco Pizarro in 1532, a small delegation from Pachacamac came to see him:

> They were given a chilly reception by Atahualpa, who asked Pizarro to throw the priest into chains . . . Atahualpa explained why he was so angry with Pachacamac and its priest. The oracle there had recently delivered three disastrously wrong predictions . . . Atahualpa concluded that a shrine which was so fallible could contain no god, and Pizarro told him he was a wise man to reach this conclusion.[14]

Delphi and Dodona have been silent for centuries and Pachacamac has long been in ruins, but that does not mean that oracles have been consigned to history. Far from it; they are alive and well and busy in many contemporary societies. The Agagibeti people who live in the Democratic Republic of Congo use an oracle known as a *diwa* on a regular basis. The oracle, which works by rubbing two boards together, usually has as its custodian an elderly man in the community. The person with the problem visits the man and pays the appropriate fee. The man then puts the question to the oracle.

> While he addresses the oracle, he rubs two flat, palm-sized, smooth-bottomed boards together with a water and medicine mix between them. Going from the general to the particular he asks if the cause is the anger of the fathers. If the boards stick or seize (*gboke*) while he addresses them, he knows that he has identified the cause. He then asks the boards who is angry with the afflicted. The recital of names accompanies the rubbing together of the boards until they stick together, thereby identifying the particular source of affliction.[15]

Another contemporary oracular practice is *Ifa*, which is practised by the Yoruba of Nigeria, Benin and Togo. Like *diwa* it has its own specialist practitioners. The process of consultation takes place against a complex religious background and requires a number of specialist items such as consecrated palm nuts, special wood dust and an assortment of symbolic objects. Reduced to its very basics, *Ifa* involves the casting of lots in order to identify one of 256 possible outcomes. 'In effect, Ifa is saying: of the 256 possible windows looking out onto Being, this is the one before which you now stand.'[16] This helpful way of characterizing *Ifa* suggests that it is a way of locating a problem within the right context. Only when it is seen correctly can it be solved correctly. This resembles the therapeutic technique known as reframing, which invites people who are stuck with a problem to look at it from a different perspective. *Ifa* helps the person who consults it to see things differently, correctly.

Perhaps the best-known oracle in current use is not a place or a person but a book. The popularity of the *I Ching* (*Yi Jing* in pinyin) continues unabated, and far beyond its ancestral home. As with much about the *I Ching* ('Book of Changes'), its origins are obscure. The name of Fu Xi, a mythical emperor who is said to have lived in the third millennium BC, is often linked with it. So is that of Weng Wan, the founder of the Zhou dynasty at the end of the second millennium BC. His son, known as the Duke of Zhou, is also said to have contributed to its development, as well as Confucius. Whatever the truth of the matter, it is clearly a work that has a long history, even if many of the details of that history are missing.

Like *Ifa*, at bottom the *I Ching* is simply a lot oracle. Traditionally, yarrow sticks were used in the process of selection, although many people now use coins. However it is done, the process involves building up a pattern of six lines (a hexagram), each of which is either broken or unbroken. This produces 64 possible hexagrams, each of which has a name and an accompanying text that constitutes the oracle. The core of each text is the part known as 'the judgement', said to be the work of Weng Wan, to which is added a commentary contributed by his son. For example, in hexagram number 62, 'preponderance of the small', the judgement reads:

> PREPONDERANCE OF THE SMALL. Success.
> Perseverance furthers.
> Small things may be done; great things should not be done.
> The flying bird brings the message:
> It is well not to strive upward,
> It is well to remain below.
> Great good fortune.[17]

This may seem obscure, but as C. G. Jung, an admirer of the work, wrote in his foreword to it, 'If the meaning of the Book of Changes were easy to grasp, the work would need no foreword.'[18] However, we should not exaggerate its obscurity, and two basic points need to be kept in mind when reading the *I Ching*. First, it is an oracle, and so it is approached through the medium of a question. The question, in turn, provides a context for understanding the answer. Second, the basic Chinese world view is a dynamic one. The world is constantly changing, and at any given time it is changing in a particular direction. Going in the same direction brings success, going in the opposite direction brings failure. The *I Ching* is designed to help those who consult it to improve their navigational skills. As a kind of map of a moving world, the *I Ching* was regarded by many Chinese philosophers as containing great wisdom independent of its oracular uses.

The *I Ching* was not the only Chinese oracle book, and many found using it to be far too much like hard work. A number of other oracle books were created that aimed at greater ease and accessibility. One such is the *Ling Ch'i Ching* (*Ling Qijing* in pinyin). Its author is unknown, but it is thought to date from about the third century AD. The name *Ling Ch'i Ching* can be translated as 'Spiritual Chess Classic', and seems to be a reference to the twelve specially inscribed discs that are used in its consultation. Throwing the discs produces one of 125 possible outcomes. For example, 'the orphan impoverished'. The core text attached to this outcome reads as follows: 'Going out from the warmth, entering the cold, with a thin jacket and unlined clothes. Departing from my beloved mother, I suffer from this unexpected misery.'[19] The *Ling Ch'i Ching* was not so accessible as to be comprehensible without its own commentaries. One of the commentators sums up what is being said here as simply: 'All affairs whatsoever are baleful.'[20]

The world of oracles yields plenty of variety. A point that cannot be overemphasized is that oracles were not necessarily concerned with predicting the future. If the only business of oracles lay in making predictions, they would doubtless not have been as successful as they clearly have been. Every prediction can turn out to be wrong, as Atahualpa learned to his cost. But how could 'Flee the very great storm, lest you be disabled in some way' turn out to be wrong? And when Cleotas enquired about whether he should keep sheep or not, what were the options? The worst possible outcome for Cleotas is that he is advised to keep sheep, buys a flock, and then loses all his money on them. But when he returns to Dodona to remonstrate with Zeus and Dione, he might receive the reply: 'But if you had not kept sheep, things would have turned out even worse!' And how is Cleotas to prove that they are wrong?

Sometimes oracles were used simply to make decisions. For example, in the ancient kingdom of Kush (present-day northern Sudan), it was apparently the custom for the oracle of the god Ammon (at the place now known as Gebel Barkal) to choose a new king from among the eligible candidates. It need hardly be pointed out that the temptation to 'help' the oracle to come up with the desired result must have been enormous for some. Even if the gods were thought to be incorruptible, they often relied on human helpers at their oracles, and human helpers always brought with them human weaknesses. One particular human weakness is the need for reassurance, and in the end that is all many people went to the oracles for.

Dreams

Was there ever a time when human beings did not have dreams? Their vividness can make it hard to believe that they are meaningless, yet their frequency makes them anything but unusual. Indeed, so prevalent is the practice of dreaming that it is difficult to believe that there has been any human society at any time that has not reflected on where dreams come from and what they mean.

In those cultures where dreams are thought to have significance, there is a temptation to actively seek them out. This practice is known as incubation, and is evidenced from many different times and places. The cult of the healing god Asclepius had incubation at its very core. Those who sought out its sanctuaries would spend the night, after all due preparation, in a special place called an *abaton*, hoping that the god would communicate with them in some way during sleep. According to the second-century AD writer and hypochondriac Aelius Aristides, Asclepius himself would sometimes appear in a dream and give instructions that needed no interpretation. On occasions such as this, what we are dealing with is simply an oracle that functions through the medium of dreams, and the dream element is secondary. If a god speaks directly through a dream, no interpretation may be required at all. What I want mainly to focus on here is those dreams that require interpretation in order to be understood, and these will mainly consist of dreams that 'just happen'.

But why do they happen? The study of dreams goes back a long way and a number of very old texts are known that seek to deal with dreams in a systematic way. The *Oneirocritica* or *Interpretation of Dreams* by Artemidorus of Daldis is not the oldest such text, dating only to the second century AD, but it has the virtue of being relatively complete and draws on materials that are a lot older. In the first part of the book he distinguishes between what he calls *oneiros* and *enhypnion*, with the former bearing on future matters, and the latter relating only to current concerns. The latter are simply a continuation of the thoughts of the day, and of no interest for divinatory purposes. If I am preoccupied with something during the day, it is not surprising if I dream about the same thing at night. On the other hand, some dreams point directly to future events, while others point more indirectly. It is the second kind here that provides the major grist for the mill of the dream interpreter's art, and Artemidorus is quite clear that it *is* an art. Works such as his own can only take the interpreter so far. The complexity of dreams means that their different elements can often be combined in different ways and so yield different meanings. It is down to the art of the dream interpreter to make the best sense of the material available:

> In this way, then, one should interpret all complicated dreams, collecting and combining each of the main points into a complete whole. In judging a dream, therefore, one must imitate the diviners. For they know how each individual sign fits into the whole and base their judgments as much on the sum total of the signs as on each individual sign.[21]

This is easier said than done because many signs have more then one possible interpretation, and all these have to be taken into account. When many signs with different possible interpretations are found in combination, many different readings are possible. This is one of the reasons why interpretation is an art. Artemidorus articulates a number of basic principles that underlie this art. First, it is necessary to have a knowledge of the dreamer as well as of the dream. Second, 'it is a basic principle that everything that appears in accordance with nature, law, customs, profession, names, or time is good, but everything that is contrary to them is bad and inauspicious.'[22]

Implied rather than stated is the idea that the sounds of the names of things are important, and a number of interpretations seem to be based on plays on words. For example, it is difficult to understand why Artemidorus should imagine that there could be any kind of relationship between fishing rods and conspiratorial plots unless it is also understood that the Greek word for one is *dolones* and for the other *dolous*.

This play on words may seem like a minor issue, but in fact it reflects a major truth about dream interpretation. For a dream to mean something there must be some form of code according to which its meaning can be unlocked. If a dream bore its meaning on its surface, it would not need to be decoded. Encoding is a means by which something is made to stand for something else. One of the ways in which this may be done is by the use of homonyms, words that sound the same but have different meanings. English has many of these, such as 'yolk' and 'yoke' or 'medal' and 'meddle'. In each case there is no difference in sound, but there is a difference in meaning. Because they sound the same, one may be used as a substitute for another (though two words that are pronounced the same in one dialect of a language may not necessarily be pronounced the same in another). There is no suggestion that homonyms are the only means by which dreams may be decoded, but it is important to note that because homonyms are specific to a particular language (or even a particular dialect of a particular language), they will usually disappear altogether in the process of translation, rendering an obvious association in one language totally obscure in another.

Artemidorus points to a basic division between those dreams that are good and those that are bad. This idea is embedded in an Egyptian dream book written some 1,500 years before his time. Confusingly, some of the interpretations offered in the book suggest that the underlying meaning is often the opposite of the surface meaning. For example, if a man dreams of himself dying violently, this is good because it means that he will outlive his father. If he dreams of himself eating excrement, this is good because it means he will enjoy his own possessions in his own home. If a man dreams of having sex with a woman, that is bad because it signifies mourning. However, if the woman is his sister, that is good because it signifies affluence. With regard to this last point, it may be noted that in ancient Egypt marriage between brother and sister was often practised by royal families, so there is doubtless a cultural element coming in here.

Another dream book survives in fragmentary form from ancient Assyria. Some connections between what is dreamt and what is foretold seem reasonably obvious: 'If a man travels repeatedly beyond the borders of his country: he will become important.'[23] Some are more difficult to fathom: 'If he eats the meat of a beaver: rebellion'; and 'If one gives him a wheel, he will have twins.'[24] It may be noted that this 'If . . . then' format is typical of the Mesopotamian way of recording omens. Indeed, much of Mesopotamian dream interpretation can be seen as simply transferring the understanding of omens to the understanding of dreams.

Simply multiplying examples of how different cultures have understood different dreams would add little of weight to the discussion. The belief that dreams contain messages about the future encoded in various ways has been widely held throughout human history, and the evidence for that is overwhelming. But dreams may contain other messages too. At the beginning of the twentieth century another book entitled *The Interpretation of Dreams* appeared, and this one was written by Sigmund Freud. Freud's study of dreams was certainly not a wholly new beginning, and he pays tribute to earlier writers on the subject, including Artemidorus. By calling his book *The Interpretation of Dreams*, Freud was self-consciously setting himself against those who insisted that dreams were meaningless. On the other hand, many of the associations that dream interpreters of the past had introduced into their art were pure fantasy. Freud believed that dreams were meaningful, but that their interpretation could and should be put on a scientific basis. The emphasis here is on the word 'scientific'. Those who visited Freud with their problems were encouraged to tell him all their thoughts, and among these thoughts were their dreams. Freud came to the conclusion that these dreams were connected to their problems. 'It was then only a short step to treating the dream itself as a symptom and to applying to dreams the method of interpretation that had been worked out for symptoms.'[25] Freud therefore concluded that dreams were *meaningful*, but what they meant had everything to do with the dreamer and nothing to do with the future. Because dreams occurred in a time and place when the conscious mind was not in control, they revealed many things the conscious mind preferred to hide.

For Freud, dreams reveal what our deepest wishes are, and these turn out to be mainly about sex. Whether Freud was right or wrong in this specific conclusion is less important than the general point that he presented dreams as a kind of mirror in which we can see ourselves. 'Know thyself!' was one of the inscriptions set up at the temple of Apollo at Delphi and that was held to encapsulate the kind of wisdom associated with the god. For Freud, dreams provided a path to this self-knowledge.

The extent to which Freud was breaking new ground is a matter of opinion. Joseph Kaster suggests that the interpretation applied by the Egyptians to the dream of dying violently, namely that the dreamer 'will live after his father dies', was

> An excellent bit of intuitive psychoanalysis, over 3,000 years before Freud. The dreamer, as a result of his unconscious and repressed wish for his father's death, fulfils in his dream the consequent wish for his own violent death as expiation for his overwhelming guilt.[26]

Whether or not this particular interpretation is correct, some of the more obscure dream interpretations to be found in the works of antiquity may make more sense if they are given a psychological twist. In the end, the desire to derive meanings from dreams may be difficult to resist, but there is plenty of room for disagreement over what those meanings actually are.

Omens

Omens are signs of future events and come in all shapes and sizes. The study of omens is the search for patterns, regularities and correlations in the way the world works, so that when we see one thing, we know what is likely to follow it. Some of these have found their way into popular sayings, so: 'Red sky at night, shepherd's delight; red sky in the morning, shepherd's warning.' A red sky in the evening is an omen of good weather to come the next day, but a red sky in the morning is an omen of bad weather to follow the same day. Although they do not have to be, omens tend to be divided into 'good' or 'bad' depending on the perceived desirability of what they portend. Clearly for those for whom the weather is important, knowing what to expect is a great boon. To the extent to which they are at all reliable, omens about the weather usually have an ultimately scientific basis that explains the connection between the sign and what it is a sign of.

The basic structure of an omen links what is known as a *protasis*, which is the sign, with an *apodosis*, which is the outcome. How the two are linked is not always clear or obvious. There is no requirement that the protasis be the actual *cause* of the apodosis, only that there be a connection of some kind, however tenuous, however remote. Many superstitions are based on a belief in omens, a belief that some things are a sign of 'good luck' and others a sign of 'bad luck' that will manifest itself in some unspecified way.

For some reason there are many British superstitions surrounding black cats, perhaps because witches were often thought to keep them. In some countries black cats were thought to be demons, or even witches who had turned into cats. This sometimes made the life of a black cat a very precarious affair, and mass killings were not unknown. However, the ways of superstition can often be unpredictable:

> At Scarborough, a few years back, sailors' wives liked to keep black cats in their homes, to ensure the safety of their husbands at sea. This gave black cats such a value that no one else could keep them; they were always stolen.[27]

This was written in 1866, and clearly refers to a golden age for black cats in the north of England. However, there seem to be as many British superstitions linking black cats to *good* luck as there are linking them to *bad* luck, which illustrates the extremely frail basis of many a superstition.

Omens played an important role in everyday life in ancient Mesopotamia. The significance attached to them led to thousands of them being recorded, catalogued and analysed. Obviously, if two notable events occurred in close proximity to each other it was tempting to see a connection of some kind between them. Because the ancient Mesopotamians were keen observers of the skies, many of their omens related to celestial events, although potentially anything that was observable might function as an omen of *something*. But omens were about more than just the conjunction of events. They revealed the gods at work in the world, and the omen was regarded as a god's principal channel of communication with humanity.

While the first collections of omens may not have had any particular shape, it soon became apparent that the materials could be catalogued in different ways. For example, it would be possible to put all omens relating to sheep into one group and all those relating to donkeys into another. Then it would be possible to divide the donkey omens into those with one donkey, those with two donkeys, and so on. Eventually, what would be produced would be a kind of catalogue of the different things in the world, along with what they signified as omens. And that is essentially what happened.

Different collections of omens might use different ways of ordering their materials (a black cat could be filed under 'black' or 'cat'), but individual omens always appeared in the same format: 'If this (protasis) then that (apodosis)'. Works on dreams follow much the same structure, which is hardly surprising since dreams can be regarded as a vehicle for omens. It is not clear how much difference was attached to whether something was seen in waking life or in a dream. What is clear from works on dreams, both Mesopotamian and Egyptian, is that omens were not regarded as the last word on anything. What they foretold was not necessarily unavoidable. Because omens were messages from the gods, it was possible for the gods to change their minds. A Sumerian text contains a prayer to the god Shamash that includes the line 'Change the dream I had into a good one!'[28] Omens could therefore be treated as warnings that something would happen unless something were done to prevent it.

This is a view articulated by Cicero in his work *On Divination*: 'unfavourable auguries . . . are not the causes of what follows: they merely foretell what will happen unless precautions are taken'.[29] Augury was a Roman institution, with its own college. The college advised on matters of state, and it was the task of the augurs to consult the god Jupiter when his views were sought on whether something should or should not be done. Perhaps because Jupiter was a sky god, the observation of the flight of birds across the sky was one of the ways in which augurs sought for the desired omen. It was not the business of the augurs to make predictions, only to ascertain whether or not Jupiter was prepared to give his approval. A special viewing platform in Rome was reserved for their use in this activity.

Roman armies were often a long way from Rome. If their leaders needed to ascertain the will of Jupiter, sending back to the college of augurs for a pronouncement was far too time-consuming, so they took sacred chickens with them. When an omen was required, they were fed and how they ate constituted the omen. Cicero wryly noted that the simple expedient of keeping the birds hungry virtually guaranteed that they would eat in a certain way. If an omen is fixed in this way, it clearly cannot be seriously regarded as a message from Jupiter. By Cicero's time (first century BC), many traditional systems of divination had evidently fallen into disrepair and disrepute in Rome.

The general term for seeking omens in the behaviour of animals is alectryomancy, and it is still practised, despite the best efforts of Roman generals to give it a bad name. Whether or not people actually believe in it, Groundhog Day is an institution in the USA. How long winter will last supposedly depends on whether or not the animal sees its own shadow on 2 February.

Cicero makes the point that omens can be either spontaneous or provoked. Like dreams, they can be things that 'just happen', or they can be intentionally triggered. There is no obvious or logical reason why omens should not manifest themselves absolutely anywhere, but clearly when people go *looking* for omens they go looking in particular places. Some oracles seem to have functioned as places where omens could be sought. Near Monemvasia in southern Greece stand the remains of the ancient city of Epidaurus Limera. Here there was an oracle of the goddess Ino, which delivered omens at the time of her annual festival. The means of obtaining omens was an unusual one. Loaves of bread were baked with barley flour and cast into a sacred pool. If a loaf sank, it was a good omen, because the goddess had accepted the offering. If it floated, it was bad because she had not.

It would be interesting to know the extent to which the skills of the local bakers influenced the outcome of this particular process. However, physical locations such as the sites of oracles were not the only places in which omens could be sought.

Looking in Unusual Places

Human beings have looked in all kinds of places for omens and oracles, including some very surprising ones. An early method of divination practised in China involved the bones of animals. Specialists in this art seem to have existed as early as the third millennium BC, but it was during the period of the Shang dynasty in the late second millennium BC that the practice really came into its own. It was also during this time that the use of turtle shells as an alternative to animal bones seems to have been introduced. The basic technique was the same in both cases: intense heat was applied and this led to cracks appearing in the shell or bone. It was the diviner's task to read the messages conveyed by these cracks. The main animal bones used were shoulder bones, and many have been preserved, often with an inscription recording the question that was asked. This method of divination, sometimes called pyromancy because of the use it made of fire, was resorted to constantly by the Shang rulers to ascertain the will of their great god Shangdi.

One of the more curious methods of divination, at least to modern eyes, is haruspicy (also known as extispicy), which involves examining the entrails of dead animals, and in particular the liver. This was widely practised in ancient Mesopotamia, while in Europe the Etruscans were credited with its invention, and they attributed it to Tages. Tages was a legendary Etruscan figure who had one day emerged from the ground, taught the people various things, including haruspicy, and then disappeared back into the ground. He was seen as the founder of Etruscan culture.

An interesting reason as to why the insides of animals seemed like a good place in which to look has been suggested by a modern writer who decided to try it out for himself: 'I discovered that if you pull the liver out of a freshly slaughtered lamb, it will act as a perfect mirror; I could see my face in it clearly for fifteen or twenty minutes, after which it went dull and ceased to be a reflector.'[30] The fact that entrails can act as a natural mirror in which things can be seen may go some way towards explaining their use in divination. However, there is clearly more to it than that. Models of livers used either in the divinatory process, or for training people in the process, have survived from both Mesopotamia and Italy. They clearly show the liver divided up into different sections, and presumably unusual features that showed up in any of these sections would have their own particular significance. Clearly the liver was not just used as a mirror, it was an object on which various messages could be written for those with the ability to read them.

If few people living today have any experience of haruspicy, the situation is quite different with aleuromancy. Although the word may be unfamiliar, anyone who has broken open a fortune cookie in a Chinese restaurant has engaged in the practice. Aleuromancy seems to have originated in China, and is a very old method of divination. In its earliest manifestations, it seems to have involved philosophical texts being baked into cakes. The divinatory aspect clearly comes from the act of choosing a particular cake and so receiving a particular text. Something similar was practised in ancient Greece. The fortune cookie is simply an updated version of the same idea. The basic idea survives in a number of customs from all over the world concerning food. To give an example from my own experience, it used to be a common practice to put one or more coins into a Christmas pudding. Being served a portion with a coin in it meant good luck. My grandmother, who may have been descended from Roman generals, used to contrive things so that *every* grandchild was *always* served a portion with a coin in it!

Another method of divination that continues to be practised in the modern world is bibliomancy. This involves picking a page and passage at random from a book and interpreting it as an omen. Although the book does not need to be a sacred one, religious texts are commonly used in this practice, and for Christians this usually means the Bible. The idea that religious texts provide guidance in life is a commonly held one, and bibliomancy is a means of identifying the specific bit of advice relevant to a particular situation. Although the Christian churches have not generally been admirers, let alone advocates, of divination, bibliomancy has been quietly tolerated, and sometimes even encouraged, for centuries. The use of the *I Ching* and other Chinese oracle texts can be seen as a form of bibliomancy.

Cartomancy is another divinatory practice in use in many places today and involves the use of cards. Although any cards may be used, specialist tarot ones are often employed. By definition, divination through the use of cards cannot have begun before their invention, and no one can agree on where or when they were invented. Claims that the tarot goes back 6,000 years jostle for position with claims that it is a relatively recent development. Whatever the truth about the tarot, it is apparent that divination through the use of cards goes back at least hundreds of years.

In aleuromancy and bibliomancy an existing text has only to be selected in some way by the enquirer. In cartomancy a 'text' has to be produced. However they are used, the cards do not speak for themselves and someone has to extract a meaning from them. The same might be said of tasseomancy. Originating in China, tasseomancy involves looking for, and interpreting, patterns made by tea leaves in a cup. Whatever the tests using inkblots that were developed by the psychiatrist Hermann Rorschach actually mean, they clearly demonstrate that people can read very different things into patterns. Depending on one's point of view, practices such as cartomancy and tasseomancy use various patterns to stimulate either the imagination or the psychic powers of the reader. In either case, more seems to depend on the reader than on the patterns.

Because anything could potentially be an omen, anything could potentially be used in a method of or as an adjunct to divination. Nevertheless, it is difficult to understand how some forms of divination were ever actually thought of, let alone put into practice. A case in point is clidomancy:

> Using clidomancy, the psychic writes a description of the crime that has been committed onto a key. The key is tied to a Bible or other holy book, and both are hung from the finger of a virgin. The movement of the key and the book, determined by a formula, forecasts the guilt or innocence of the accused.[31]

It hardly seems necessary to add that this method of divination only worked when the sun or moon was in Virgo! Yet, however unlikely it may seem, clidomancy was practised in medieval Europe.

Many more examples could be given, but I think enough have been put forward to demonstrate the variety of methods that have been devised and used in divination, and some of the odd places in which people have decided to look in their pursuit of omens and advice. While I have no reason to believe that clidomancy has any living practitioners, and haruspicy has at most a few, many other practices not only survive but thrive.

Shamanism

From methods and places I turn now to a special group of people who are associated with divination. The word 'shaman' comes from the Tungus language of Siberia. The term 'shamanism' has been invented to try and capture a set of beliefs and practices associated with shamans, although to do so is difficult. While the word may come from Siberia, recognizable forms of shamanism can be found scattered across the world and history. The extent to which these may have shared or separate origins is a matter of speculation. There is evidence of shamanism surviving from the Stone Age. The paintings discovered at the Lascaux grotto in France in 1940 are thought to depict scenes connected with shamanism, and they are conservatively dated to 14,000 BC. Clearly shamanism had plenty of time to expand its influence before recorded history began.

There is no shamanism without the shaman, and the role of the shaman is 'to journey to other worlds and to use revealed knowledge for a positive outcome. In this way, the shaman is an intermediary between the gods and mankind.'[32] The shaman is portrayed as a traveller between worlds, but how he (it is usually a 'he') does so is another matter. The sceptic would deny that the shaman ever actually goes anywhere, while the believer would insist that his travels are not imaginary but very real. In some cultures, shamanism is closely associated with the use of certain psychotropic drugs such as mescaline (derived from the peyote cactus) and psylocibin (the active ingredient in what are popularly known as 'magic mushrooms'). Both the cactus and the mushrooms grow in Mexico, a part of the world with strong shamanic associations. The use of the word 'trip' to describe some drug experiences may suggest a similarity to the shaman's altered state. In one sense the drug taker does not actually 'go' anywhere, but because of some drugs' ability to alter perceptions, the experience is one of being in another place, another world.

Aldous Huxley experimented with mescaline and wrote of his experiences in *The Doors of Perception*: 'What the rest of us see only under the influence of mescaline, the artist is congenitally equipped to see all the time. His perception is not limited to what is biologically or socially useful.'[33] The title of his book is taken from some lines written by William Blake in 'The Marriage of Heaven and Hell':

> If the doors of perception were cleansed every thing would appear to man as it is, infinite.
>
> For man has closed himself up, till he sees all things thro' narrow chinks of his cavern.[34]

And this in turn is an allusion to the story of the cave told by Plato. It must be stressed that while the shamans of some cultures certainly make use of drugs, this is by no means always the case. What *does* always seem to be the case is that the shaman is able to enter an altered state of consciousness akin to the religious ecstasy reported by mystics. Chemicals provide one means of entry to this state, but not the only one.

However it happens, the shaman is a person who somehow sees more than other people do, who is aware of, and in contact with, dimensions of existence that other people are not. Whether understood metaphorically or literally, the shaman goes on a journey to a realm that is inaccessible to other people. This other realm is far from empty. On the contrary, it is full of spirits, and shamans usually have their own spirit guides to help them navigate their way through it. These spirit guides often take on animal form. Sometimes the shaman himself takes on animal form for his journeys through the spirit world.

The purposes of these journeys may vary, and largely depend on the shaman's role in a particular society. Typically the shaman is a healer, but healing may not be his only function. The shaman may also go to the spirit world as a representative of his community. The ability of the shaman to bring messages from the spirit world back to his community gives him a role similar to that of the culture hero. The resemblance of the shaman to the hero goes much further than this. Joseph Campbell suggests that the typical structure of the heroic adventure has three basic parts. First there is the departure (which is usually subsequent to a call of some kind), then there is the initiation, then there is the return.[35] The departure and return is the basic structure of the shamanic experience, while the call followed by initiation seems to be how people become shamans. Sometimes 'the call' is little more than the expectation that the son will follow in his father's footsteps. Sometimes it comes in a very different and much more dramatic way. Black Elk, a shaman of the Oglala Sioux, tells of seeing two human figures descending from the sky summoning him to his vocation. But the summons is usually only just the beginning. There is usually a process of initiation to go through in order to become a shaman, and this may involve a ritual death and rebirth. Among the Aranda of Australia, a candidate for shamanship has to wait outside a particular cave. He then goes through a ritual in which he is 'killed' and taken into the cave. Once inside the cave, spirits replace his internal organs with new ones. He emerges from the cave literally a new man.

Interest in shamanism received a major boost in the late 1960s and early 1970s when two very different books appeared. *The Teachings of Don Juan* by Carlos Castaneda purported to be the author's adventures with a shaman in Mexico, while *Shamanism: Archaic Techniques of Ecstasy* certainly was a weighty academic treatment of the subject by Mircea Eliade. Opinions continue to be divided over the accuracy and authenticity of Castaneda's book (and those that followed it), but Eliade's work has been extremely influential in making shamanism a subject for serious study. Michael Harner's *The Way of the Shaman* (1980) is more practical than either and acknowledges its debts to both. For Harner, shamanism is above all about healing, even though his initial drug-induced visions and experiences among the Conibo people of Peru had nothing to do with healing. To tie this in more specifically with wisdom, it might be said that the shaman has access to sources of wisdom, but what he does with that wisdom is another matter. Similarly, the subtitle of Eliade's book emphasizes techniques of ecstasy, not uses of ecstasy.

When we turn from means to ends, the figure of the shaman becomes less exotic and more familiar. Many societies have their 'wise men' and 'wise women' to whom people turn for healing, advice and help of all kinds. Shamans perform all these functions, but in a rather more dramatic way than many of their counterparts.

Divination Today

Although it has a long history, divination is not just about remote places and distant times. In all kinds of ways it is still very much part of everyday life for millions of people all over the world. Two case studies may illustrate this basic point. Both come from the late twentieth century and give some insight into how the consultation process can work.

The first comes from Chichicastenango, a town in the highlands of Guatemala. Linda Schele was invited to visit Sebastian Panjoj, who is an *Ah Q'ij*, or diviner, as well as a local magistrate. On two tables he has a variety of objects including candles, coins, flowers and odd bits and pieces such as a broken watch. There were also several stones of all shapes and sizes. Most of them were quite small and dark, but some were crystals. He had acquired many of them during the 260 days he spent going through the initiation process to become an *Ah Q'ij*. (The period of 260 days is an important one for the Maya.) There was also a quantity of red beans. He asked for a question, and a fee of 5 quetzals (about one U.S. dollar).

> He gathered all the beans together in a single pile and pushed them around by running his fingers through them with a turning motion of his wrist. Then he gathered a group of them with his fingers and pulled them away into a second pile. He did not count them, but seemed to *feel* when he had enough. He arranged the beans and crystals in groups of four until he had two rows lined up on the table.[36]

Apart from asking a few questions, nothing more was done other than gathering the beans together and spreading them out into patterns again, an act that was repeated a few times. Then he gave his response to the question that had been asked, which was 'utterly unexpected, but eminently satisfactory'. He also offered to conduct a ritual at a later time 'to counteract the problems he had detected through the beans'.[37] The whole process took only a few minutes. Another took much longer, mainly because the *Ah Q'ij* asked a lot more questions then. While certain powers seem to have been ascribed to the stones, it is not clear that the beans constituted anything more than something physical to work with.

The second comes from the Wourbira area of Burkina Faso, where some of the Lobi people live. The client visits a *buor*, or diviner, and is shown to a special room. The *buor* opens his divining bag and takes out various objects, including a bell and cowrie shells. He invokes God and the spirits and asks if he may proceed. Unlike the Guatemalan example, the *buor* asks the client no questions. The questions are addressed to the spirits. The *buor* holds the client's right hand in his left one, and the movement of the hands signify the answer to the question. Most questions are designed to be answered by a 'yes' or a 'no', so much depends on the *buor*'s skill in asking the right questions. The diviner uses his right hand to toss cowrie shells onto the floor from time to time in order to check that he has understood things correctly. The way they fall determines whether he has or not. Most possible ways in which the shells can fall mean a 'no' answer, so the checking process is rigorous. 'After the diviner has gathered the most important information, he turns the questioning over to the client, who until then has remained silent.'[38] The client may have to remain silent for quite some time, because in a typical consultation the *buor* may ask hundreds of questions. The outcome of the session is normally that the *buor* will pass on to the client specific commands that have been issued and confirmed by the spirits. Whether clients choose to obey them is entirely for them to decide.

I do not propose to go into any deep analysis of these examples, but a few basic points may be noted. On the face of it, the approach taken by the *Ah Q'ij* is more intuitive and that taken by the *buor* more systematic. While the divination carried out by the *Ah Q'ij* certainly takes place within a religious context, the *buor* explicitly addresses the spirit world in a way that the *Ah Q'ij* does not. The method of the *Ah Q'ij* is opaque, that of the *buor* transparent. And the *Ah Q'ij* can deliver answers before the *buor* has even found out what the question is! But the *Ah Qi'ij* takes on a continuing role in trying to help fend off any negative anticipated outcomes, whereas the concerns of the *buor* end as soon as the client walks away from the consultation. It seems that both continue to do good trade.

People resort to divination for many different reasons. Often it is for little more than reassurance, and that demand is easily met. But for millennia many human beings have wanted more than that. They have resorted to divination in order to give themselves an edge in dealing with the vagaries of fate. Knowing what to expect makes it easier to deal with whatever happens, and if something undesirable lurking in the future can be avoided altogether, so much the better. More than that, insights into the future can be highly profitable. The long-standing human desire to be ahead of the game continues, and there are plenty of people who are happy to feed that desire.

> Today the predicting business is a multibillion-dollar industry providing employment to hundreds of thousands of people . . . Each year the prediction industry feeds us with $200 billion in (mostly erroneous) information. The forecasting track records for all types of experts are universally poor.[39]

As a matter of fact, most of those who make forecasts get them wrong most of the time. No wonder Cato found it difficult to understand how two soothsayers could meet in the streets of Rome without bursting out laughing. The fact of the matter is that those who write newspaper columns offering expert tips on the stock market or horse racing have about the same success rate as those who write the astrology columns. It would be interesting to see how well an *Ah Q'ij* or *buor* would do against the tipsters.

Those who have written about divination from a social anthropological point of view emphasize the role that diviners play in society. Where divination is respected and valued, those who control the machinery of it inhabit positions of considerable influence. If decision-making is guided by divination, the diviner's hand can be seen in many things. The influence of ancient institutions such as the oracle of Apollo at Delphi can be gauged by the number and size of the treasuries various Greek cities built in the vicinity of the temple there. The prestige was immense, the power was immense, and the wealth was immense. It was not the fact that the Reagan White House had consulted an astrologer that worried Americans. Lots of them do the same in one way or another. The worry was over the potential influence the astrologer had on government policy.

Divination can also play an important role in reinforcing and defending a society's *values*. This was certainly one of the functions of the *huacas* in the Inca empire. When a diviner is asked what someone should or should not do, then they are clearly being asked to give reassurance on what is acceptable as well as advice on what is possible. The word of a diviner who purports to bring a message from a god or spirit cannot be dismissed as mere opinion. Diviners in some societies are as influential in shaping people's sense of what is and is not appropriate behaviour as agony aunts are in some others.

Divination does not necessarily have to depend on the idea that gods and spirits of various kinds are sending us messages. Some practices and cultures rely more on the idea that there is an order at work in the world, and that parts can tell us about the whole. But whether we are thinking of messages from the divine, or an understanding of how the world works that penetrates far below surface level, we are still in the world of wisdom.

Pythagoras. This depiction of Pythagoras in discussion with a shepherd is by the 16th-century Italian artist Giulio Bonasone. There was a long-standing belief that Pythagoras invented the term 'philosopher', putting him at the very beginning of the history of philosophy. Many different traditions claimed him as one of their own. It is highly unlikely that he had anything to do with the celebrated theorem of geometry to which his name has become attached.

6
Wisdom and Philosophy

There was an ancient tradition that the term 'philosopher' was invented by Pythagoras. It literally means 'a lover of wisdom', and the lover of wisdom was devoted to 'the contemplation and discovery of nature'.[1] Although it may not have been the only thing that occupied their minds, we know that many of the earliest figures from the history of the Western philosophical tradition devoted much of their time to trying to understand the basic principles underlying how the world worked. Because the Greek word for nature is *physis*, the study of nature became known as 'physics'. Although we now regard this as a science, for centuries it was a part of philosophy, and was sometimes known as 'natural philosophy'.

According to Cicero, Socrates 'was the first to call philosophy down from the heavens . . . and compel her to ask questions about life and morality and things good and evil'.[2] Although Socrates was certainly not the first to do this, we know he took an interest in questions about how people should live their lives. This area of enquiry became known as 'ethics', from a Greek word meaning 'character'.

Many of those who came after Socrates divided philosophy into three parts. To 'physics' and 'ethics' they added 'logic' (from a Greek word meaning 'thought' or 'reason'). This third part of philosophy was concerned with how we can know things, and with how we can reason and argue correctly. Different philosophers had different views on which of these three was the most important and how they fitted together. However, between them 'physics', 'ethics' and 'logic' were for a long time widely agreed to cover what philosophy was.

To amplify this point, it may be noted that philosophers have frequently disagreed with each other over what philosophy is, and that makes philosophy a somewhat unusual area of study. Furthermore, although 'philosophy' means 'the love of wisdom', not all philosophers have even been interested in wisdom, let alone in love with it. It can come as a surprise to discover how often 'wisdom' fails to get into the indexes of books about philosophy. It was not always so.

Pythagoras, Heraclitus and Empedocles

Western philosophy is often said to have begun with Thales of Miletus, one of the Seven Sages of Ancient Greece, but some said it began with Pythagoras. A book of Greek wisdom literature declares: 'The first philosopher is Pythagoras. He was one of the ascetic learned men, one of the great philosophers, and one of the most eminent ancients.'[3] Despite his undoubted importance, so many stories and legends grew up around Pythagoras that in time even his very existence came to be doubted. However, it seems certain that he was born on the island of Samos and around 530 BC moved to southern Italy, where he spent the rest of his life. He attracted a community of followers around himself, and so Pythagoreanism may be regarded as the first genuine organized school in the history of Western philosophy, although in modern terms it might resemble something more like a sect or a cult. Like many cults, it had a reputation for secrecy, making an accurate reconstruction of its beliefs particularly difficult.

The name of Pythagoras is best known today because of the theorem in geometry to which it has become attached. In fact, it is highly unlikely that he had anything to do with it. On the other hand, it is not in itself implausible, because the belief that numbers were the key to understanding the basic principles and nature of the universe was a distinguishing feature of Pythagoreanism. The Pythagoreans also believed in the transmigration of souls, and it is said that Pythagoras himself could recall several of his previous human lives. A soul that inhabited a human body might return to an animal one, however, and this may be why the Pythagoreans practised vegetarianism. Some of their other dietary practices are a little more difficult to fathom, and there has been a great deal of speculation over the centuries as to why

Pythagoras might have prohibited his followers from eating beans. Some of their non-dietary practices seem to amount to little more than superstition: 'Putting on your shoes, start with the right foot; washing your feet, with the left.'[4]

The idea that Pythagoras was an ascetic is not unreasonable, given the number of prohibitions, dietary and otherwise, associated with his school. The reputation for being learned is also attested to by one of his younger contemporaries, Heraclitus. While acknowledging that Pythagoras was extremely widely read, Heraclitus nevertheless also criticized him for being a dilettante. The implication seems to be that while Pythagoras may have possessed a breadth of knowledge, there was a lack of depth. It seems that Heraclitus saw in Pythagoreanism a certain degree of eclecticism that left him unimpressed. He also accused Pythagoras of certain unspecified misdemeanours. Exactly what he had in mind is unknown, but the early Pythagoreans were certainly not always popular with their neighbours. Indeed, Pythagoras and his followers seem to have been thrown out of Croton, the first place where they established themselves in southern Italy, and were forced to move elsewhere.

Pythagoras is said to have written nothing, but many sayings came to be attributed to him. Some of these dealt with wisdom, including the observation that 'Wisdom is the medicine of souls.'[5] Such a view, if Pythagoras held it, was certainly not unique to him. On the contrary, the saying sums up the view of many ancient philosophers. What is far more distinctive about Pythagoreanism is its emphasis on number, and the belief that the order of the world is essentially a mathematical one. Whether or not he deserves the credit for it personally, the name of Pythagoras has long been associated with this truly revolutionary idea about how the world works.

Whatever he may have to tell us about Pythagoras, Heraclitus deserves a mention in his own right. He came from Ephesus and seems to have led a largely uneventful life there. A number of sayings are attributed to him, some of which are easier to understand than others. He clearly enjoyed making his points in a paradoxical way, for example: 'Sea is the most pure and the most polluted water.'[6] But the hidden meaning of this observation is soon revealed: sea water is palatable and healthy for fish, but undrinkable and unhealthy for humans. What appears to be a contradiction on the surface is revealed not to be one when things are looked at a little more deeply. The most famous observation attributed to Heraclitus also concerns water. The statement that we can never step into the same river twice is again puzzling on the surface. But if by 'the same' we understand 'identical', the meaning quickly becomes plain. Water does not stand still in a river bed but flows along it, so that at any given point it is constantly changing. If we twice step into a river at the same place, the water we step into the second time is not the same water we stepped into the first time. This celebrated image encapsulates a central idea in the philosophy of Heraclitus: the world we live in is constantly changing. In another sense, however, we do step into the river twice, because the ever-changing water flows between banks and over a bed that remain constant, so it is true to say that 'We step and we do not step into the same rivers.'[7] Just because the world is constantly changing does not mean that it is chaotic.

It may be said that the world according to Heraclitus is one of constant change within the limits of order, and the limits of order are also the limits of reason. In one of his more obscure sayings, Heraclitus observes that 'the wise is one, grasping the knowledge of how all things are steered through all.'[8] It is clearly possible to interpret this saying in more than one way, but I am tempted to see in it the idea that wisdom is connected with understanding the fundamental process of ordered change that underlies and drives everything in the world. That would bring the philosophy of Heraclitus close to the world view of the *I Ching*. In another obscure saying he states that 'One alone is wise, unwilling and willing to be called by the name of Zeus.'[9] Part of this seems to suggest that wisdom is divine; the real problem lies in understanding what the other part means. Is there a human wisdom that is, by definition, not divine? Or is there a wisdom that lies beyond divine wisdom? The answer seems to me to be the former. Although translations differ, another saying attributed to Heraclitus is 'Men who are lovers of wisdom must be inquirers into many things indeed.'[10] If humans could never approach wisdom, surely such enquiries would simply be futile?

Finally in this section I shall turn to another ancient philosopher, Empedocles (*c.* 494–*c.* 434 BC). He came from a town in Sicily called

Acragas (now known as Agrigento) and was a younger contemporary of Heraclitus. Although the evidence is at best inconclusive, some thought him to have been a follower of Pythagoras. There was a tradition that not only had he been one, but also that he had betrayed the school's secrets. While this is not impossible, what we know about Empedocles suggests that he was far too much of an individualist to become a member of anyone else's movement. He also seems to have possessed an unusually wide variety of skills: 'Empedocles represents . . . a very old type of personality, the shaman who combines the still undifferentiated functions of magician and naturalist, poet and philosopher, preacher, healer and public counsellor.'[11]

Many colourful tales are told about Empedocles, including how he met his death by jumping into the crater of Mount Etna. His reputation as a philosopher, however, derives from fragments of two major works by him that have survived. The first, entitled *On Nature*, seeks to explain the world in terms of four basic elements: earth, fire, air and water. Alongside these elements are two basic principles, which he calls 'love' and 'strife'. While love unites, strife divides, and these seem to be understood as dynamic forces that either bring together or disperse the elements. The second work, called *Purifications*, attributes human woes to the practices of animal sacrifice and meat-eating. These contaminated the human race and made it impure. As with Pythagoreanism, the source of his vegetarianism is a belief that souls can be, and are, reincarnated in a variety of life forms. Like Pythagoras, he recalls some of his own previous incarnations, which included a fish, a bird and a bush.

If the human condition is understood as one of impurity, then escape from it comes through a process of purification, hence the title of his second work. Empedocles suggests that it is possible for souls eventually to go beyond all these reincarnations and become immortal gods. He also suggests that this is what has happened to him. In what are thought to be the opening lines of *Purifications* he refers to himself as 'an immortal god, no longer mortal', someone who is 'revered by men and women' who follow him 'in their thousands' seeking advice, prophecies or healing.[12] Empedocles seems to believe that the way to immortality is through purification and the way to purification is through wisdom. Through a profound understanding of the situation in which we find ourselves, we can work out how to escape. Understood this way, I believe there are significant similarities between the philosophy of Empedocles and both Buddhism and Gnosticism.

It is possible to agree with Cicero that Pythagoras, Heraclitus and Empedocles were all concerned with 'the contemplation and discovery of nature'. What each of them sought to do was to get below the surface of nature and see what really made the universe tick. Number, change, love and strife emerge as possible answers. Although our knowledge of all these early philosophers is at best sketchy, they were clearly concerned with more than just accumulating scientific knowledge about the world. Understanding how the world works gives us our best chance of living in harmony with it. This seems to be at the heart of what they took to be wisdom.

Socrates, Plato and Aristotle

Three of the most famous philosophers in the history of Western philosophy are Socrates, Plato and Aristotle. According to the oracle of Apollo at Delphi, Socrates (469–399 BC) was the wisest person of his time. Socrates came to two conclusions. First, if he was the wisest person of his time then human wisdom was not up to much. Second, such wisdom as he had seemed to be based on an awareness of his own limitations, especially where knowledge was concerned. It may be noted that 'Know your limits!' is one of the interpretations that has been attached to the famous 'Know thyself!' inscribed on the temple of Apollo at Delphi. Self-enquiry may be expected to reveal what we are not as well as what we are. The wisdom of Socrates becomes humility when applied to himself, but when applied to others it is a challenge either to defend a claim to knowledge or abandon it.

Because Socrates wrote nothing, most of what we think we know about him comes from the writings of others, and in particular his own pupil Plato (*c.* 428–*c.* 348 BC). Plato depicts a man who is constantly questioning and frequently irritating. The dialogues of Plato are full of episodes where someone confidently engages Socrates in a discussion, only to walk away after a while, totally deflated.

Unlike Socrates, Plato wrote a lot, and over a long life. His views on many matters have to be pieced together from various observations scattered across his works, and different people tend to piece them together in different ways. On the subject of wisdom, two important points stand out in Plato's philosophy. First, he seems to have been the first to think of wisdom as one of the four 'cardinal virtues'. The other three were courage, moderation and justice. Those who possess these stand out as exemplary and highly developed human beings. Of the four, wisdom is the most important. Second, wisdom is also what brings human beings closest to the gods. By becoming as godlike as possible, we escape as far as is possible the limitations and dark side of the human condition. It is easy to see how some of those who took their inspiration from Plato, such as St Augustine of Hippo (AD 354–430), developed a very spiritual understanding of wisdom.

Plato's pupil Aristotle (384–322 BC) took things in a different direction. A central idea that runs through his thinking is that 'wisdom is knowledge of certain sorts of principles and causes.'[13] So wisdom is a kind of knowledge, but it is not to be confused with ordinary factual knowledge. Wisdom, we might say, is more about the 'why' than the 'what'. When Aristotle says that the wise person 'has knowledge about all things as far as possible',[14] he is not thinking of some kind of amazing encyclopaedic knowledge stored in a vast memory. Far from it. What he is thinking of is a profound understanding of how the world works, or, to repeat a phrase I have used before, what makes it tick. A simple example may help to make the point. It would be possible for someone to memorize *pi* (π) to 100 decimal places (and people have done it). For someone who understands the *principle* of *pi*, however, it is not necessary to memorize 100 digits, because the sequence of numbers can always be created anew. Once basic 'principles and causes' are grasped, any number of particular facts or phenomena can be understood as deriving from or produced by them. This does not happen automatically, however, and some may understand principles in an abstract way without grasping what they mean in practice. For Aristotle, wisdom requires *both* the understanding of the principles *and* the ability to derive practical conclusions from them.

For Aristotle, the wise person is unusually self-sufficient in life. The study of the basic principles and causes that make the world tick is essentially its own reward and brings a level and kind of psychological satisfaction that cannot be found elsewhere. It is perhaps in the writings of Aristotle that we first find a clear and explicit link made between wisdom and contentment. Wisdom is not just useful or interesting, or something with which to impress other people, it is also what makes life most worthwhile and satisfying. This seems to me to be a significant development in the philosophical approach to wisdom. By making the possession of wisdom something *enjoyable*, Aristotle seems to make it something a bit more human, and at the same time provide an obvious reason why we should seek it.

Because we rely heavily on the writings of Plato to understand the thought of Socrates, it is not always easy to know where one ends and the other begins. However, if Socrates thought of wisdom as something that really belongs only to the divine, and Plato thought of it as becoming godlike, for Aristotle it seems to have been something much more human, however rare. Finally, it may be noted that later generations found Socrates, Plato and Aristotle convenient names to which to attribute a multiplicity of supposedly wise sayings, whether or not they were consistent with the philosophies they espoused.

Antisthenes, Zeno, Epicurus, Pyrrho and others

A handful of philosophical movements dominated thinking about wisdom for hundreds of years. Apart from those founded by Plato and Aristotle, the most famous were Cynicism, Stoicism, Epicureanism and Scepticism. Although these terms are still familiar today, they have changed in meaning somewhat over the centuries. The aim here is to go back to the beginnings of these movements and focus mainly on their founders. It has been noted that wisdom was sometimes called 'the medicine of souls'. Following through with this metaphor, it may be said that each of these four philosophical movements produced its own diagnosis of the human condition, and its own cure for it. It may be helpful to keep that in mind as we look at their ideas, beginning with the Cynics.

Antisthenes came from Athens and was a younger contemporary of Socrates, with whom he was friends. 'People, he concluded, live as if in a constant state of intoxication, immersed in a thick and darkening cloud of fog.'[15] Like many who have contemplated the human condition before and since, Antisthenes was convinced that we are often led astray by our desires and instincts, which have the ability to drown out or dominate the more rational side of our nature. The distinctive dimension that he brought to bear on this problem, however, was a distrust of customs and conventions. Antisthenes believed that we often act on the basis of what custom and tradition say we should do, but he also believed that custom and tradition often point us away from what reason and human nature would have us do. These beliefs go to the heart of what became the Cynic philosophy. Because custom and tradition are in many ways the warp and weft of social life, the Cynic philosophy is often seen as an anti-social one, and it is true that Cynics tended to live on the edges of society, because that is where they felt most comfortable.

The term 'Cynic' derives from a Greek word meaning 'dog', and 'the dog' seems to have been a nickname given to Antisthenes. Even though we know the ancient Greeks kept dogs as pets, it is not assumed that this nickname was ever intended to be a compliment. At least two possible interpretations of the term suggest themselves. First, a dog that is a pet brings animal behaviour into a human context. Second, a dog that is a scavenger lives on the fringes of human society, neither at the centre nor too far removed from it. The Cynics, it might be said, did both. They lived like animals within human society, but at the same time criticized it from the fringes. They were in society, but not of it. Later Cynics developed the literary genre known as the diatribe, in which they launched their attacks on those who went astray by thoughtlessly following social convention.

An early convert to Cynicism (and according to some the first real Cynic) was Diogenes of Sinope who reputedly said: 'Ever since Antisthenes set me free, I have ceased to be a slave . . . He taught me what was my own, and what was not my own. Property is not my own. Kindred, relations, friends, reputation, familiar places, association with others, all these are not my own.'[16] In the Cynic philosophy we can see the association that Aristotle made between wisdom and self-sufficiency taken to new and extreme lengths. Over time the Cynics developed a kind of minimal uniform, consisting of just a cloak, a staff and a leather satchel, by which they outwardly demonstrated their inner indifference to what most people valued. Diogenes famously lived in a barrel for several years, spurning any kind of home comforts. According to one story told about him, he used to carry a cup and a bowl around, but came to see that they were surplus to his requirements and threw even them away. It is tempting to see in the Cynics' attitude towards property and possessions echoes of New Testament teachings in which a life of poverty is commended. The comparison is not a fanciful one and it is entirely possible that Jesus had encountered Cynic teachings. The town of Gadara, which lay no more than 25 miles from Nazareth as the crow flies, produced a number of celebrated Cynics.

Crates of Thebes (*c.* 365–*c.* 285 BC) was a follower of Diogenes, and he seems to have been the originator of what became a kind of Cynic slogan: 'Life in accordance with nature'. This could mean different things to different people, and to Crates and his wife Hipparchia one of the things it meant was not respecting any social conventions relating to sex. Not surprisingly, this led to the couple being at the centre of a good deal of scandal. One of the people Crates influenced was Zeno of Citium (334–262 BC), although he seems to have been unimpressed by the more anti-social elements of Cynicism. But he took the slogan 'Life in accordance with nature' and used it as the foundation for a new philosophy. This philosophy acquired the name of 'Stoicism' because Zeno used to teach at a building in Athens known as the painted stoa. Zeno himself was originally from Cyprus, and according to one story told about him arrived in Athens as the result of a shipwreck.

For Zeno, life in accordance with nature certainly did *not* mean behaving like animals. He believed that life in accordance with nature was only possible for those with an extensive knowledge of nature, so whereas the Cynics largely turned their backs on learning, the Stoics embraced it. According to a later Roman Stoic, Seneca (*c.* 4 BC–AD 65), it was vital to have 'learned the laws of life as a whole and . . . worked out a proper judgment about everything'.[17] This echoes Aristotle's observation that the wise person 'has knowledge about all things as far as possible', and is to be interpreted in much the same way. What is required is not a detailed knowledge of every minute fact but a fundamental understanding of how everything fits together, how the world works, and, crucially for the Stoics, what leads to what. Such knowledge is at the heart of the Stoic conception of wisdom, but acquiring it is not an end in itself.

Zeno substantially accepted the Cynics' diagnosis of the human condition, but proposed a different cure. For Zeno, the point of studying nature was in order to find out what was impossible, what was inevitable, and what fell between the two. For him 'nature' was not how animals lived and behaved but rather how the world worked. The practical purpose of acquiring this knowledge was aptly and succinctly summed up by another Stoic, Epictetus (*c.* 55–*c.* 135): 'Some things are up to us and others are not.'[18] For Zeno, human misery was the result of wanting what we cannot have and not wanting what we do have. He came to the conclusion that events in the world unfold according to a cosmic plan and that our role in these events is essentially a passive one. Very little of what happens in the world is actually 'up to us', but it is very much up to us to decide how to react internally to these external events. Put very simply, if we are pleased by what happens we are happy, if we are displeased by what happens we are unhappy. These reactions are up to us, so each of us has a personal choice between happiness and unhappiness. The point of gaining knowledge of how the world works is in order to be able to anticipate what is going to happen next, and so be in a position to welcome it. Knowing what is going to happen does not in itself do away with unhappiness, but knowing that what is going to happen is *inevitable* makes acceptance of it the only rational response. Stoic wisdom lies not only in knowledge of how the world works, but also in the optimal management of the emotions in the light of that knowledge. Just as Diogenes claimed to have been set free by the philosophy of Antisthenes, so the vocabulary of slavery and liberation can also be applied to Stoic philosophy. Perhaps the most succinct summary of Stoic philosophy came from Spinoza (1632–1677): 'when a man is a prey to his emotions, he is not his own master.'[19]

Like the Stoics, the followers of Epicurus (*c.* 340–*c.* 270 BC) believed in the value of knowledge, but they had a different kind of knowledge in mind. Epicurus was convinced that a great deal of human suffering was the direct result of human ignorance. People are upset by things that they fear, but they fear things because they do not understand them properly. For example, in a letter to a friend, Epicurus addresses a common human fear, that of death: 'Get used to believing that death is nothing to us . . . since when we exist, death is not yet present, and when death is present, then we do not exist.'[20] This may sound like a play on words but Epicurus was entirely serious. Death is not something that happens to us, because by the time death comes we have already gone. More than 2,000 years later Ludwig Wittgenstein (1889–1951) made the same point in much the same way: 'Death is not an event in life: we do not live to experience death.'[21]

For Epicurus, death was but one of many things that, once understood, could be faced with equanimity. The most compact summary of the Epicurean philosophy was produced by Philodemus of Gadara (*c.* 110–*c.* 35 BC) and goes as follows:

> Concerns about gods and death you must scorn;
> The good can be had, the bad can be borne.

This pithy observation is known as the *tetrapharmakon* (a Greek word meaning 'four-part cure'), and was the remedy put forward by Epicurus to address the human condition. Perhaps because he suffered from very poor health, he understood 'the good' and 'the bad' very much in terms of the absence or presence of pain. 'The good can be had' because it is possible to organize our lives in a suitably sensible way so that we encounter no more pain than is absolutely necessary. Epicurus founded a community called The Garden, and perhaps the organization of one's life along these lines is easier if it is done in a community of like-minded individuals. And 'the bad can be borne', because whatever pain is unavoidable can be dealt with. Epicurus distinguished the physical sensation of pain from the mental anguish that routinely accompanied it. The point he was trying to make was dramatically illustrated in a scene from the film *Lawrence of Arabia*. Lawrence (played by Peter O'Toole) puts out a match with his finger and thumb. When another person asks him how he does it, he replies, 'It's a trick.' When the other person tries it himself, he exclaims 'It hurts!' To which Lawrence replies: 'The trick is not minding that it hurts.' And it seems that Epicurus himself may well have been a master of this 'trick', having declared that the wise man can be happy even when undergoing torture. We see here something very different from the kind of wisdom that Socrates thought could belong only to a god. In the hands of both the Stoics and the Epicureans, wisdom is primarily about managing one's life in such a way that suffering is reduced to an absolute minimum.

The final founder of a philosophical movement I want to look at here is Pyrrho of Elis (*c.* 360–*c.* 272 BC). The movement is sometimes known as Pyrrhonism in his honour, but Pyrrhonism tends to be seen as a particular case of a more general philosophical outlook known as Scepticism. It may be noted that Zeno and Epicurus were close contemporaries of each other, whereas Pyrrho was a little older and more a contemporary of Aristotle. There is another more specific possible connection between Pyrrho and Aristotle because Aristotle was the tutor of Alexander the Great (356–323 BC), and Pyrrho may have travelled with Alexander's army on its campaign through Persia and India. Indeed, it has been suggested that Pyrrho's thinking was much influenced by the Indian, and specifically Buddhist, thinkers he met along the way. The suggestion is entirely plausible, but also unproven. It is also recorded that Pyrrho was a painter for part of his life, although not a particularly successful one.

By all accounts Pyrrho himself wrote nothing, but he had a prolific pupil in Timon of Phlius. Timon seems to have embraced the role of polemicist and propagandist, and wrote works that both praised Pyrrho and poured scorn on others. He famously dismissed Zeno as being no better than a stupid Phoenician fishwife (Zeno's family originally came from Phoenicia). Piecing together what Pyrrho actually thought, as opposed to what others thought he thought, is not easy, but the general position with which he has clearly become associated is this: we should suspend judgement on any matter regarding which we cannot be certain; and we are rarely, if ever, entitled to be certain. The cry of the Sceptic is always 'Yes, but . . .'. For every opinion there is a contrary one, and for every piece of evidence there is a conflicting one. The Sceptics set great store by the fact that things can seem different to different people at different times in different places and under different conditions. So, out of all these different appearances, who is to say how things really are? Consequently, the role of the Sceptic was never to assert but always to question, never to propose but always to challenge.

Scepticism is still around, but today it tends to be seen as something that is concerned only with raising doubts about claims to knowledge. For Pyrrho and his followers, however, that was nothing more than a means to an end. Pyrrho's diagnosis of the human condition was that a great deal of suffering had its origins in attachments to beliefs. If we believe a thing to be true and it turns out not to be, we are upset as a result. If we suspend judgement as to whether things are true or not, we make ourselves immune to this kind of upset. This is the therapeutic dimension of ancient Scepticism. The wisdom of the Sceptic lies in declining to believe whatever is not established beyond doubt, including the evidence of one's own senses. Unless there are compelling reasons to do so, the Sceptic declines to hold any fixed views on anything. An amusing story is told about Pyrrho. It is said that his friends had to follow him around to make sure he came to no harm, because if he came to a cliff he might doubt whether it was really a cliff at all and walk straight over it. The fact that he lived a long life makes it unlikely that this story is true. Or else he was incredibly lucky.

Antisthenes, Zeno, Epicurus and Pyrrho taught and embodied four different philosophies, but they all had the same basic outlook on the world. For all of them, the point of philosophy was to address the problem of human suffering, and for each of them wisdom, however understood, was the solution.

Wisdom and Islamic Philosophy

It comes as a surprise to many to discover that Islamic philosophy is essentially 'Western'. Some of the territories outside Arabia into which the armies of Islam first ventured (in West Asia and North Africa) were those in which the philosophical heritage of Greece remained strongest. Over time a substantial process of intellectual assimilation took place, assisted by translations of Greek and Latin texts into Arabic. A good example of how Islamic and 'Western' philosophy were intertwined can be found in the case of Ibn Rushd (1126–1198). Known outside the Islamic world as Averroës, he produced a string of commentaries on the works of Aristotle during the twelfth century. Translated into Latin, they had a significant influence on the thought of Thomas Aquinas (*c.* 1225–1274) in the thirteenth. And while Aquinas is thought of as indisputably 'Western', he came from near Naples, which lies some way to the east of Cordoba, the home town of Ibn Rushd. However, like Aquinas, Ibn Rushd approached philosophy from within a religious tradition founded on monotheism, and this gave both of them a significantly different outlook from the earlier Greek philosophers who lived in a world inhabited by a wide variety of gods and spirits.

Muslim philosophers never had a single settled view on wisdom (philosophers do not do unanimity well), but there were some widely shared ones. While a few broadly identified philosophy (*falsafa*) and wisdom (*hikma*), most did not. For those who did not, wisdom was seen either as being in parallel with philosophy or as superior to it in some way. And for those who saw it as superior, it was either different but better, or else something broader of which philosophy was itself a part. For many, wisdom was connected in some way or another with mysticism. As a subject in its own right, mysticism will be discussed in the next chapter. Here it will be considered only in the context of what a selection of Muslim philosophers thought of the relationship between philosophy and wisdom.

One of the greatest of Muslim philosophers was Abu Hamid al-Ghazali (1058–1111). He was a man of great learning, born in what is now Iran. By the early age of 34 he had become a professor of theology in Baghdad, and enjoyed an enormous reputation as a scholar. The more he studied, however, the more convinced he became that reason could only take the human mind so far in the pursuit of the profoundest truth. This led to him going through some form of personal crisis, as a result of which he abandoned his post and became a recluse and religious ascetic. Years of withdrawal were followed by years of wandering and teaching, and for a while he was once again a professor, this time at Nishapur.

Both during his teaching and his itinerant years he produced many substantial works on which his fame now primarily rests. The title of the most famous is usually translated as *The Incoherence of the Philosophers* (although Henri Corbin has suggested it would be better translated as *The Self-destruction of the Philosophers*). The basic quarrel of al-Ghazali with the philosophers can be summarized as follows:

> Many of their particular arguments are logically false and the various positions that they take in their system as a whole are inconsistent with one another, but, above all, because some of their basic assumptions are unfounded.[22]

As criticisms go, these are pretty damning ones. It is important to note that al-Ghazali was not against philosophy as such, and he was certainly not against reason as such. What he was against was bad philosophy and bad reasoning. At bottom, his main argument against philosophers is that they try to make reason go too far, they try to make reason prove what it cannot possibly prove. Their desire to do so is what frequently leads them into making unfounded assumptions.

Fortunately, reason is not the only route to knowledge. Alongside it al-Ghazali puts faith, but this too has its limits. The route to the highest form of knowledge is through direct experience, and by this is meant not *sense* experience but *mystical* experience. It is through mystical experiences that the profoundest truths of the universe are revealed. Ibn Rushd responded to *The Incoherence of the Philosophers* with a work known as *The Incoherence of the Incoherence*, but others were to find al-Ghazali's ideas more palatable. One of these was Shihab al-Din Suhrawardi (*d.* 1191), who made fully explicit the connection between mystical experience and wisdom.

Suhrawardi also came from what is now Iran. His most celebrated work was entitled *Wisdom of Illumination*, which deals with the wisdom revealed through mystical experience. Suhrawardi does not claim this wisdom to be anything new. On the contrary, he lists many names from the past of others who have attained it. Originally revealed to Hermes (or Enoch, or Idris), it was passed down through chains of sages that included Pythagoras and Empedocles, Asclepius, Zarathustra, a number of Persian kings, Plato and Aristotle. The idea that esoteric knowledge *has* to be directly transmitted from one person to another is often encountered, and Suhrawardi produced an extremely impressive, and eclectic, list of predecessors.

Given the number of philosophers on the list, it is evident that Suhrawardi had no problem with philosophy as such, but simply wanted to put it in its proper place. The highest knowledge cannot be attained through philosophy alone, but neither, it seems, can it be attained by mysticism *alone*. There are levels of illumination, and more is seen by those (like Pythagoras, Plato and Suhrawardi himself) who are adepts in both philosophy and mysticism than by those who limit themselves to one field or the other. The movement started by al-Ghazali and developed by Suhrawardi was sometimes known as the 'new wisdom' school, reflecting a new synthesis in Islam of philosophy and mysticism.

The last philosopher I shall consider in this section is Sadr al-Din Shirazi (*d.* 1641), usually and better known as Mulla Sadra. Again from Iran, he became famous as the head of the School of Isfahan. It is said that he died when returning from his seventh pilgrimage to Mecca, having walked all the way there and back each time. Like Suhrawardi, his approach was naturally eclectic. He 'believed in the unity of truth transmitted in an unbroken chain from Adam down to Abraham, the Greeks, the *Sufis* of Islam, and the philosophers'.[23] However, he introduced an interesting twist as far as the Greeks were concerned, because he identified two quite distinct traditions within their philosophy: 'one initiated by Thales of Miletus and culminating in Socrates and Plato; the other initiated by Pythagoras, who received instruction in wisdom from Solomon, whom he met in Egypt'.[24] The idea of Pythagoras and Solomon meeting in Egypt to discuss wisdom is, to say the least, a fascinating one, however historically unlikely. Mulla Sadra was also influenced by Ibn al-Arabi, whom he regarded as the most important of the Sufis. It was a matter of faith for Mulla Sadra that the 'beacon of prophecy' had played a crucial role in leading all the sages on his list to wisdom.[25] In this way it was possible to maintain that a fundamental unity underlay the apparent diversity displayed by the list.

I have been unable to do adequate justice to the imagination, erudition and sophistication of the three thinkers mentioned here, but I hope some sense has been gained of their significance and how they advanced the thinking on wisdom within the Islamic tradition. All three came from places that fall within the borders of present-day Iran. A very different philosophical tradition flourished further east.

Wisdom and Chinese Philosophy

I have used the pinyin system to transliterate Chinese names and terms in this book, but Confucius and Mencius are too well known in those forms for there to be any point in changing them here. However, it may be noted that in their pinyin forms, Kongzi and Mengzi, the *zi* element is not a name, but a title meaning 'Master'. And where other names or terms may be commonly encountered in transliterations other than pinyin, I have indicated the principal alternative form.

Just as in English the words 'sage' and 'wisdom' have two quite different origins, so in Chinese there is *sheng* (sage) and *zhi* (wisdom). Because Chinese philosophy tends towards the concrete and the practical, it also tends to take a greater interest in the sage as an embodiment of wisdom than in the abstract concept of wisdom itself. Because *sheng* and *zhi* have different roots, however, we cannot simply say that the sage is the person with *zhi* (*chih*). It may also be noted that the Chinese character for wisdom includes the character for knowledge. So wisdom is related to knowledge, but not identical with it. It goes without saying that different Chinese philosophers and philosophical schools had different ideas concerning both *sheng* and *zhi*, and no more can be done here than to give an overview of the topic along with a handful of examples.

Probably the most famous Chinese philosopher is Confucius (551–479 BC). He came from near the town of Qufu, where there is still a temple dedicated to him. Tradition had it that he had a hand in the development of the *I Ching*. Many sayings were attributed to him, although it is impossible to know how many actually originated with him. Among his observations on wisdom we find the following: 'The man of wisdom delights in water; the man of humanity delights in mountains. The man of wisdom is active; the man of humanity is tranquil. The man of wisdom enjoys happiness; the man of humanity enjoys long life.'[26] This needs some careful unpacking because the Chinese word *ren* (*jen*), which is translated here as 'humanity', is not without its difficulties. Other translators have used other English terms such as 'benevolence', 'perfect virtue', 'man to manness' and 'human heartedness'. It is not easy to extract a common core from this range of alternatives, but perhaps *ren* is better understood as something that embraces all these things and more: 'Its meaning is far wider than mere benevolence or even altruism; rather, it is the root of them.'[27] Understood as a kind of love for all humanity, *ren* seems very similar to what Buddhists would recognize as compassion (personified in Chinese Buddhism as the goddess Guan Yin). For Confucius, the acquisition of wisdom is not in itself sufficient for someone to become a sage; there has to be compassion as well. Whatever the differences between 'the man of wisdom' and 'the man of humanity' may be, they are not irreconcilable because they are synthesized in the sage.

Mencius (fourth century BC), a later follower of Confucius, articulated what he called the theory of the 'Four Beginnings' to explain why wisdom was one of the things within the grasp of every human being. 'The feeling of commiseration is the beginning of humanity; the feeling of shame and dislike is the beginning of righteousness; the feeling of deference and compliance is the beginning of propriety; and the feeling of right and wrong is the beginning of wisdom.'[28] So while few may become sages, all human beings have the potential to do so, because that potential is part of human nature. This belief in the fundamental goodness of human nature was a key and distinguishing feature of the philosophy of Mencius, and it may be noted that for him wisdom was intrinsically connected with the notions of right and wrong.

But if we are all potentially sages, why do we not all actually become sages? A much later Confucian, Wang Yangming (1472–1529), sought to answer this question: 'The reason is that, while the original substance of the mind is originally correct, incorrectness enters when one's thoughts and will are in operation.'[29] Over the course of our lives we acquire various opinions and develop various preferences. These help to distort our perceptions of the world and make us act in all kinds of unwise ways. The solution to the problem is to make the mind 'free from selfish desires' and 'completely identical with the Principle of Nature'.[30] By the 'Principle of Nature' Wang Yangming means a kind of innate knowledge that is part of human nature and possessed, however deeply it may be buried under our accumulated mental junk, by all. When we have cleared away everything that obscures it, the Principle of Nature shines through and naturally shapes and guides our actions. The way to wisdom lies within.

Confucianism was but one of many ancient Chinese philosophies. Another that is far less well known today is usually called Moism after the name of its founder, Mozi (Mo Tzu). In Moism, the notion of the will of heaven plays an important role: 'The sage kings of the Three Dynasties . . . were those who obeyed the will of Heaven and obtained rewards. The wicked kings of the Three Dynasties . . . were those who opposed the will of Heaven and incurred punishment.'[31] The era of the Three Dynasties spanned the period between roughly 2500 BC and 250 BC, and many of the figures from that time belong to legend rather than history. It was a common practice in Chinese philosophy to associate wisdom with specific past rulers, and the further in the past they were the better, because their antiquity enhanced their authority.

Mozi did not share the optimism of the Confucians concerning human nature. While Mencius (who may have been a contemporary) believed that the beginnings of wisdom lay within, Mozi believed that they lay without. While it is not entirely clear how Mozi understood 'the will of heaven' in metaphysical terms, its practical function was to provide an external source of moral values, and it was the will of heaven that everyone should love everyone else. Those who followed the will of heaven acted correctly and compassionately. The sage kings both enacted laws and conducted their foreign policy according to the will of heaven. This meant that inside the state there was justice and outside the state there was peace between it and its neighbours. Furthermore, because following the will of heaven was not only the right thing to do but also the most beneficial thing to do, those who followed it did well while those who went against it did badly. Because following the will of heaven was what transformed a king into a sage king, it must be presumed that it was also what transformed an ordinary person into a sage.

If Mozi is now largely forgotten, the names of Laozi (Lao Tzu) and Zhuangzi (Chuang Tzu) are rather better known. Their names are also the titles of the books the two men are said to have written, although the work attributed to Laozi is more often known as the *Tao Te Ching* (also as the *Laozi*). Of Laozi himself nothing is known, but Zhuangzi is thought to have been a contemporary of Mencius. Together they are the regarded as the founding philosophical fathers of Taoism.

The *Tao Te Ching* is a notoriously difficult text, densely written and subject to many different interpretations. In it we find the following lines:

> When the great Tao declined,
> The doctrines of humanity and righteousness arose.[32]

It is curious to see humanity and righteousness discussed in terms of decline, but they have to be seen in the context of the Tao. The notion of the Tao is an elusive one, even though it is at the centre of all Taoist thought. The word literally means 'way', and the imagery of water is often used to give expression to it. Just as a river naturally finds its way between its banks and along its bed without having to make any effort to do so, so the Taoist sage effortlessly and instinctively follows life's path. When people develop the doctrines of humanity and righteousness, it means that they are having to think about their actions instead of just doing things spontaneously. That is why the very existence of those doctrines is seen as a symptom of decay.

The same point is made in a more explicit way by Zhuangzi: 'My description of being wise has nothing to do with benevolence and righteousness, it is that one should be led by one's innate nature, nothing more.'[33] At least one way of interpreting this is that wisdom comes through self-knowledge, and self-knowledge brings knowledge of the Tao. This bears some similarity to the teaching of the *Upanishads* and the belief that what the sages experience is *Brahman* as known through, or as, *atman*. There are also echoes of the cry of the Cynics and Stoics that we should seek a 'Life in accordance with nature'. For Zhuangzi there is something artificial and forced about benevolence and righteousness, and they serve as distractions from the real thing, which is the Tao.

Because the Tao itself is such an elusive concept, many Taoist writings focus on the more concrete figure of the sage. A work known as the *Huainanzi* (of unclear authorship but probably from the second century BC) contains a number of observations about sages that help to fill this figure out a little. 'When everything goes naturally, what does a sage have to do?'[34] Because the sage has no personal desires or ambitions, there is no reason to intervene in events. The sage adapts to events, but does not seek to shape them. Sages 'are not wedded to conventional customs and are not influenced by people'.[35] However, the actions of sages are not without their effects: 'When sages do good, it is not as a means of seeking honor, yet honor follows; it is not in hopes of gain, yet gain results.' But they tend to remain shadowy figures: 'Sages conceal their good deeds and keep their benevolence anonymous.'[36]

This brief discussion has been sufficient to show something of the variety that exists within Chinese philosophy concerning both sages and wisdom. Perhaps the only common theme to emerge from the Confucian, Moist and Taoist writings is the esteem in which the figure of the sage is held.

Wisdom and Indian Philosophy

There are a number of problems to be faced in exploring the world of wisdom and I want to use the specific context of Indian philosophy to explore one particular problem. This is the problem of translation. In assembling materials from many different times and places, many different languages are encountered. It would have been possible, but probably unhelpful, to reproduce all these materials in their original languages and let the reader try to make sense of them. In some cases, I could have made my own translations, but in most cases I have had to rely on the translations of others.

Translation has always been an art as much as a science. Such are the obstacles facing translators that their successes are far more surprising than their failures. Anyone who has encountered the howlers and gibberish that may emerge from computer translation software knows all too well how easy it is to get a translation wrong. One of the problems facing translators is that words in one language rarely map neatly onto words in another. Furthermore, words do not exist in isolation, but belong to networks of associations of various kinds. It has already been observed that the interpretation of dreams may draw on associations that exist between words that sound the same but which have quite different meanings. The way in which words are linked in this way will vary from language to language. This is one of the reasons why the translation of puns is so difficult.

In Indian philosophy *Prajnaparamita* means 'perfection of wisdom', with the *prajna* element meaning 'wisdom'. However, *prajna* is not always translated as 'wisdom'. It can also be found translated as 'intelligence', 'direct intuition' and 'conscious intensity'. On the other hand, *prajna* is not the only word that translators render as 'wisdom'. It sometimes appears as a translation of *vidya* (which can also be rendered as 'philosophy' or 'knowledge') or *viveka*. A more common translation of *viveka* is 'discrimination', which is to be understood in its original sense rather than in the prejudicial sense it often carries with it today. Discrimination is the ability to distinguish between things that are different. In the context of Indian philosophy it may specifically mean 'the spiritual knowledge which discriminates between spirit and non-spirit',[37] or between the real and the unreal, or between the permanent and the impermanent. If *prajna* can be translated as 'intuition', it is easy to see why *viveka* can be translated as 'wisdom'. There is a shared sense of a profound knowledge of the nature of reality (however that is to be understood) that is achieved through some kind of direct insight or intuition (whatever that process is). This seems to be the core of what the Indian philosophers regarded as wisdom. And once we can identify the *kind of thing* Indian (or other) philosophers think wisdom is we can look for the *same* kind of thing elsewhere, irrespective of what people may call it.

It is also important to remember that words have histories. Just because *prajna* meant something at some time does not mean that it meant the same thing all the time. This is not just a fact about the languages we translate from, it is also a fact about the language we translate into. The meaning of the English word 'wisdom' itself is not fixed. Perhaps this is best illustrated by one of its cognate terms, 'wit'. Both words have exactly the same etymological root, and this can be seen in words like 'witless', which can mean 'lacking in wisdom'. However, 'witless' may also be used to suggest a more generalized form of stupidity that is not specifically linked to the absence of wisdom. Altogether a more positive term is 'witty', but this is now most often used as a synonym of 'humorous', although traces of its connection with wisdom sometimes linger in the background. In contemporary usage, a witty person has to be amusing, but does not have to be wise.

The lessons that can be learned from Indian philosophical works can apply equally to other traditions. The difficulties involved in translating *prajna* also arise when dealing with *hokma* (Hebrew), *sophia* (Greek), *hikma* (Arabic), *sapientia* (Latin), *sagesse* (French), *Weisheit* (German) and so on. While these difficulties should not prevent us from studying and comparing other traditions, they should also make us approach them with due caution. Even the best translations are problematic, inferior ones even more so.

Wisdom and the Renaissance

Like all historical periods, the European Renaissance had no clear beginning and no clear end, but it certainly includes the fifteenth and sixteenth centuries. How much earlier it began and how much later it ended are matters on which there is less agreement. Although Italy may have been its centre, it extended far beyond its boundaries. Artistically and philosophically it was a period of great creative activity, and came after a period of a thousand years during which Christian thinkers and preoccupations dominated European thought. The Renaissance was not *anti*-Christian, but it rejected many of the limitations that Christianity had imposed on culture and thinking. The result was often an exuberant eclecticism, and the study of wisdom was one of the beneficiaries of this. If Socrates called down philosophy from the heavens, then the Renaissance called down wisdom from the heavens. Unsurprisingly, the medieval Christian theologians had tended towards an understanding of wisdom that emphasized its connection with the divine. While this connection did not disappear during the Renaissance, the thinkers of that period were much more likely to stress the human dimension of wisdom. Some even felt able to leave the divine out of the picture altogether. Renaissance thought is sometimes referred to as 'humanist', reflecting this shift in emphasis. Three different Renaissance thinkers have been chosen to illustrate the variety on offer during this period.

Giovanni Pico della Mirandola (1463–1494) managed to cram a lot of learning into a short life. He studied Greek, Latin, Hebrew and Arabic, wrote a number of important works, and sought to found a new school of thought that would bring together all the valuable insights of preceding ones. His early death at the age of 31 put paid to many of his ambitions, but his legacy remains significant.

In his best-known work, the 'Oration on the Dignity of Man', he assembles an enormous cast of characters in support of his cause. In it, Greek, Islamic and medieval philosophers rub shoulders with the likes of Moses and Zarathustra, Apollo and Asclepius. Nevertheless, underpinning all the bewildering variety is a single common theme: 'all wisdom has flowed from the East to the Greeks and from the Greeks to us.'[38] Moreover, this wisdom has an essentially esoteric character, and Pico approvingly cites the example of Pythagoras as someone who refused to write down his most important teachings. Pico himself wrote the 'Oration on the Dignity of Man' in order to help defend himself against charges of heresy, so the role of Moses is important in bolstering his bona fide Christian credentials. However, his appeal to the authority of Moses takes a surprising turn: 'Moses on the mount received from God not only the Law, which he left to posterity written down in five books, but also a true and more occult explanation of the Law.'[39] Wisdom appears here not only as something that is possessed by very few, but also as something that is *actively hidden* from the many. Perhaps the most surprising twist comes when Pico identifies this wisdom with magic. Magic itself will be looked at in the next chapter, so here I shall simply note that Pico acknowledges that there are different types of magic and is at pains to stress that the kind he is talking about works by 'calling forth into the light as if from their hiding-places the powers scattered and sown in the world by the loving-kindness of God'.[40] But this is not done merely for its own sake, because there is an important ulterior motive: 'For nothing moves one to religion and to the worship of God more than the diligent contemplation of the wonders of God.'[41]

The idea that knowledge of the world can lead to knowledge of the world's creator is not new. However, it is important to understand that the kind of knowledge that Pico is talking about here is primarily mystical. It is the kind of knowledge that is acquired after years of contemplation rather than after years of experimentation. And because this knowledge offers a profound insight into the nature of the world, the power it brings with it can be considered as a form of magic.

Although the European Renaissance is perhaps associated most of all with Italy, the next two thinkers to be discussed here both came from France. Like Pico, Charles de Bovelles (often known by the Latinized form of his name 'Bovillus') was an eclectic. His *Book on the Sage*, which appeared early in the sixteenth century, draws on many different traditions. For him the acquisition of wisdom can be understood as a process of transformation. The wise person is humanity brought to perfection, and because human beings are superior to all others, the wise person is effectively 'a terrestrial god'.[42] Wisdom is essentially knowledge, but knowledge has two different aspects, an outward-facing one and an inward-facing one. The wise person seeks not only knowledge about how the world works, but also self-knowledge. Ultimately the two seem to be one: 'In the soul's knowledge of itself man knows all things in the world.' But the story does not end there: 'By knowing angels and God as well, he perfects and widens this knowledge to a knowledge of the universe.'[43] Although normally self-effacing and living on the edges of society, if not actually apart from it, the wise person would be the ideal ruler: 'He alone has the capacity to govern kingdoms because, knowing all things, he respects the natural order and the rank of every man, rendering to each his own and thus maintaining equality and justice.'[44] It is not difficult to imagine Mozi agreeing with those sentiments.

Every human being seems to have the potential for wisdom, but only some fulfil this potential. The way in which the transformation occurs is fascinating. The seeker after wisdom 'appropriates the nature of all things to himself, sees all things, and resembles the entirety of nature. Swallowing and consuming whatever is in the nature of things, he becomes all those things.'[45] According to Bovelles, the human soul has the intellectual ability to squeeze the essence out of our perceptions of the world and absorb them. Just as flamingos can become pink because of what they feed on, so human beings can become wise on account of their intellectual diet. Perhaps Ludwig Feuerbach (1804–1872) had Bovelles in mind when he observed that 'Man is what he eats.' For Bovelles, it was possible to absorb everything and so become everything, with the result that the wise person is also a microcosm, a reflection and replication in miniature of the whole universe.

The final thinker to be considered here is Pierre Charron (1541–1603), a friend of the rather better known Michel de Montaigne with whom he shared a taste for Scepticism. For a sceptic, knowledge is always problematic, and where Bovelles sought to bring knowledge and wisdom together, Charron insisted on keeping them far apart. Where some saw knowledge as human and wisdom as divine, Charron was inclined to see things the other way round. Knowledge was divine, because it was beyond the reach of the meagre intellectual faculties that human beings possessed. Wisdom, on the other hand, when properly understood, was definitely within a human being's reach. The life of the sage is a life of virtue, and we all have the power to choose that life. Like the Cynics and the Stoics he believed in the principle of 'Life in accordance with nature', and believed that 'nature' pushes us in the direction of virtue. Like Plato he believed that there were four cardinal virtues, and regarded the practice of each virtue as part of what it meant to live in accordance with nature. While we all have the potential for virtue, we are also beset by any number of temptations and distractions that lead us away from fulfilling it. These have to be overcome if we are to attain wisdom.

Charron's major work *Of Wisdom* sets out the way to be followed by the one who would be wise, and it is divided into three books. The first is dedicated to self-knowledge, because only if we understand where we are and what we are can we make progress. The second teaches how to develop self-discipline, which is the means whereby we may make progress. The third discusses the four cardinal virtues, which is where the path to wisdom ends.

In this chapter I have sought to convey something of the variety of views concerning wisdom that can be found in the philosophies of different times and cultures. It is only fair to point out that not all philosophers have taken a keen interest in wisdom, and most modern (since, say, 1700) Western philosophers have shown no interest in it at all. It is perhaps surprising that something that is absolutely the essence of philosophy according to some is not even worth a mention in the opinion of others. However, philosophers have held many different views concerning what philosophy is, and have therefore held different views on what philosophy may or may not be related to. There has been a strong tendency within modern philosophy to try and forge links between philosophy and science, and it can be difficult to find room for wisdom in a scientific view of the world.

Alchemy. This drawing by the 17th-century Dutch artist Vincent Laurensz. van der Vinne appears to show an alchemical experiment being conducted, to the clear alarm of some of the spectators. Many depictions of such experiments exist, which helps modern scholars to reconstruct some of the processes and equipment the alchemists used. The minaret in the background reflects an association of alchemy with the Arab world.

7
Wisdom, Mysticism and Magic

It is fair to say that while a great deal has been written about both magic and mysticism, much of it is of dubious quality. The world of wisdom has had more than its fair share of people proclaiming themselves to be practitioners of the occult or enlightened beings who have turned out to be nothing more than charlatans and false prophets. While the test of time can help to distinguish the genuine article from the fake, it is not guaranteed to do so. In the end, lasting fame is proof only of itself.

In looking at magic and mysticism, one of the problems to be faced is that neither of the two terms is particularly well defined. For example, some would regard divination as a kind of magic, and at least in the popular sense of the word a 'mystic' is often thought of as one who can see into the future. More than that, for those who do not believe in it, to call something 'magic' is to dismiss it as either superstitious nonsense or a clever conjuror's trick. Similarly, many regard mystical experiences as so many forms of self-delusion. Nevertheless, there are sufficiently strong and historical associations between magic, mysticism and wisdom to make them worth exploring.

The Nature of Magic

Before getting into specifics, I want to address the more general question: 'What is magic?' I would suggest that the essence of magic is *power*, understood as the ability to influence events. Immediately there is a problem, because unless we are the helpless victims of fate, we are *all* able to influence events. Magic is therefore a *special kind* of power to influence events, one that is usually understood as the possession of only a few. Where everyday methods are sufficient to achieve what is desired, there is no need to resort to magic. The supernatural begins where the natural ends, and different societies will have different ideas on where the line between the two is to be drawn. What seems magical to some may appear quite mundane to others.

Eliphas Levi was a pseudonym used by Alphonse Louis Constant (1810–1875) under which he wrote some celebrated works about magic. In them, he suggested that there were three basic principles underlying all magical practice. First there was the Law of Correspondence, the belief that a human being is a microcosm, a universe in miniature. According to this view, each part of the human body corresponds to a part of the universe. The second principle concerned the human will. For Levi, magic was literally an exercise in willpower, and the human will is a natural force. Finally there was the principle of the Astral Light. This was a mysterious substance that permeated the whole universe. In its normal state it was invisible and totally formless. However, through the exercise of the human will it could be gathered and shaped into visible forms.

Whether or not we agree with the particulars of Levi's theory, I think there are some useful general points that can be extracted from it. First, magic is presented as essentially a process. In magic, things do not 'just happen'. Second, although we may think of it as in some way 'supernatural', there is nothing in magic that is either contrary to or outside nature. However miraculous it may seem, an act of magic is not a miracle. Seen in this light we may think of magic as a more advanced way of manipulating nature, but a way that few manage to master.

The traditional distinction between 'white' and 'black' magic is generally seen in terms of ends rather than means. It is the distinction between the use of magic for 'good' and the use of it for 'evil'. Wisdom is overwhelmingly associated with white magic. Whether wisdom is actually incompatible with black magic is a moot point. Since the distinction between 'good' and 'evil' is neither as clear-cut nor as absolute as many would wish it to be, much the same can be said about the difference between black magic and white magic.

Having considered some of the basic principles of magic, I will now look at some examples. A good place to begin is in Egypt, a place accorded special significance by many writers on magic.

Magic in Ancient Egypt

The origins of magic are lost in the mists of time and likely to stay there. However, the evidence for it is very old indeed. The earliest artefacts found in Egypt that seem to be associated with magic are around 6,000 years old. These are amulets, of which there were literally hundreds of types. Egypt not only produced them but also exported them, and they have been found in huge numbers both in their country of origin and elsewhere. Ancient Egyptians of all classes seem to have felt the need for them for century after century. The primary function of an amulet is to protect its wearer. Clearly the more permanent the protection the better it is: 'Perpetual amulets were likely to be in the form of jewellery. It is hardly an exaggeration to say that most Egyptian jewellery had amuletic value.'[1] It is also no exaggeration to say that providing protection was one of the primary purposes and functions of Egyptian magic. A work of instruction that purports to contain the advice of King Khety (who ruled Egypt around 2150 BC) to his son Merikare succinctly describes magic as 'a weapon to resist the events that happen'.[2] It is a gift from the gods to use as and when appropriate.

One of 'the events that happen' to everyone sooner or later is death, so it is not surprising to find that a considerable amount of Egyptian magic concerned itself with this. The ancient Egyptian texts commonly known as 'books of the dead' were mainly collections of spells designed to protect the soul after the death of the physical body. The oldest known such book dates to the middle of the second millennium BC, but some of the contents of these books are at least 1,000 years older and appear in writings known as the 'Pyramid Texts'. These, as the name suggests, were inscribed on the walls of royal tombs. The earliest known example of such a text can be found at Saqqara, in the tomb of King Wenis (his name sometimes appears as Unas), who died around 2330 BC.

Unsurprisingly, given the long period of time over which they came together, the collections found in books of the dead bring together a wide variety of spells to be used in a wide range of circumstances. One of the shortest ones is designed to be used when threatened by a snake: 'O Rerek-snake, take yourself off, for Geb protects me; get up, for you have eaten a mouse, which Re detests, and you have chewed the bones of a putrid cat.'[3] Geb, the god appealed to here, was a very ancient one, and his name often appears in spells from the 'Pyramid Texts'. He was closely associated with healing and was thought to have magical powers over spirits that caused diseases. The nature of the spell itself is quite curious, appearing to contain elements of a threat, an injunction and an insult. Presumably it was thought to be efficacious, though it is not entirely clear why. The invocation of Geb looks as if it might be the most important part, but it cannot be assumed that any parts of the spell were regarded as superfluous or redundant. On the contrary, a spell is usually understood as a sequence of words that has to be recited in full and absolutely correctly in order to achieve its end. A belief in the power of words, whether spoken or written, can be found in many cultures, and it is clear that ancient Egypt was one of them. The idea that knowing the name (or the 'real' name) of someone or something brings power over that person or object is also widespread. The story of Rumpelstiltskin is a well-known and relatively modern illustration of it.

The Egyptian god most closely associated with magic was Heka, who was so powerful that even the other gods feared him. His power lay behind the creation of the world, and his power prevented it from falling back into chaos. He was seen as the personification of a power, also called *heka*, and which is often translated as 'magic'. Certain people were thought to have, or be a channel for, or be able to direct *heka*. Women in general were believed to have *heka* when they were lactating, presumably because of magical properties attributed to milk. The Egyptians used the word *hekau* to denote a magician, but it does not seem that this was a profession as such. Rather, a number of people might be *hekau* sometimes. The closest thing the Egyptians had to a professional practitioner of magic was probably the individual known as the lector priest. Lector priests were temple officials whose main function was to recite texts on formal occasions. A lot of their work would probably be taken up by the regular programme of rituals performed in the temple, but they would also be called upon to recite texts (including spells from a book of the dead) while a corpse was being mummified, for example. They also had a reputation for being interpreters of dreams.

At least in the popular imagination, lector priests were thought to have powers that we might more readily recognize as 'magical'. A story dating back to at least 1600 BC tells of a lector priest called Ubainer who discovered that his wife was being unfaithful. He made a small crocodile out of wax and told his steward to drop it into the pool where his wife's lover was bathing. Once it hit the water the model became a full-size living crocodile that dragged the man down into the depths. This seems to be an illustration of the kind of powers that many believed the lector priests possessed. Crocodiles also feature in a story told by Lucian of Samosata about an Egyptian scribe from Memphis called Pancrates who possessed magical powers. He liked 'riding about on crocodiles and going for swims with them'. He was also able to 'take a broom, or a rolling-pin, or the bolt off the door, dress it up and then, by saying a spell, make it walk about just like a human being'.[4] If this is beginning to sound familiar, it is probably because the story developed into the earliest known version of the one later called 'The Sorcerer's Apprentice', which became part of Walt Disney's *Fantasia*. The durability of the story is quite remarkable in itself. It is not known whether Lucian (*c.* AD 115–200) ever visited Egypt, but he evidently saw it as a credible setting for this incredible story.

Perhaps the most famous name in the world of Egyptian magic is that of Hermes Trismegistus. With him, it is quite impossible to free the historical core from the layers of legend that surround it. There clearly *is* a historical core because writings attributed to him exist, whoever may have written them. The legends are inconsistent as to whether he was a god or a human being, and if a human being, when and where he lived. Not all the legends even made him an Egyptian. There were competing traditions that he might have been a Babylonian or Phoenician. The strongest tradition, however, said he was from Egypt and the author of a collection of writings known as the *Hermetica*.

There are many different opinions as to who composed them, where, when and why. Some were philosophical, some magical, and some just plain incomprehensible. There is now a broad, although not universal, consensus that they were probably written in the early centuries AD. What is indisputable is that for centuries they were generally believed to have come from ancient Egypt, and that makes this the natural place to consider them. Many believed Hermes Trismegistus to have been an Egyptian sage and priest who was a contemporary of Moses. Consequently, when Cosimo de' Medici (1389–1464) procured copies of the Hermetic writings, he instructed his translator, Marsilio Ficino (1433–1499), to drop everything and pay attention to them. Because the writings themselves were strongly eclectic, drawing on different philosophical and religious traditions, they proved to be an important channel through which ideas from antiquity could be rediscovered. Ficino believed that the *Hermetica* contained a philosophy and theology that encapsulated the essence of an ancient wisdom. Many agreed with him, and the *Hermetica* had a significant influence on the development of Renaissance thought.

The most obviously 'magical' of the *Hermetica* is the 'Asclepius', supposedly disclosed by Hermes Trismegistus to a grandson of the Greek healing god. In it can be found the revelation that as well as celestial gods, there are terrestrial ones, who are deified human beings. These gods 'see to things one by one, predict events by means of sacred lots and divination, foresee what is coming and render aid accordingly'.[5] The gods can also be summoned through the use of various substances to take up residence in statues through which they can exercise their powers. It seems to have been this idea in particular that fired the magical imagination of Ficino and others, and much of the practice of magic in the Renaissance can be regarded as a conscious attempt to emulate and revive what was believed to be an authentically Egyptian tradition. Whether or not the *Hermetica* are genuinely Egyptian writings, the idea that gods inhabit and at least sometimes animate cult statues is an authentically Egyptian belief, and one that underpinned the operation of many ancient Egyptian oracles.

Magic in Ancient Greece and Rome

The place of magic in the world of the Greeks and the Romans was a complex one. There is plenty of evidence to suggest that many so-called practitioners of magic were regarded as frauds and charlatans, but there is also plenty of evidence to indicate that magic was taken sufficiently seriously to be the object of legislation. In this section I shall first look at two particular kinds of association made between magic and wisdom in the Graeco-Roman world, and then look at two case studies of individuals as illustrations of two very different views of magic.

There was a strong tradition linking Pythagoras and his followers with magic, and a number of stories told about him bear a strong resemblance to those told about shamans. Similar stories were told about a number of other characters, such as Empedocles, Abaris the Hyperborean (sixth century BC?), Aristeas of Proconessus (seventh century BC?) and Zalmoxis (sixth century BC). There are recurrent themes in their stories such as the ability to work miracles, the ability to fly, and the ability to appear in two different places at the same time. Zalmoxis is also said to have turned into a wolf, in keeping with the close connection between shamans and animals. It need hardly be said that solid evidence of their magical achievements is difficult to find, but there is clear evidence that people believed in them. The philosopher Porphyry (third century AD) wrote in his essay on the life of Pythagoras:

> In brief, there is no one of whom more achievements or more extraordinary achievements have been suspected. He is recorded as making infallible predictions of earthquakes and promptly averting pestilences and fierce winds. He checked hailstorms and calmed the waters of rivers and seas so that his companions could enjoy a gentle passage over them.[6]

While Abaris, Aristeas and Zalmoxis are very shadowy figures, Pythagoras and Empedocles are firmly historical. But Porphyry was writing nearly a thousand years after the time of Pythagoras, and his essay reflects the body of legend that grew up around the famous philosopher over the intervening centuries. The original 'lover of wisdom' seems to have become a magnet for stories about magical accomplishments.

A very different kind of association between wisdom and magic can be found in the practice of necromancy. Necromancy involves conjuring up the spirits of the dead in order to converse with them. It seems to have been taken for granted that the dead possessed a wisdom that the living lacked, and this led to the development of all kinds of ways and means whereby they might be put into contact with each other. Some places that were thought to be entrances to the underworld became renowned as oracles of the dead, of which there were several in the Graeco-Roman world. The one at Heracleia ad Pontus (near modern Eregli on the Black Sea coast of Turkey) was said to have been founded at the place where Hercules himself made his descent to Hades and dragged Cerberus, its canine guardian, back up with him. Tainaron, at the southern tip of the Mani peninsula in Greece, also claimed to be the place where this happened, and there was an oracle of the dead there too.

Necromancy was not just about special places, it was also about special people. Necromancers were the experts in dealing with ghosts, whether summoning them or exorcising them. The Romans tended to take a rather dimmer view of necromancy than the Greeks did, and calling someone a necromancer almost became a slander. Unhealthy dealings with the dead were sometimes attributed to unpopular emperors as a kind of black propaganda. On the other hand, people regarded as miracle-workers often had some necromantic skills in their repertoire. An example of this can be seen in our first case study.

Apollonius of Tyana (first century AD) was clearly an exceptional individual, even if only a fraction of the stories told about him are true. Our main source of information is a lengthy account of his life written by Flavius Philostratus, but his name crops up in other places as well. Some early Christian writers were keen to disparage him, which is perhaps not surprising given that his followers seem to have regarded Apollonius as a semi-divine miracle-working saviour figure. He is also credited by some with being the author of texts on alchemy, and in this role can appear under the Arabic name of

Balinas. Whatever the historical value of the narrative put together by Philostratus, it is clearly designed to entertain. It contains:

> sudden supernatural omens, minidialogues on the favourite topics of the day, colourful bits of archaeological lore, plenty of magic, rapid action scenes, amazing descriptions of fabled, far-off lands, occasional touches of naughty eroticism, and a whole series of favourite 'philosophical' scenes.[7]

He is also said to have called up the ghost of Achilles at the site of his tomb. It is clearly impossible to give more than a flavour of such a thrilling tale here, although much of it actually feels more formulaic than authentic.

Apollonius came from Cappadocia, in what is now central Turkey. From an early age he showed a scholarly aptitude and studied under a variety of teachers before finding a Pythagorean one. This stage in the narrative clearly and explicitly links Apollonius to the Pythagorean tradition. When his father died he gave away his inheritance and took a vow of silence for five years (as well as a lifelong vow of chastity). After this, he went on a long journey. This meant that on his return he could claim to be the heir to the learning of the Persians, Indians and Egyptians. When he came back from his travels he seems to have taken up the life of an itinerant teacher, miracle-worker and healer. A typical story about him tells how the people of Ephesus sent for him because they were suffering from the plague. Literally in an instant he was there, and immediately realized that the disease was the work of a demon disguised as a beggar. He persuaded the Ephesians to pelt the beggar with stones, and they were amazed to see him change into a massive and ferocious hound!

While his displays of magical powers are clearly an integral part of the story of Apollonius, they are no more than a part, and they are set within a broader spiritual and philosophical context. The outward displays of magic are just one kind of evidence of a deeper power within. With the charlatan there are only the outward displays of magic, and they are nothing but tricks. One such charlatan seems to have been Alexander of Abonoteichos (second century AD). He is also best known because of his appearance in a literary work, but he is portrayed very negatively there: the reader is invited to 'picture to yourself a mixture of deceit, cunning, and general wickedness, reckless audacity and executive ability, combined with a plausible manner'.[8] According to Lucian, Alexander set up a fake oracle in his home town with the aid of a large snake, a few accomplices and a handful of props. The scam worked so well that Alexander was able to keep it going for years and amass a significant fortune. Lucian says he tried to expose the fraud himself, but failed. Alexander had enough friends in high places, and enough people who believed, or wanted to believe, that the oracle was real, to maintain the deception until he died. As far as Lucian was concerned, Alexander was simply a professional con man preying on the gullible.

Whether or not there is any truth in any of these stories, what these case studies present is an illustration of two stereotypes that the readers are clearly expected to recognize. Apollonius is wise, chaste, disciplined and able to work genuine miracles. Alexander is clever, dishonest and able to fool people. One gives magic a good name, the other gives it a bad one. One is wise, one is merely cunning in the most negative sense of the word.

Alchemy

Another stereotype encountered across the ages is that of the alchemist. In the popular imagination, an alchemist is someone who claims to be able to transform base metal into gold, and is therefore a fraud because such a thing cannot be done. Ben Jonson's comedy *The Alchemist* (first performed in 1610) does much to reinforce this stereotype. The alchemist, called Subtle, is indeed a fraud. On the other hand, it is also difficult to have much sympathy for some of his victims, such as Sir Epicure Mammon, whose greed makes him an easy target. However, although alchemy was very much a live issue when Jonson wrote his play in the early seventeenth century, its history goes back much further. Or perhaps we should say 'histories', since there seem to be at least two independent traditions.

One tradition goes back to Hermes Trismegistus, and therefore implies a link between alchemy and the teachings found in the *Hermetica*. There was a legend that when his tomb was discovered the corpse was found to be clutching an engraved emerald plate, which has come to be known as the 'Emerald Tablet'. In it he declares: 'I am called Hermes Trismegistus, because I hold three parts of the wisdom of the whole world.'[9] Exactly where and when this discovery was made is a matter of some dispute and is credited to as wide and diverse a group of people as Sara (the wife of the biblical patriarch Abraham), Alexander the Great and Apollonius of Tyana. Densely expressed, the 'Emerald Tablet' is susceptible to many different interpretations, insofar as it can be understood at all. Perhaps its most important observation is: 'That which is above is like to that which is below, and that which is below is like to that which is above, to accomplish the miracles of the one thing.'[10] This seems like a variation on the Law of Correspondence identified by Eliphas Levi as a basic principle underlying all magic. What the Law of Correspondence means in practice is that something done to one thing has an effect on another thing because of some kind of sympathetic relationship between the two. Although great antiquity is claimed for the 'Emerald Tablet', scholars have been unable to unearth any solid evidence to substantiate that claim. The first attested mention of it seems to date from as late as the ninth century AD.

Rather earlier is a collection of alchemical texts assembled in Constantinople in perhaps the seventh century. The earliest writings in it are sometimes attributed to Bolus of Mendes (third century BC?), and they comprise a set of 'recipes' for 'making', among other things, gold and silver. For the alchemists the *colour* of something was very important, and clearly it is possible to make things that are silver or gold *in colour* but that are not actually, or only partly, silver or gold in nature. (All that glisters may not be gold, but it is significant that the words for the colour and the metal are the same.) Whatever its origins, it is clear that alchemy became centrally concerned with how one substance might be changed into another. This was sometimes achieved through the use of a third substance, and the idea developed of a kind of 'super third substance' that could effect all kinds of changes in things, and this elusive substance came to be known as 'the Philosopher's Stone'. Clearly, there was little practical point in devoting a massive amount of time and effort to changing something expensive and rare into something common and cheap, so alchemy came to be associated above all with the transmutation of base metals into gold.

There was, however, another dimension to alchemy that developed in a different direction. The idea that one thing can become another does not have to be restricted to our thinking about material substances. The conversion of the base into the refined has a parallel in the conversion of the sick into the well, so a medicinal aspect of alchemy emerged. And the materially impure becoming pure could be seen as an analogy to spiritual development, so a spiritual aspect of alchemy emerged too. These ideas are eloquently brought together by Henry Vaughan (1622–1695), who described Christianity as 'the true Medicine, rectifying and transmuting that which is no more into that which it was before corruption, and into something better by far, and that which is not into that which it ought to be'.[11] And making the connection with wisdom explicit, Mary Anne Atwood (1817–1910) describes alchemy as 'the finding of the Sophia in the mind'.[12]

A completely separate alchemical tradition seems to have developed in China, and here too we find that it developed different dimensions. In Taoism there is an explicit and clear distinction made between 'outer alchemy' (*wai-dan*) and 'inner alchemy' (*nei-dan*): 'If outer alchemy aims at purification of various materials to produce life-prolonging medicine, inner alchemy aims at the purification or refinement of the adept's body-mind unit, also hoping to conquer death.'[13] The ends may be the same, but the means are definitely different. Although there are early records of people seeking to create gold, this never became a preoccupation of Chinese alchemists. Immortality was by far the most important goal. The main interest of Chinese alchemists in gold was as an ingredient in their elixirs for immortality.

The most important ingredient in Chinese alchemy was cinnabar, a sulphide of mercury that is used to produce the colour vermilion. So important was this substance that it became synonymous with alchemy (the *dan* element in *wai-dan* and *nei-dan* means 'cinnabar'). Clearly, its colour was connected with its importance, but there was more to it than that. According to Ge Hong (Ko Hung), author of an early text on Chinese alchemy, 'Cinnabar becomes transformed when heated. The longer the period it is heated, the more miraculous the transformation it undergoes.'[14] Since the production of elixirs seems to have involved heating things together in a cauldron over a fire, how something reacted to heat was clearly important. The application of heat is often used as a method of purification, and this seems to have been the purpose behind heating cinnabar. In its purest, most refined form it was believed to make anyone who swallowed it instantly immortal.

The inner alchemy (which may, but does not have to be, combined with the outer alchemy) operates on a very different basis. While the outer alchemy may deliver physical immortality, the inner alchemy aims at something that might be characterized better as enlightenment. As such, the inner alchemy has a much stronger connection with philosophical Taoism than the outer alchemy does. Just as the processes associated with the outer alchemy seek to purify through heat, so the processes associated with the inner alchemy seek to purify through yogic practices. Clearly there were different schools of thought as to what was efficacious. While the beneficial effects of breathing exercises and meditation seem to have been taken for granted, some also advocated certain sexual practices or physical routines as well. The theory was that all these could help to push forward a process of inner purification that ended with a final transmutation into pure unfettered spirit.

Alchemy of all kinds is associated with transformations that are beyond the attainment of most, and so appear magical to the majority. Ben Jonson's alchemist may have been a fraud, but credulous and greedy people like Sir Epicure Mammon were not the only ones who took alchemy seriously. Jonson's contemporary Robert Fludd (1574–1637) was one of the towering English intellects of his time, and he took alchemy seriously too. It has also been seen that alchemy concerned itself with much more than the transmutation of metals. Both Christianity and Taoism found in alchemy a vocabulary and vehicle for spiritual transformation. This moves us from magic to mysticism, which is the other main theme of this chapter.

The Nature of Mysticism

There is no agreed definition of mysticism but this one provides a useful start: 'Mysticism is the quest for firsthand intimacy with God, the Divine, the Source, the Ground. Often defiant and heretical, it accepts no substitutes and refuses all intermediaries.'[15] Even if this quest takes place within the context or confines of an established religious tradition (and it usually does), it is nonetheless irredeemably personal in nature. It is this that makes mysticism a potential source of heresy, because if an experience is profound enough and strong enough it makes it difficult to accept the opinions of others that seem to be in conflict with it. As a result, whatever the reverence in which individual mystics are held, organized religions sometimes find it difficult to deal with them collectively, and the more dogmatic and institutionalized the religion, the greater the difficulty. On the other hand, a profound and strong experience does not guarantee infallibility, and it is by no means the case that all mystics agree with each other. Comparative studies of mystical traditions reveal clear differences. Some argue that the differences are only superficial, merely matters of interpretation, and that ultimately all religions are one. Others argue that different religious traditions deliver different spiritual experiences, and they should not be confused with each other. Later in this chapter I shall sketch out a few mystical traditions and readers may begin to draw their own conclusions as to how similar or different they are.

The origins of words never tell us everything, but they usually tell us something. The English words 'mystic', 'mystery' and those related to them have their origin in a family of Greek words concerned with initiation. Many divinities have had special mystery cults attached to them, including those of Isis and Mithras. However, by far the most celebrated mystery cult in the Graeco-Roman world was that of Demeter and Persephone based at Eleusis, near Athens. Demeter was a goddess generally associated with crops and fertility while Persephone, her daughter, spent half the year in the underworld and returned to the surface each year in spring. The general nature of their cult is therefore obvious, but the 'mysteries' associated with them formed a kind of cult within a cult. Initiation into the Eleusinian mysteries clearly involved some kind of revelation, but initiates had to swear not to reveal anything about it to others. Remarkably, this secret was extremely well kept for centuries and there is still a great deal that remains unknown about what went on during the initiation process. The word 'esoterism' is sometimes used as a synonym of mysticism, and this too emphasizes the idea of something known only to a few. It derives from a Greek word meaning 'inner' and points towards something that is kept within a small number of people. It is often believed that what is esoteric has to be directly passed from one person to another.

If mysticism is the 'quest for firsthand intimacy' with the divine, then it is easy to see the connection between mysticism and wisdom if wisdom is thought to be in some way an aspect or property of the divine. Sometimes this 'intimacy' is understood in terms of an actual union with the divine, sometimes as becoming 'godlike' rather than becoming god.

Yoga

Although there is no logical reason why some kind of union with the divine might not just happen unbidden, mystical traditions tend to assume that this happens rarely, if at all. The far more common scenario is that it is actively sought, and this search involves some kind of practice. The term 'yoga' is often used to refer to such practices. While the term itself arose within the specific context of Hinduism and Indian philosophy, it is now often used more broadly. The root sense of yoga involves a union of some kind, but different understandings and interpretations take different views on what is united with what and how. What yoga is thought to be able to achieve depends on what one believes is possible.

Many people think of yoga in terms of twisting one's body into complicated (and often painful) postures. This is not a complete misunderstanding, but it is a long way from being a full or accurate picture. The kind of yoga that makes use of complicated postures is more correctly known as *hatha* yoga (*hatha* means 'force' or 'strength'), but the postures form only one part of its physical discipline. There are also various breathing and cleansing exercises that are all designed to purify the body in one way or another. Another kind of yoga, *raja* yoga, places a greater emphasis on controlling the mind: 'When the agitation of the mind is stilled, supra-mental perceptions or visions appear, and with them comes the perception of the fundamental unity of all that exists.'[16] While different mystical traditions might disagree as to what is actually perceived when 'the agitation of the mind is stilled', the basic point is that what is learned through yoga is learned through direct experience. Underlying this basic point is the belief that our everyday busy, conscious, discursive, analysing mind gets in the way of our search for wisdom. The analogy of a reflecting pool is sometimes used. When the water in a reflecting pool is stirred up, it reflects badly and presents a distorted image of how things are. When the water is still, it reflects well and presents an accurate picture of how things are. Stilling 'the agitation of the mind' makes the mind an accurate mirror of reality, enabling us to see how things really are.

In the *Bhagavad Gita*, a small part of the *Mahabharata*, three different kinds of yoga are discussed. These are usually known as *bhakti* yoga, *jnana* yoga and *karma* yoga. What they point to is the idea that people of different types and temperaments may need to take different paths to arrive at the same destination. *Bhakti* means 'worship', and the person who takes this path leads a life of devotion. *Jnana* means 'knowledge', however; what is meant is not some kind of bookish leaning, but rather the acquisition of experiential knowledge through the contemplative life. Finally, *karma* means 'action', but the yoga associated with it involves a particular *quality* of action. The practice of *karma* yoga means a total lack of self-interest, such that nothing is done for any personal gain or benefit. The point of all this, and the reason why I mention it here, seems to be that no one is prevented from following the path of yoga because there is a path that is suitable for everyone. Not following any path is always a choice. If we do not enjoy the fruits of yoga it is because we have denied them to ourselves. This makes an interesting counterbalance to the idea that mysticism is by its nature restricted to a handful of initiates.

Kabbalah

Kabbalah (or Kabbala or Cabala or various other spellings) has recently become better known than it was due to a number of people in the public eye associating themselves with it. Before the 1990s relatively few people had heard of it, although it has been around for a very

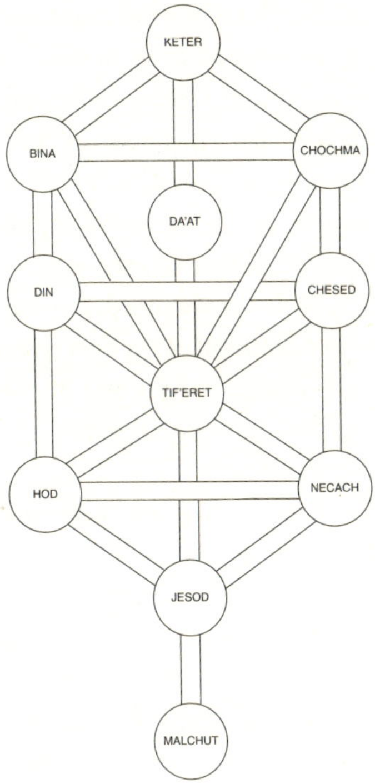

The Sephirot.

long time. The term Kabbalah 'is used to designate Jewish mystical teaching, which being considered secret, was not written down but communicated by word of mouth'.[17] The origins of an oral tradition are notoriously difficult to date and many different claims are made as to when Kabbalah first emerged. There is a tradition that it was first taught to Adam by the angels, making it a part of the whole of human history. There is, however, also a written dimension to Kabbalah, and its most important text is known as the *Zohar*. This dense and difficult work first appeared in Spain at the end of the thirteenth century. A mystic and teacher called Moses de Léon (1250–1305) claimed to have rediscovered it after it had been lost for centuries, although it seems much more likely that he wrote it himself. He attributed its authorship to a Rabbi Simeon bar Yohai, a genuine figure who lived in the second century AD. Not everything about the book is as authentic. Its author cites a number of works in support of his position, some of which seem to have been invented by him entirely for this purpose.

On the face of it, the idea of a written text within an oral tradition makes little sense. The whole point of an oral tradition is that things are not written down. However, the contradiction is only apparent, and is not unique to Kabbalah. In a mystical tradition like Kabbalah, written texts are thought to conceal as much as they reveal. Their surface meanings are never the whole story. Indeed, on the surface they may sometimes seem to mean very little. The full, true, secret meaning can be read only by the initiated. It is rather like a cipher that has two keys. Those in possession of the text possess only one key, and the other key can only be 'communicated by word of mouth'. Both keys are required in order to unlock the meaning. The uninitiated can only guess as to what lies within.

The most distinctive feature (at least to the uninitiated) of Kabbalah is the idea of the *sephirot*, which might be described as an attempt to draw a kind of map of the divine. The *sephirot* can be thought of as 'the potencies and modes of action of the living God',[18] and in Kabbalah there are always ten of them. They are often presented in a diagrammatic structure that links them together in various ways. The diagram is actually a stylized tree, and the symbol of the tree plays a significant role in Kabbalah. At the top of the tree are the three *sephirot* known as Crown, Wisdom and Understanding. At the bottom are the two usually known as Kingdom and Foundation. Between them are the other five. Translations may vary, but I shall give them here as Judgement, Mercy, Beauty, Firmness and Splendour. There are many ways of reading this diagram, and I shall give just three here. In this discussion I shall talk about 'the divine' rather than 'God' because like many mystical traditions (whether they do it implicitly or explicitly), Kabbalah tends to downplay the idea of a personal deity.

If the diagram is read from the top, it can be seen as an account of how many different aspects of the universe came into being. However, this did not happen all at once, and the diagram represents the sequence the process follows. The placing of Wisdom near the top of the tree recalls the biblical words: 'The Lord created me at the beginning of his work.' Some readings of the diagram treat it as a kind of metaphysical, genealogical tree, with pairs of *sephirot* combining to produce new ones. At the end of the process is Kingdom, and it is Kingdom that touches the world in which we live.

If the diagram is read from the bottom, it shows paths that can be taken from Kingdom to Crown. If we read the diagram from the top downwards as representing the descent of the divine, then we can read it from the bottom upwards as the ascent of the mystic. The diagram represents the route to take and the stages to go through in order for the mystic to experience 'first-hand intimacy' with the divine. As with yoga, different paths are possible. But at least some mystics may discover that wisdom, rather than cleanliness, is next to the Crown of godliness.

A third way of reading the diagram goes in no particular direction, but simply explores it as a way of revealing the different ways in which the divine can manifest itself, and therefore of ways in which we can begin to discern its presence. Ultimately, Kabbalah does not believe that the divine can be captured in language or properly described, but we are more likely to catch a glimpse of it in some directions than in others.

Just as alchemy could be associated with mysticism, so Kabbalah could be associated with magic. This most famously happens in stories about golems. In medieval Europe, it was believed that certain powerful mystics could actually bring human effigies to life, and such creatures were called golems. For example, it was said that Rabbi Judah Loew of Prague (sixteenth century) made a golem to work for him. The idea of the golem became more widely known in the twentieth century thanks to a novel by Gustav Meyrink and a silent film by Paul Wegener, both simply entitled *The Golem*. The origins of such stories are unclear, but they clearly go back a long way and may be connected with Kabbalistic ritual. If the aim of the mystic is somehow to become like, or even part of, the divine, then what better proof of having achieved this than by demonstrating the power most associated with the divine, that of creation? However, stories of the golem often had unhappy endings. Human creators are still only human. They make mistakes, and these mistakes may come back to haunt them. In their mistakes, they reveal that ultimately their wisdom is only of the human variety.

Gnosticism

For centuries the early Gnostics lay buried in obscurity. We knew the names of some of them, such as Carpocrates and Valentinus (both second century AD), but for information about what they thought and taught we had to rely mainly on the words of their ancient enemies. Many early Christian writers regarded Gnostics as dangerous heretics, and sought to destroy both their reputations and their writings. In this they were very successful. However, and totally unexpectedly, the situation changed in 1945 when a cache of Gnostic writings was discovered near the town of Nag Hammadi in Egypt. For the first time for a very long time, the ancient Gnostics were suddenly able to speak for themselves again. But what did they have to say?

No one would want to pretend that Gnostic texts make for easy reading. As with Kabbalah, there is a sense that many texts are meant to reveal their true meanings only to the initiated. Unlike Kabbalah, however, the context within which Gnostic texts are meant to be understood is not clear. Although there may be aspects of it with which the orthodox are uncomfortable, Kabbalah clearly and firmly sits within Judaism and its texts are written against a background of Judaism. With Gnosticism it is different. While many Christian writers clearly regarded Gnosticism as a deviant movement *within* Christianity, and many scholars have portrayed it as a kind of reaction *against* Christianity, others have seen it as 'a movement, or, more precisely, tendency, which was wider and older than Christianity. The product of syncretism, it drew upon Jewish, pagan and Oriental sources.'[19] There are numerous different sects and movements that can be brought under the Gnostic umbrella, but if we think of them all as being rebellious in nature, then they were not necessarily all rebelling against the same thing. What follows is an attempt to bring together the most important and most recurrent ideas associated with the Gnostic 'tendency'.

The Gnostics always seem to have thought of themselves as a kind of elite 'who had knowledge of the divine spark planted deep within them and who could follow it from their body through the entire cosmos to a mystical union with God'.[20] They believed that they were literally 'lost souls', trapped in a physical world, and many of their texts were attempts to explain how this situation had arisen. This led them to develop various narratives explaining how everything had come into being. One of the problems they faced was that they generally thought of the physical world, including their own bodies, in very negative terms, and could not accept that the divine being they sought union with had created it. This usually led them to postulate intermediaries who could take the blame, and Wisdom was sometimes put in this role. The biblical book of Proverbs provides one possible source of inspiration for this idea, but in Gnosticism it is given a very different spin. The figure of Wisdom (Sophia) is never actually evil in Gnosticism, but she is often fallible, and her shortcomings are sometimes regarded as the reason why the world is a very imperfect place.

Once it had been understood that each human being was a divine spark trapped within a physical body, and how this had happened, the next and most important step could be taken. The Gnostics were not prepared simply to accept their predicament. The more negatively they characterized the physical world, the more imperative it was to try and separate themselves from it. Ultimately, the only escape lay in death and a final liberation from the physical body, but there were other interim options. Like many mystics, Gnostics believed it was possible to achieve at least a temporary separation of the soul from the body while the body was still alive, and this typically happened during prayer or meditation. Outside prayer and meditation, all Gnostics could live lives that in one way or another reflected their rejection of the physical world. Asceticism was one possible route, antinomianism another. In asceticism, the physical body is disciplined into submission so that it is no longer a source of distraction. In antinomianism, the conventions regarding the physical body are flouted as a demonstration of indifference to it. Since many of these conventions often relate to sexual activity, antinomians tend to be the subjects of considerable gossip.

As a 'tendency', Gnosticism is not limited to any particular time or place. Medieval Europe saw the emergence of a number of movements that can be regarded as Gnostic in nature. One of the best known of these was Catharism, which prevailed for some time in the Languedoc region of France, and which became the target of what is known as the Albigensian Crusade. The suppression of a sect whose members welcome death is always going to be difficult, and the Cathars proved to be very durable. One of their last stands took place in 1244 at the castle of Montsegur, in the foothills of the Pyrenees. Its impressive remains can still be seen as a monument to Gnosticism.

Sufism

Sufism has many monuments. The tombs of famous Sufis are to be found scattered over many parts of the Muslim world. Sufism may be regarded as the mystical aspect of Islam, and some famous individual Sufis have already been encountered. The term 'Sufi' derives from the Arabic word *suf*, which means 'wool'. The connection seems to be that many early Muslim ascetics wore plain clothing made from wool. Some also claim to hear in the word 'Sufi' echoes of *sophos*, the Greek word meaning 'wise'. There are many different orders (or sects, or brotherhoods) of Sufism, each with its own particular emphases and traditions. Probably the best-known Sufis are the so-called whirling dervishes, or Mevlevi, who are celebrated for their special spinning dance. A number of different explanations have been given for this ritual. It is said that it can induce a state of mystical ecstasy, although this is by no means guaranteed or necessary. Rumi, the thirteenth-century founder of the order, put it this way: 'Why do I have to dance in the glow of His sun? So that when the speck of dust dances He may remember me.'[21]

The notion of remembering, however, works two ways in Sufism. While the dancing dervish may wish to be noticed and remembered by his God, all Sufi practices are examples of what is known as *zikr* (or *dhikr*), an Arabic word meaning 'remembrance'. Sufis like to think of themselves as 'God's friends, perpetually engaged in remembrance of him'.[22] Some remember through dancing, some remember through shouting God's name, some remember through quiet meditation, and so on. The act of remembrance also finds its way into Sufi literature, where the theme of longing for the loved one is frequently encountered. In Sufi poetry there is often an expression of something that goes far beyond simple friendship.

If 'Mysticism is the quest for first-hand intimacy with God', what happens when people think they have actually achieved this? One of the reasons I have chosen to discuss Sufism is in order to introduce the cautionary tale of al-Hallaj (*c.* 858–922). Al-Hallaj was born in what is now Iran and died in what is now Iraq. As a child he learned the Qur'an by heart, and as a teenager he sought out the great Sufi masters of his day. He finally became a student of Abu al-Qasim al-Junayd in Baghdad. When he was about 40 years old he began to travel, making three pilgrimages to Mecca, teaching in various countries and spending some time as a missionary in India. Unfortunately, he lived at a time when Sufis in general were viewed with some suspicion, and his tendency to talk publicly about his mystical experiences meant that even many Sufis viewed him with some suspicion. Al-Hallaj is sometimes seen as an 'intoxicated' Sufi, one who is prone to talk recklessly of his experiences. He is said to have declared 'I am the Truth', which was interpreted as a claim not only to be intimate with God, but actually to *be* God. As a result of this, he was arrested and executed in Baghdad in 922.

Many of the details concerning the trial of al-Hallaj are confused and contested, and the fact that it happened in a time of political intrigue has to be taken into account. Nevertheless, it may be said that even if the story is untrue, it is believable. Mystics who proclaim the closeness of their personal intimacy with God will often run the risk of being misinterpreted, and the personal consequences of this may be severe. The mystic who claims to be able to bypass all human institutions and hierarchies and make direct contact with the divine wisdom is not always a welcome figure. From an organizational point of view, the mystic is always liable to be perceived as a heretic, or at least as a troublemaker.

I also want to use Sufism as an illustration of how mystical movements often stress that their most important teachings are 'communicated by word of mouth'. The different orders of Sufism all have their own lineages that demonstrate how teachings have been passed down through a succession of masters and pupils. It is through this lineage that the authenticity of the teaching is preserved and assured. Sufi orders, whether large or small, look back to a founder and usually the name of the order is derived in some way or other from how the founder was known. For example, the Yeseviyya look back to Ahmed Yesevi and the Mevlevi dervishes look back to Rumi. Ahmed Yesevi himself looked back to Yusuf al-Hamadani (1048–1140), who was regarded as the founder of the Khwajagan order. The Khwajagan order (literally 'The Order of the Masters') evolved into a number of different ones including the Naqshbandiyya, named after Baha al-Din Naqshband (1318–1389). The emergence of the Naqshbandiyya and Yeseviyya is a simple illustration of how a movement could fragment as new groups formed around new teachers. Because the Yeseviyya, Naqshbandiyya and others could all trace their lineage back to al-Hamadani, they could all claim ultimately to belong to a common tradition, even if it evolved in different ways in different places at different times. The Arabic term translated as 'order' here is *tariqa*, which can also mean 'way' or 'path', so the different orders were not in competition with each other; they were just following different paths to 'intimacy with God'.

The tombs of famous Sufis are not just monuments to the dead, they may also form focal points for the popular devotions of the living. When I lived in Khartoum in the 1980s, a popular destination on a Friday was the tomb of Hamed al-Nil on the edge of Omdurman. Large numbers of devotees would meet there in the late afternoon and dance until the sun went down.

In the popular imagination perhaps mysticism and magic amount to much the same thing. Many societies have their wise men and/or women who are sought out to perform various services. These people seem to have special powers, although it is not always clear where these powers come from. But as long as they prove to be efficacious, perhaps that question is often left unasked, let alone unanswered. As discussed here, however, mysticism and magic can be seen to focus on different things. We might say that magic is primarily outward looking, in that it seeks to influence events, whereas mysticism is primarily inward looking, in that it is about making personal spiritual progress. The major overlap comes when spiritual progress manifests itself in the power to influence external events. Seen in the other direction, the miraculous is frequently interpreted as evidence of the holy.

Many people are dismissive of magic and mysticism, but even from the modest selection of materials gathered together here it is apparent that both have played a significant role in the history of wisdom and, indeed, the history of the world. A belief in the power of magic has influenced the lives of millions and the great mystics have helped to shape the world's religions. And in their heyday, many of the rich and powerful beat at least a metaphorical path to the alchemists' doors. Whatever views may prevail today, a great deal of people have believed in magic and mysticism for a long time in many different places. And a great deal of people believed that in one way or another they were connected with wisdom.

Solomon. Seventeenth-century Flemish print designed by Erasmus Quellinus, showing Solomon as an old man. The symbolism used here is both complex and eclectic, but all the items surrounding Solomon seem designed to reinforce the idea that his accomplishments were many and varied.

8
Wisdom and Proverbs

It may seem very generous to give proverbs a whole chapter to themselves and apparently put them on a par with whole disciplines like philosophy and history. This, however, will be a relatively short chapter, and as a matter of fact the study of proverbs *does* count as a discipline in its own right. It carries the name of paroemiology. If collecting proverbs counts as one way of studying them, then paroemiology is a very ancient discipline indeed because the oldest known collections of proverbs were assembled and written down before 2500 BC. However, this statement immediately requires some qualification. Ancient Sumerian works such as 'The Instructions of Shuruppak to his son Ziusudra' contain more than just proverbs, as does the biblical book of Proverbs, which was compiled many centuries later. There are all kinds of overlaps between proverbs, instruction literature and fables, and while modern scholars continue to debate where one genre ends and another begins, ancient compilers probably did not care. Their main concern was with bringing together words of wisdom in whatever format they might be found. While the result might be regarded as a work of literature, literary values were of secondary importance. The point of such collections was to produce something from which people could *learn*. The didactic function was explicit in instruction literature, but it was implicitly there in fables and proverbs too. By way of contrast, a modern collector of proverbs prefaced his book with the observation that its purpose was 'to trace, so far as may be possible, the history of English proverbs'.[1] Here there is no ulterior motive, nor even an ulterior aspiration. Readers may be interested in the book's contents, but there is no expectation that they will actually derive any benefit from them. We should not expect to find proverbs treated in the same way in all societies at all times.

There is no agreed definition of what a proverb is, and that immediately makes the study of proverbs problematic. The fact that proverbs seem to crop up in so many different cultures makes it difficult to come up with a single definition that is equally applicable in all contexts. Modern paroemiologists have taken a variety of approaches to this problem. For example, a substantial amount of scholarly ink has been expended on trying to identify a common structure that proverbs all share. Given that languages have many different structures, such an approach is unlikely to deliver anything except a high level of generality. For example, the conclusion that 'proverbs must have at least two words' does not really get anyone very far.[2]

The primary 'structural' fact about a proverb is that is it short, and on that there is general agreement. A second feature of the proverb may best be summed up in the words of Alexander Pope in his 'Essay on Criticism':

> True wit is Nature to advantage dress'd;
> What oft was thought, but ne'er so well express'd.[3]

A proverb is something that is 'well express'd', there is an aesthetic dimension to it. In literary terms a proverb is like a tiny polished gem. The same point could always be made at greater length and in a different way, but the proverb is a triumph of economy and imagery. By way of example, 'A stitch in time saves nine' manages to pack into six words a graphic image of the benefits of preventive maintenance that has an application far beyond the world of needlework. It would, however, be meaningless for someone who had no knowledge of needlework at all, and clearly the imagery of a proverb has to resonate in some way with its intended audience. We would also expect the imagery used in a proverb to reflect the world of its origins, and this seems to be the case: 'The dominant imagery of the Sumerian proverbs reflects agriculture and animal husbandry, a life-style which formed the basis of Sumerian culture.'[4] Similarly, 'A stitch in time saves nine' belongs to a culture where clothes are mended rather than thrown away.

But why does a single stitch save precisely *nine* other stitches? Why not four? Or seventeen? The only remotely plausible explanation is the similarity in sound between 'time' and 'nine'. This leads to another dimension of the proverb: it is memorable. 'Memorable' can mean both 'worth remembering' and 'easily remembered', and both senses are applicable here. The use of rhyme, alliteration or assonance can make a proverb easier to remember, but just because something can be easily remembered does not mean that it deserves to be. However, to call something a proverb is to credit it with an authority that makes it worth remembering. The reason for attributing thousands of proverbs to Solomon, whether or not he had any connection with them, was in order to give them authority. A proverb is not just a saying, it is a saying that has something special to offer, and that something special has traditionally been recognized as wisdom. Proverbs were not attributed to Solomon because of his political or architectural achievements, but because he was renowned for his wisdom. In ancient Greece, the Seven Sages performed a similar function.

Even where particular people with a reputation for wisdom are not credited with producing them, proverbs can still carry a certain authority. To quote a proverb is not to make a personal statement, but to appeal to something that has stood the test of time and been passed down from generation to generation. Proverbs can constitute a kind of collective cultural wisdom. In some traditional African cultures, being able to quote a proverb in support of one's position can be almost like citing a legal precedent. This introduces another dimension of paroemiology: proverbs can be studied in terms of how they are *used*. What is regarded as the embodiment of wisdom in one culture may function as nothing more than a throwaway line or literary embellishment in another. Those who study proverbs on a comparative basis have to take into account not only text but also context. One of the more unexpected contexts in which to find proverbs being used is in the diagnosis of mental illness, but an inability to interpret proverbs correctly has been seen by some as a symptom of schizophrenia.

Although there is no agreed definition of what a proverb is, there are many different definitions on offer. One that works better than most is that of Moses Ibn Ezra, 'A proverb has three characteristics: few words, good sense, and a fine image.'[5]

Proverbial Wisdom

According to Lord John Russell, a proverb is 'The wit of one man and the wisdom of many.'[6] In the end, the reputation enjoyed by proverbs as a vehicle for wisdom must come down to their content. It would be relatively easy to compose something that had 'few words' and 'a fine image', but without also having 'good sense' it would not be a proverb. 'A stitch in time never saves nine' is brief and makes good use of imagery, but it fails the 'good sense' test and does not work as a proverb. Although 'good sense' sounds much more mundane and commonplace than 'wisdom', in proverbs they can amount to much the same thing. The wisdom of proverbs is above all the wisdom that comes from experience. Throughout history people with a reputation for wisdom have been sought out for their advice, and the proverb may be regarded as a vehicle in which the advice of the wise is preserved and transmitted so that it remains accessible.

Not every proverb is constructed or can be read as an explicit piece of advice. On the face of it, 'A stitch in time saves nine' might just be taken as an observation about how the world works. It is, however, an observation that can become the basis of a piece of advice because it has practical implications. Where the advisory nature of a proverb is only implicit, it becomes evident (to those able to see it) when the proverb is approached within a context that makes it relevant. And only when we follow the advice and see that it works do we really understand the proverb. As John Keats put it, 'a proverb is no proverb to you till your life has illustrated it'. The illustration does not have to be a positive one. We may appreciate the truth of a proverb after we have failed to follow its advice and suffered the consequences.

The extent to which human nature is fixed or constant has been the subject of a great deal of debate, and we would expect climate and culture to influence people's outlook on the world to at least some degree. Nevertheless, the study of proverbs suggests that some things change very little from age to age or from place to place. Here are three examples taken from collections that circulated in ancient Sumer thousands of years ago: 'You don't return borrowed bread'; 'Flies enter an open mouth'; 'The income never suffices. The expenditure never ceases.'[7] Although we do not know how the Sumerians used them, in their translated forms it is not difficult to understand their meanings, or to think of contexts in which we might use them today.

It has often been observed that proverbs can sometimes contradict each other: 'Absence makes the heart grow fonder' and 'Out of sight, out of mind' provide an obvious instance of two proverbs pulling in opposite directions. This phenomenon reflects a fundamental fact about the written word, which is that once it has been produced it is to all intents and purposes fixed and frozen for all time. Until the relatively recent inventions of Edison and others, the spoken word vanished as soon as it was uttered, but the written word lived on potentially forever. When the words of the wise were written down they lost control of them, and lost control of the context in which they might be approached and appreciated. 'Absence makes the heart grow fonder' and 'Out of sight, out of mind' are like two different prescriptions written by a physician for two different patients with two different ailments. If each patient takes the prescribed medication, all will be well. But if they swap prescriptions and each takes the wrong medication, all will not be well. A drug that alleviates headaches does not 'contradict' a drug that lowers blood pressure, it just does something different. In the same way, a proverb that is applicable in one context may not be applicable in another. Understanding when particular proverbs are applicable and when they are not may itself require some of the wisdom that gave rise to them in the first place. And even understanding the proverb itself may be beyond the ability of some: as an African proverb puts it, 'When a fool is told a proverb, the meaning of it has to be explained to him.'[8]

One of the strengths of the proverb is also one of its limitations. Being brief helps the proverb to be memorable, but it also sets a limit to what it can convey. A proverb can offer a flash of insight, but it cannot carry a sustained discussion. Bringing lots of proverbs together simply creates a collection of self-contained items. While such a collection may reflect a coherent and unified outlook on the world, it is unable to articulate that outlook in a systematic and comprehensive way. Proverbs are not to be confused with philosophy.

Helena Petrovna Blavatsky. Blavatsky (1831–1891) was the undoubted intellectual powerhouse behind the movement known as theosophy. However, she was also a divisive figure and while many are impressed by her writings, others suspect that a lot of what she claimed to have been learned from various mysterious teachers she simply made up herself.

9
Wisdom and the Present Day

The approach taken in this book has not been a chronological one. To some extent that is inevitable because so much of the chronology is either unknown or at best speculative. Furthermore, although some of the materials that have been presented in these pages relate to a specific period in the past, others have a lifespan that continues up to the present day. Whenever it originated, astrology is still practised, and however ancient they may be, the gods of Hinduism are still worshipped in India and elsewhere today. To weave such a vast array of materials together into a single coherent historical narrative would be impossible. However, before moving to the book's conclusion I want to use this chapter to focus on some recent developments. In a survey that takes in at least 4,500 years of human history, 'recent' is interpreted relatively loosely here, and some of the discussions in this chapter will take us back as far as the nineteenth century. But I shall begin in the twentieth with what became known as the New Age movement.

New Age

The New Age movement may be thought of as the spiritual offshoot or dimension of the counter-culture that developed in the 1960s and 1970s in North America, Europe and elsewhere. Under its umbrella sheltered a vast array of beliefs and practices, some new, some old, and some new but claiming to be old:

> Esoteric or mystical Buddhism, Christianity, Hinduism, Islam and Taoism enter the picture. So do elements from 'pagan' teachings including Celtic, Druidic, Mayan and Native American Indian. An exceedingly wide range of practices – Zen meditations, Wiccan rituals, enlightenment intensive seminars, management trainings, shamanic activities, wilderness events, spiritual therapies, forms of positive thinking – fall under the rubric.[1]

And this list could be extended easily. If a counter-culture is understood as an act of rebellion, then it is easy to see what all the items on the list are not. They are not institutionalized Christianity, which was by far the most dominant religious tradition in those places where the New Age movement took root and flourished. Just as the broader 1960s counter-culture rebelled against 'the establishment', so its spiritual dimension rebelled against the religious 'establishment'. New Agers might disagree as to where wisdom (and the word crops up frequently in New Age writings) *could* be found, but were unanimous on the subject of where it could *not* be found. To some extent, then, the identity of the New Age movement is a negative one. It is defined by what it is not.

However, there is a bit more to it than that, and it is possible to see at least the outlines of a more positive identity as well. Two ideas in particular recur relatively frequently throughout New Age thought and literature. The first is that of a *philosophia perennis*. The basic notion of the *philosophia perennis* is relatively easy to pin down. It is the belief that there is some kind of universal truth (often capitalized as 'Truth') that has been recognized and grasped by enlightened beings throughout the ages. The actual content of the *philosophia perennis* is more difficult to identify. Those who write about it frequently emphasize the point that the Truth can only be known through direct and immediate experience, and that this is possible only for 'those who have chosen to fulfil certain conditions, making themselves loving, pure in heart and poor in spirit'.[2] While many may speak of it, few actually know it. Words may convey some sense of it, or help to point us towards it, but they cannot capture it.

One exponent of the *philosophia perennis* was Frithjof Schuon (1907–1998), although the New Age came rather late in the day for him. Born in Switzerland, as a young man he read the *Upanishads*; in his twenties he was initiated into an order of Sufism; in his fifties he was adopted into the Sioux nation; and late in life he had visions of the Virgin Mary. Along the way he wrote a number of books and acquired many followers. His first work, *The Transcendent Unity of Religions*, sets out in both its title and contents the idea of the *philosophia perennis*. In it he states: 'The evidence for the transcendent unity of religions results not only from the oneness of Truth but also from the oneness of the human race.'[3] Different religions may follow different paths, but in the end we are all human beings living in the same reality. Ultimately, and most importantly mystically, all religions are one. Seen from this perspective, outward differences between religions are of no real importance. Those who fail to grasp this (which is to say, most people) reveal only the superficiality of their religiosity. In the philosophy of Schuon we find a form of rationalized eclecticism: in the end differences do not need to be resolved because in the end they do not exist. Such an outlook found a ready audience among New Agers. Schuon and his followers sometimes referred to his work as 'sapiential philosophy', clearly indicating the connection they believed it had with wisdom.

The other recurrent idea to be found permeating the New Age movement is what has been termed 'Self-spirituality'. The idea that the divine lies within can be found in many different places, from the *Upanishads* to Gnosticism. For New Agers, 'The inner realm, and the inner realm alone, is held to serve as the source of authentic vitality, creativity, love, tranquillity, wisdom, power, authority and all those other qualities which are held to comprise the perfect life.'[4] This embracing of the inner may be seen as an implicit rejection of the 'outer', and it is possible to see in it echoes of the old Cynic philosophy that rejected the life of convention in favour of the 'Life in accordance with nature'. However, the danger of believing that the divine lies within is that it may lead to the belief that whatever lies within is divine, which is a very different (and far more dangerous) matter. The idea that each and every aspect of a person's 'inner realm' is to be identified with, or is part of, our 'true' or 'divine' nature, which carries a universal, absolute and unchallengeable value, can be a recipe for psychological disaster.

While the *philosophia perennis* and Self-spirituality may be important, and even dominant, themes of the New Age movement, it would be wrong to paint too tidy a picture of what in the end amounted to an enormous number of unrelated individual movements, large and small, old and new, scattered over many different countries. What can be said is that the New Age movement was founded on a huge spiritual demand, and that this demand was met by a wide variety of suppliers.

Any number and combination of New Age figures could have been chosen for particular consideration, but I have decided to focus here on two very different ones. Bhagwan Shree Rajneesh (1931–1990) was born as Chandra Mohan and died as Osho. During the 1970s his ashram in India became a magnet for many from Europe and North America. Whereas almost all his initial followers had been from India, they were rapidly outnumbered by those who came from elsewhere, first to Pune and then later to a new ashram in Oregon. His orange-clad followers became a familiar sight in many towns and cities around the world. Some of the antics of some of the Rajneesh movement's members in the U.S. brought it a considerable amount of unwanted publicity, and significantly damaged its reputation. Rajneesh's own fondness for acquiring Rolls-Royces left many unimpressed. Behind all the bad publicity, however, was a genuinely charismatic, eclectic and innovative teacher who could give improvised talks on a wide range of spiritual topics and traditions. Behind all the variety and novelty, however, there was ultimately one very simple and very old message: 'The purpose of life is to become conscious . . . [and] pure consciousness is the aim of yoga.'[5] Rajneesh borrowed and taught a wide variety of meditative techniques, as well as devising some new ones to go alongside them, but the different techniques were only so many different ways of achieving the same goal. While Rajneesh was undoubtedly original in many ways, he was also undoubtedly very traditional in others.

T. Lobsang Rampa (1911–1981) came to prominence before the New Age movement began when his first book, *The Third Eye*, appeared in 1955. In it he recounted his experiences growing up in Tibet. It sold well and many more books followed, the last of which was published in 1980 when the New Age movement was well under way. Over the years he acquired a considerable readership, but not all his readers were equally impressed. Some questioned his authenticity, and investigations revealed that T. Lobsang Rampa was in fact Cyril Hoskins, a plumber from Devon. Hoskins insisted that his body had been taken over by the spirit of a Tibetan lama and that everything in his books was true. Today there are websites dedicated to Rampa's work that still accept him as genuinely Tibetan and from which the name of Cyril Hoskins is entirely absent. As one seasoned observer noted: 'We may admire his direct punchy style, his imagination and his sheer cheek. But compared with what the [Tibetan Buddhist] tradition itself has to offer, it is weak stuff.'[6]

Rajneesh and Rampa were both colourful characters, and both attracted devoted followers. Both were controversial, but in very different ways. However unorthodox he might have been, Rajneesh was definitely the real thing whereas Rampa was regarded by many as a total fraud. But for those looking for something 'different', each had something to offer.

As a movement, theosophy long pre-dated the New Age, but it was taken up by a number of New Agers with enthusiasm. The movement had at its heart the Theosophical Society, which was founded in New York in 1875 by Helena Petrovna Blavatsky (1831–1891), Henry Steel Olcott (1832–1907) and others. Shortly after, they established a new headquarters for the organization in Adyar, near what was then called Madras (now Chennai) in southern India. During the course of its history it has both spread and divided. After the deaths of Blavatsky and Olcott, Annie Besant (1847–1933) became the movement's undisputed leader, but her promotion of Jiddu Krishnamurti (1895–1986) as the new 'world teacher' alienated some, including Rudolf Steiner (1861–1925), who founded his own Anthroposophical Society partly in protest. Another theosophist who left to found an independent movement was Alice Bailey (1880–1949), who set up the Arcane Society. Krishnamurti, Steiner and Bailey all became New Age favourites.

Intellectually, the leading light of the Theosophical Society was undoubtedly Blavatsky, whose writings formed the core of the society's teachings. A curious and controversial figure, she wrote two major works, *Isis Unveiled* and *The Secret Doctrine*, along with a number of others. In *The Key to Theosophy* she provides a late, useful and relatively brief summary of her work, along with responses to a number of her critics. Theosophy is a 'wisdom-religion', preserved and transmitted over the centuries by a mysterious secret brotherhood composed of many Masters of Wisdom, or Adepts. Blavatsky claimed to have been taught by such an Adept, although her works suggest a wide range of other sources. In *The Secret Doctrine* she claimed to have seen and translated mysterious writings in a previously unknown language, a claim that did little to convince the sceptics.

In terms of content, theosophy is highly eclectic, and one of the aims of the Theosophical Society was 'to vindicate the importance of old Asiatic literature, namely of the Brahmanical, Buddhist and Zoroastrian philosophies'.[7] However, one of the main inspirations behind theosophy may have been African. Ammonius Saccas (second/third century AD) taught in Alexandria for many years, although it is not known if he actually came from Egypt. He wrote nothing himself, but is known through his pupils such as Plotinus and Origen. Plotinus (second/third century AD) is generally regarded as the founder of Neoplatonism in which the philosophy of Plato is taken in a more, and more explicitly, mystical direction. Ammonius Saccas is not presented as the founder of the wisdom-religion, merely as one of the most important links in the chain of its transmission. But even this is somewhat surprising given that Blavatsky claimed to have acquired her esoteric knowledge through travels in Asia.

The long list of names and traditions scattered throughout Helena Blavatsky's writings makes it possible to see theosophy as one more variant on the *philosophia perennis*, while the suggestion that the dominant theme of Neoplatonism is 'the need to detach the soul from the body and external existence, and turn inwards' may also suggest a link with 'Self-spirituality'.[8] It is not too difficult to see why New Agers might find theosophy interesting and attractive. As to theosophy itself, what it offered was its own particular eclectic blend of many diverse elements. Whether or not she ever met any Masters of Wisdom on her travels, by writing *The Secret Doctrine* Blavatsky can reasonably claim to have introduced many in Europe and North America to Asian traditions of thought with which they were unfamiliar.

Sophiology

The New Agers who were in rebellion against institutionalized Christianity might have been surprised to know about some of the developments that had been taking place within it. In 1875 a young Russian man arrived in London 'in order to study the Gnostic, Indian and Medieval philosophies'.[9] This was Vladimir Solovyov (1853–1900), on a travelling fellowship from the University of Moscow. At the age of nine he had had a vision of Sophia, the Divine Wisdom, in the university's chapel. Now, in the Reading Room of the British Museum, he had another, and it summoned him to Egypt. In the desert on the outskirts of Cairo he had a third and final vision of the Divine Wisdom. Unsurprisingly, these visions had a significant influence on his thinking, and Sophia is a subject to which he continually returns in his writings. What he actually means by it, however, is problematic: 'Sophia is variously represented as the substance of God, of the Trinity, as the archetype of creation, as the substance of the Holy Spirit. In addition, Sophia appears as the "eternal Feminine" and is also associated with the Theotokos, Mary the Mother of God'. To these may also be added 'world-soul' and 'ideal humanity'.[10] It is difficult to extract from or impose on this any kind of unity, and it is difficult to know whether Solovyov changed his position or simply struggled to articulate the position he held. The importance of Sophia in his thought is clear, but much is not. If we look at what Sophia does in the thought of Solovyov, then it seems to me that its primary function is as a unifying force, something that can bring together the human and the divine, which is what Solovyov's own experiences of Sophia did.

Solovyov laid the foundations of Russian sophiology, which others built on in different ways. Pavel Florensky (1882–1943) managed to combine the roles of priest, philosopher and scientist before ending his days as one of the many victims of Stalin. As a student he encountered the thought of Solovyov, and this helped to shape his own intellectual development. As with Solovyov, he was able to interpret Sophia in a number of different ways. As a priest, his interests naturally revolved around Orthodoxy as an institution as well as a theology. Florensky reflected on how Sophia related to the Church, liturgy and its icons. He was also able to draw on Sophia as a symbol and source of hope in times of difficulty: 'With the background of the social cataclysms of the beginning of the [twentieth] century . . . the widely accepted image of Sophia could, it seemed, be a guarantee of salvation and perform the function of a connecting element and embody the unity and wholeness of the world.'[11] As something that brought the divine and the human together, Sophia could also serve as an assurance that the human had not been abandoned by the divine.

While Florensky stayed in Stalin's Soviet Union and suffered the consequences, many other philosophers left, whether willingly or unwillingly. One of those was Sergei Bulgakov (1871–1944), who made his way to Paris. In the hands and pen of Bulgakov, sophiology was pushed further than it had been before, and rather too far for the tastes of some. In 1935 there occurred what became known as the Sophia Affair when Bulgakov was accused of heresy by both the Moscow Patriarchate and the Russian Orthodox Church Outside Russia (an organization established by and supporting Russian exiles). Fortunately, Bulgakov's own bishop was more sympathetic. A panel was set up to investigate the matter, but the investigation never formally came to a conclusion. Nevertheless, it was clear that sophiology was moving in directions that made some people extremely nervous.

The problem facing sophiologists like Florensky and Bulgakov was that Orthodox Christian theology is Trinitarian, accepting and insisting that the divine manifests itself in three different persons, or hypostases, namely Father, Son and Holy Spirit. Florensky actually talked about Sophia in connection with a 'fourth hypostasis', but Bulgakov rejected that. The problem remains how close Sophia can be brought to the divine without actually becoming part of the divine. In his major work, *The Bride of the Lamb*, Bulgakov has this to say:

> The Divine Sophia contains the entire fullness of divine being . . . The Divine Sophia is God's *exhaustive* self-revelation, the fullness of divinity . . . The divine All belongs to the Divine Sophia; she is the all-unity of the divine All . . . The Divine Sophia (also known as the divine world) is therefore a *living* essence in God.[12]

The impression here is that Bulgakov is trying desperately hard to maintain at least *some* distance between Sophia and the divine, but not doing a particularly good job of it. It is not difficult to see why some might feel nervous.

Russian sophiology represented a new, and radical, attempt to address the issue that had been bothering Jewish and Christian theologians for centuries: just what *is* the relationship between wisdom and the divine?

Sage Philosophy

If the relationship between wisdom and the divine is a very old topic, sage philosophy is a relatively new one. The term 'sage philosophy' originated in a very particular context, and it is necessary to begin by filling in some of the background. During the colonial era in Africa, many Europeans questioned whether 'the African' was capable of rational or abstract thought. Not surprisingly, the post-colonial period gave rise to a number of responses to this fundamentally racist question, and the idea of sage philosophy was one of them. It may be noted that many of those who questioned the nature and quality of African thought were Christians, who presumably did not doubt that theologians such as Augustine of Hippo (born and died in Africa) were rational. Neither were doubts cast on the intellectual integrity of institutions such as the universities of Cairo and Cape Town. The discussion concerned itself mainly with *oral* cultures and was not particularly interested in the contents of libraries. It was also concerned with traditional communities rather than academic ones. So the basic question addressed by sage philosophy was whether the kind of wisdom encountered in traditional African societies can be regarded as a kind of philosophy. As such, this is an interesting question and one with a relevance well beyond the borders of Africa.

The issue about oral cultures can be resolved very quickly. I see no reason for even beginning to think that philosophy is intrinsically connected with literacy. Some of the major figures in the Western philosophical tradition, such as Pythagoras, Socrates and Ammonius Saccas, seem to have committed nothing to writing, and the 'works' of Epictetus are in fact notes taken by his pupil Arrian. Few would question the philosophical credentials of any of these people. It has also been observed more than once that the written word has certain disadvantages compared to the spoken one. It is true that all those mentioned lived in literate societies, but perhaps that just makes their gestures more pointed? If literacy is essentially an *aide-memoire*, there is no reason why philosophy requires it.

A far more interesting question concerns whether what might be termed 'folk wisdom' is comparable to philosophy, and, if it is not, what the difference between the two might be. Henry Odera Oruka (1944–1995), who was largely responsible for bringing the term 'sage philosophy' into play in this context, put it this way:

> Sage-Philosophy in my usage consists of the expressed thoughts of wise men and women in any given community and is a way of thinking and explaining the world that fluctuates between *popular wisdom* (well known communal maxims, aphorisms and general common sense truths) and *didactic wisdom*, an expounded wisdom and a rational thought of some given individuals within a community. While the popular wisdom is often conformist, the didactic wisdom is at times critical of the communal set-up and the popular wisdom.[13]

What Oruka seems to be suggesting is that the purveyor of folk wisdom (which he calls 'popular wisdom') should be seen almost as a communal resource, as a person who safeguards and pronounces on the basic values of the community. Such a role is a quasi-legal one, in that the folk sage may be implicitly called upon to judge whether or not something is in accordance with established and acceptable ways. This may sometimes involve deciding which proverb is applicable on which occasion. Judging is an area of activity strongly associated with wisdom in many societies, and it is entirely understandable that people should wish their judges to be wise people.

Oruka argues that while the wisdom of the folk sage is authentic wisdom, it is not a form of philosophy. Unfortunately, I do not think that his choice of words is particularly helpful here. His use of 'rational' is understandable, given the colonial-era debates concerning the nature of African thought. However, it is unclear why he seems to suggest that 'popular wisdom' is not used for didactic purposes. The opposite seems to me to be more likely to be true. Nevertheless, I think he is trying to make two valuable points. First, it is possible to string together any number of 'communal maxims, aphorisms and general common sense truths' but they will not add up to a system of thought. What we have in folk wisdom is a lot of individual observations, but no underpinning theory to bind them all together. Second, folk wisdom is inherently conservative whereas philosophy has to be critically reflective. If not exactly an enforcer of the status quo, the folk sage nevertheless represents the values of the status quo in much the same way that the culture hero does. The philosopher, however, must be prepared to challenge the status quo and if necessary reject it. The argument that 'it has always been done this way' is of little philosophical value, although it carries great weight in a traditional society.

Oruka claims that both folk sages and philosophers are to be found in traditional African societies, sometimes in the same person. This is put as a factual claim and I see no reason why it should not be true. In the end it is only by questioning people that it is possible to establish why they hold the views they do, and this is the method used by students of sage philosophy. Outside the specific context in which the debate about sage philosophy arose, it has helped to prompt a re-evaluation of the nature of philosophy, and of the relationship between philosophy and wisdom.

Towards a Science of Wisdom

If not actually inexhaustible, the topic of wisdom certainly provides plenty of opportunities for research, and many different disciplines can be brought to bear on it. Here I want to give a brief overview of some areas of research in which scholars have been engaged over the past 30 years or so. Broadly speaking, this research has addressed three fundamental questions. The first question is: how can we define wisdom? The second question is: how can we recognise wisdom? And the third question is: can wisdom be measured? Not everyone has been equally interested in all three questions, but between them they help to give a kind of unity to a number of different projects. Much (but by no means all) of the recent literature has come from people whose primary discipline is psychology, broadly understood. Other disciplines include sociology, philosophy and neurobiology.

When *Wisdom: Its Nature, Origins, and Development* appeared in 1990, it proved to be a significant event in the modern study of wisdom. Its editor, Robert J. Sternberg, pulled together a wide variety of contributions to tackle the extensive areas covered by its title. For those of us interested in the study of wisdom, the book's appearance read like a message saying 'You are not alone!' However, reading the book itself conveyed a rather different message: 'We cannot agree what wisdom is!' Over a dozen different (and some very different) understandings of wisdom emerged from its pages, and since then even more have been added to the range of options available. Wisdom itself has also become divided into general wisdom, personal wisdom, theoretic wisdom, transcendent wisdom, and so on. Even the most fanatical eclectic would struggle to extract any kind of coherent picture from all this. While some disagreements are on matters of detail, some are absolutely fundamental. Is wisdom a kind of knowledge? Or is it a kind of skill? Or is it a kind of perception? Or is it a kind of personality trait? Or is it a combination of some or all of these things?

One of the most influential characterizations of wisdom in recent years has been connected with what is known as the Berlin Wisdom Paradigm. This grew out of work done at the Max Planck Institute for Social Development by Paul Baltes and others. This homed in on five factors that were thought to be central and crucial to wisdom: 'Rich factual knowledge about life; Rich procedural knowledge about life; Lifespan contextualism; Relativism of values and life priorities; Recognition and management of uncertainty.'[14] This is meant to function not only as a statement of what wisdom *is*, but also as an indication of how it can be recognized. For example, we might reasonably expect people's knowledge of how the world works, or their ability to deal with uncertainty, to manifest themselves in some way in their behaviour.

Although five factors are identified, it is possible to reduce them to two more basic ones. The first two factors are about knowledge and the last two are about adaptability, while the middle one contains elements of both. What emerges from the Berlin Wisdom Paradigm is essentially a kind of understanding free from dogmatism.

However, many have felt uncomfortable with what the Berlin Wisdom Paradigm leaves out, and in particular with its lack of any emotional dimension. One of these is Monika Ardelt, who has developed what she calls the Three-Dimensional Wisdom Scale, the three dimensions being the cognitive, the reflective and the affective. The 'cognitive' dimension is very close to what appears in the Berlin Wisdom Paradigm. The 'reflective' dimension relates to the capacity for self-examination and self-awareness, and the 'affective' dimension involves the feelings we have towards other people. It may be useful to spell out what the affective component means in more detail.

> [It] consists of a person's sympathetic and compassionate love for others. The transcendence of one's subjectivity and projections through (self-)reflection is likely to reduce one's self-centredness. This in turn will permit deeper insights into one's own and others' motives and behaviour, which enable a wise person to interact with people in a more constructive, sympathetic, and compassionate way.[15]

The trend towards a more scientific approach to wisdom manifests itself in part in contemporary research attempting not only to define wisdom but also to measure it. With this aim in mind, Ardelt has developed a 39-item questionnaire, which is used to assess where people fall along the Wisdom Scale. However, while the Wisdom Scale clearly measures something, not everyone agrees that it measures wisdom.

Another kind of approach has been taken by Carolyn M. Aldwin and others, and this argues that 'wisdom is thought to develop through a process of self-knowledge, nonattachment, integration, and self-transcendence, or decentering from the self.'[16] This approach has been influenced in part by my own earlier work on wisdom, which was more influenced by philosophical, psychological and mystical traditions than any scientific ones.[17] In 2008 Aldwin, Ardelt and others worked to come up with an agreed definition of wisdom that would bring a number of different strands together. This was the result:

> Wisdom is a practice that reflects the developmental process by which individuals increase in self-knowledge, self-integration,

> nonattachment, self-transcendence, and compassion, as well as a deeper understanding of life. This practice involves better self-regulation and ethical choices, resulting in greater good for oneself and others.[18]

Needless to say, unanimity has not yet broken out, and there is much more work to be done. What is encouraging is an emerging sense of common purpose, aligned with a recognition that wisdom is multi-dimensional. The different disciplines that are contributing to the contemporary study of wisdom are helping to shine light on its different aspects.

Finally, it is worth noting that wisdom has also become an area of study for neurobiologists. If wisdom is analysable in terms of certain mental capacities, whether cognitive, reflective, affective or whatever, then it might be possible to identify the neurobiological infrastructure associated with it. There is clearly much more work to be done, but it is exciting that a whole new front seems to have been opened up.

Perhaps the main message to be taken out of this chapter is that interest in wisdom is alive and well, and to be found in some surprising places. As an umbrella term, 'New Age' shelters some uneven ground beneath it. New Agers found their inspiration in a variety of movements. Some came with an impeccable pedigree, but some were definitely mongrels. In some parts of the New Age world new life was breathed into old traditions, in some parts charlatans preyed on the vulnerable. Any number of books with 'wisdom' in their titles appeared, but while some offered the genuine article some barely rose above the banal. What the New Age movement did most successfully was to open up many different avenues of spiritual development for those who found more conventional religious movements unappealing.

In their own ways, both sophiology and sage philosophy pushed against the limits of long-established traditions, but in constructive ways. The fact that Bulgakov was accused of heresy is sufficient evidence of the radical nature of sophiology, but finding a satisfactory place for the figure of Wisdom first within Judaism and then within Christianity had long been problematic. Sage philosophy challenged the notion of what philosophy was or could be, and although this challenge took place within a particularly post-colonial setting, the questions posed had a far wider resonance.

The most recent developments have sought to put the study of wisdom on a more scientific footing. First the social sciences and now the natural sciences are taking an interest. This can only be a plus, and it is hoped that there will be interesting and important developments within these disciplines in the years to come.

St Sophia. Statue by Georgi Chapkanov in Sofia, Bulgaria, erected in 2000 on the site where another statue – of Vladimir Lenin – once stood; it is 8 metres (26 feet) high, set atop a plinth 14 metres (46 feet) high. The owl perched on Sophia's arm is a traditional symbol of wisdom.

Conclusion

In the opening pages of his *Nicomachean Ethics*, Aristotle remarked that not every discipline was capable of the same level of precision, but what was required in each was to achieve the level appropriate to the subject matter under consideration. It just had to be accepted as a fact that certain disciplines were more prone to uncertainty than others. In the preceding chapters I have sought to heed that advice. In particular, I have not tried to impose on the materials presented in them a single unifying narrative or pattern. Because different ages and cultures have been allowed to speak for themselves, many different voices have been heard. That has been part of the point of the exercise, and I have tried to put on display something of the variety that can be encountered in the world of wisdom. Even though wisdom itself is sometimes associated with order, the world of wisdom itself can seem like a rather untidy place. Given how big that world is, perhaps some measure of untidiness is only to be expected.

There are two obvious ways of responding to this situation. The first is to argue that the untidiness is only apparent, and that underneath or behind it all there lies order, clarity and unity. The second is to accept the untidiness as genuine, but look for themes and threads that run through it and give it some cohesion. In this way the untidiness remains, but things are saved from being a total mess.

For those who believe in a fundamental unity underlying the apparent untidiness, there are two obvious routes to take: tradition and definition. In the narrowest understanding of the tradition route, wisdom is something esoteric that has to be passed on from one person directly to another. Only an established line of transmission from an authentic source is admissible as evidence. Obviously, this poses some problems. The further back in time the tradition goes, the more difficult it becomes to produce satisfactory evidence of an unbroken line of transmission. On the other hand, if the tradition is only of recent origin, does it count as a tradition at all? And if a tradition can begin at any time, does that not undermine the need for a tradition? Why go searching for an old tradition if a new one can be started now?

Among those who subscribed to the narrowest understanding of the tradition route were those such as the Kabbalists who felt obliged to trace their own tradition back to the very first man, Adam. Suhrawardi and Mulla Sadra were among those who took the same route and compiled imaginative genealogies that went back into the remotest past and linked philosophers, kings and prophets. But at the beginning of such genealogies there was usually some kind of divine revelation, sometimes with the assistance of angels. These and similar outlooks on wisdom seem to share a common structure. First, wisdom is regarded as essentially divine. Second, humanity may receive it by revelation and preserve it by direct transmission from one person to another. Thirdly, the age of revelation is over, so wisdom is only accessible through tradition.

If the understanding of the tradition route is broadened out, it leads to the idea of the *philosophia perennis*. Here there is still a belief in a *common* wisdom, but there is less emphasis on direct transmission. It is allowed that different cultures at different times may have discovered it independently, because it is believed that it underlies all genuine religions. The *philosophia perennis* might be regarded as the mystical core of religion generalized. Because divine revelation is not required for the *philosophia perennis*, the emphasis on tradition can be weaker, and a multiplicity of traditions can be accommodated. However, there is still a considerable respect for tradition as a vehicle for the secure transmission of wisdom, and many advocates of the *philosophia perennis* are keen to locate themselves within one tradition or another.

A general feature of the tradition route is that it tends to be strongly esoteric, which means that the *content* of the wisdom that travels along it remains obscure to the outsider. However, it usually seems to be equated to a special and profound kind of knowledge that can only be gained through direct experience.

In turning to the other route taken by those who want to argue for the unity of wisdom, that of definition, this is also home to advocates of the idea that wisdom is a kind of knowledge. From at least the time of Aristotle onwards there was an association of wisdom with a kind of knowledge that was either particularly broad or deep or both. Some thought of it in encyclopaedic terms, others more in terms of an understanding of first principles. Knowledge of one kind or another is also well to the fore in the Berlin Wisdom Paradigm, constituting two of its five elements. The other three elements, however, take wisdom beyond the range of knowledge alone. Whatever the precise meaning to be attached to 'Recognition and management of uncertainty', it seems to have more to do with perception and skills than with knowledge as such. This line of development is taken further by Monika Ardelt who explicitly brings the reflective and the affective under wisdom's wing. Finally, the definition arrived at by Carolyn Aldwin and others explicitly defines wisdom as a *practice* that incorporates a number of different elements.

A practice to which I have devoted a significant amount of space in this book is divination, but that is not the kind of practice Aldwin and others have in mind. The *kind* of definition of wisdom they are working towards is one that has no place for divination within it. Yet the association of divination with wisdom seems to me to be too well established and too strong simply to ignore. But if divination is a part of wisdom, and a definition of wisdom can find no room for divination, then the definition cannot be adequate. Ludwig Wittgenstein observed that if we try to define what a game is, we are faced with the problem that there is no one characteristic, let alone a set of characteristics, that is common to all games. What we find is 'a complicated network of similarities overlapping and criss-crossing: sometimes overall similarities, sometimes similarities of detail'.[1] Or to put it another way, even if there is no actual unity underneath the untidiness, at least it may be possible to identify some of the themes and threads that run through it.

A number of themes have cropped up from time to time that seem to me to shed light on different aspects of wisdom. One recurrent theme is that of creativity, and this has emerged in a number of different ways. In Zoroastrianism, Judaism and Christianity there are traditions of a personification of wisdom playing a role in the creation of the world itself. A number of culture heroes are also credited with this achievement. The famous judgement of Solomon demonstrates creativity of a different kind, namely the ability to think imaginatively and come up with a solution to a problem that is not remotely obvious. The value attached to solving riddles in certain cultures may be seen in the same light. In many cultures, those who are thought to have laid the foundations of civilization are credited with a special wisdom. Sometimes, like the *apkallu*, they seem to be just messengers bringing gifts from the gods, but others are credited with being the creators of these things themselves. Even modern-day inventors like Thomas Edison may be regarded as performing feats that verge on the miraculous.

A second theme is that of relativism. It has been noted that what passes for wisdom in one culture (or subculture) may not pass for wisdom everywhere. The insistence of the Maharaja of Gwalior that shooting various things, but tigers in particular, was required behaviour on the part of rulers' children reflects the customs and practices of his time, class and place. But even had guns existed in ancient Egypt, it cannot be assumed that Ptahhotep would have encouraged his son to blast away at wildlife with them. Literary works belonging to the instruction genre typically assume a particular kind of world that is to be lived in, and while some advice may be very generic, some can be very specific. The theme of relativism also emerges in the phenomenon of what is known as folk wisdom, which tends to be conventional and conservative. Because conventions vary from culture to culture, so does the content of folk wisdom. On the other hand, wisdom may also be ascribed to those who challenge conventions, such as the Cynic philosopher and the trickster.

The other side of relativism is universalism, and this too has been evidenced. Although proverbs like 'Where there is hunger, there are no bad tortillas'[2] have a specific place of origin (Mesoamerica in this case), the sentiment and truth they express can nevertheless be recognized anywhere: if you are starving, you will eat anything. The fact that we can not only understand but also appreciate proverbs that originated hundreds, and sometimes thousands, of years ago in cultures and places very different from our own is an important one. There are many things we struggle to understand about other cultures both ancient and modern, but on the whole proverbs generally make sense to us. They make sense to us because in some ways human life has changed very little over the millennia. We still need to eat, drink and sleep. We still fall in and out of love. We still need to figure out ways of getting on with each other. And so on. If something was a good solution to one of life's basic problems 4,000 years ago, and the same problem still besets us today, it seems only reasonable to give it a try. If it works, then it speaks for a certain universal core at the heart of proverbial wisdom.

The connection between wisdom and advice is another recurrent theme. Those deemed wise have frequently been sought out for their advice. Presumably this is because it was believed that they had something of practical value to offer, and it may be noted that this is not a trivial point. Wisdom has not always been associated with practical matters, as evidenced by the figure of the other-worldly mystic. The connection between wisdom and advice seems to work in two ways. First there is a link via knowledge. The idea that the wise somehow know more than others has already been met with. And although it has more than one function, gaining access to knowledge not normally accessible is part of the purpose of divination. The idea that divination involves some kind of contact with the divine serves only to enhance its association with wisdom.

Second, there is a link via perception. It has been observed that the sage may be seen as a figure who transcends partisanship and that selfishness is an obstacle to wisdom. It was also seen that the Three-Dimensional Wisdom Scale lays a strong emphasis on the affective dimension and highlights the importance of reducing self-centredness. This all seems to me to point in the direction of a conclusion I came to some time ago.[3] Self-interest introduces a bias into how we apprehend the world we live in. If we can remove that bias, our apprehension of the world will improve. Because we respond to how we think the world is, the more accurate our thoughts about it are, the more appropriate and effective our reactions to it are. This seems to me to be the basis of Buddhist teachings on compassion. We cannot make ourselves compassionate, but we become compassionate when we understand the world properly. Whether we use the term literally or metaphorically, the wise person 'sees' the world better than others do and so is in a better position to give advice about how to live in it.

Perhaps the notion of self-interest (or its absence) can also help to articulate the difference between black magic and white magic. Rather than thinking of magic as 'good' or 'bad', perhaps the distinction is better understood as between the use of magic for self-interest and the use of magic for other purposes.

All of these themes seem to me to shine some light on the complex phenomenon that is wisdom, but without actually yielding a definition of it. Attempts to arrive at a definition may help to clarify some parts of the picture, but I doubt that they will ever succeed in capturing all of it.

I indicated at the outset that in my own opinion the study of wisdom is principally about people because it is in wise people that we principally encounter wisdom. That is why this book has such a large cast of characters. While some have their homes in mythology or legend, most have been figures of flesh and blood. On a number of occasions the idea has been encountered that in the world of wisdom the written word needs to be treated with some distrust. Some teachers committed nothing to writing on principle, some believed that a text could never be more than half a teaching. It is perhaps in the context of the proverb that the limitations of the written word are easiest to see. Because a proverb is only an insight into a little bit of life, it needs to be used appropriately. Someone who quoted 'A stitch in time saves nine' on every imaginable occasion would be quite the opposite of wise. The wisdom of proverbs lies both in their contents *and* in their deployment, and deployment is always by *someone*. Even where we apparently have wisdom encapsulated in a timeless format, it still requires the personal touch to bring it alive.

Postscript: A Century of Wisdom

The century is an old literary genre. In its original form it consisted of a collection of 100 short sayings. Each saying provided the reader with something to reflect on. They were often used and carried around by monks to aid them in their spiritual progress. Here I have assembled 100 short sayings about wisdom to give the reader of this book something to reflect on. They are taken from a wide variety of sources, and some of the sayings are proverbs attributed to no one in particular. They come from different times, traditions and places and are not meant to represent or articulate a single outlook on wisdom. As in the rest of this book, one of the aims is to give a sense of the variety on offer. However, each in its own way makes an observation on wisdom from one angle or another. For ease of navigation I have arranged them into a number of different sections, but many of them could have found their way into more than one. It will become apparent on reading them that although many are entirely compatible with each other, some of them point in distinctly different directions. It will also be noticed that some are rather more universal in application than others.

With respect to proverbs, a number of different sources and versions are often available, and it is not always obvious whether someone is using, or adapting, an earlier saying or producing a new one. It may be that I have failed to give someone credit where it is due, or given someone credit where it is not. Any item that appears with no attribution is presumed to have been in circulation in the English language for a sufficiently long time for it to have become part of the common currency and credited to no one in particular.

There is a particular problem with items that have been translated from other languages, because different translators may render the same saying in distinctly different ways. In such cases I have taken a purely pragmatic approach and trusted the instincts of the translator. If translators have used 'wisdom' or 'wise' or 'sage', then I have given them credit for knowing what they are doing, even if others might disagree with them. While the results of taking this line may fall short of perfection, I think no real harm is done.

Proverbs

By wisdom peace, by peace, plenty.

'Tis wisdom sometimes to seem a fool.

A wise man begins in the end; a fool ends in the beginning.

Wise men in the world are like timber-trees in a hedge, here and there one.

Early to bed and early to rise makes a man healthy, wealthy and wise.

He is not wise that is not wise for himself.

He is wise that follows the wise.

The wise man is deceived but once, the fool twice.

Who is wise in the day can be no fool in the night.

Wise men care not for what they cannot have.

Fools ask questions that wise men cannot answer.

A word to the wise is enough.

Loss teaches wisdom. – Arab proverb

A wise man seeks wisdom; a madman thinks he has found it. – Persian proverb

Poets

After the event even a fool is wise. – Homer

Wisdom is the conqueror of fortune. – Juvenal

Where ignorance is bliss, 'tis folly to be wise. – Thomas Gray

Oppression makes the wise man mad. – Robert Browning

To love is wise. – Robert Bridges

The days that make us happy make us wise. – John Masefield

Where is the wisdom we have lost in knowledge?
Where is the knowledge we have lost in information?
– T. S. Eliot

Who knows useful things, not many things, is wise.
– Aeschylus

The Italians are wise before the deed; the Germans in the deed; the French after the deed. – George Herbert

Ask, who is wise? – you'll find the self-same man.
– Thomas Moore

A sage in France, a madman in Japan. – Thomas Moore

The invariable mark of wisdom is to see the miraculous in the common. – Ralph Waldo Emerson

I love Wisdom more than she loves me. – Lord Byron

Politicians

Neither a wise man nor a brave man lies down on the tracks of history to wait for the train of the future to run over him.
– Dwight D. Eisenhower

History teaches us that men and nations behave wisely once they have exhausted all other alternatives. – Abba Eban

Learn all the time; do not wait in the faith that old age will bring wisdom by itself. – Solon

It is a wise man who can keep silent in an argument, even though he is right. – Cato

Government is a contrivance of human wisdom to provide for human *wants*. Men have a right that these wants should be provided for by this wisdom. – Edmund Burke

There is in human nature generally more of the fool than of the wise. – Francis Bacon

Nature is always wise in every part. – Edward Thurlow

Philosophers

Nothing is closer to wisdom than truth. – Sextus

Claim anything except that you are wise. – Sextus

The wise man neither rejects life nor fears death. – Epicurus

Harm from other men comes either as a result of hate or envy or contempt, which the wise man overcomes by reasoning. – Epicurus

Fools are tortured by the recollection of bad things, while wise men enjoy past goods kept fresh by a grateful recollection. – Epicurus

No one was ever wise by chance. – Seneca

Wisdom must be intuitive reasoning combined with scientific knowledge. – Aristotle

They call him the wisest man to whose mind that which is required at once occurs. – Cicero

Science robs men of wisdom and usually converts them into phantom beings loaded up with facts. – Miguel de Unamuno

It is difficult to conceive the sage without a kind of harmonious equilibrium which he cannot but feel as happiness. – Gabriel Marcel

Wisdom is awareness of the real nature of things. – Chaungo Barasa

Wisdom denotes the pursuing of the best ends by the best means. – Francis Hutcheson

Wisdom accompanies brevity of speech. – Sextus

Buddhism

Buddhist Wisdom is not contemplation, nor existent or non-existent mind. It is not concerned with large or small, enlightenment or illusion. – Dogen

In the man lacking wisdom, the wrongs of others only provoke impatience; but for the wise, they call his patience into play and make it grow even stronger. – *Brahmajala Sutra*

The wise man does not cling to existence or non-existence. – *Mulamadhyamakakarika*

The wise investigate a situation carefully
Before taking action on what needs to be done.
– Sakya Pandita

Even as a great rock is not shaken by the wind, the wise man is not shaken by praise or blame. – *Dhammapada*

Wise people fully accept good advice
Even if it comes from children. – Sakya Pandita

Wisdom is what achieves happiness. – Sakya Pandita

Novelists

We do not receive wisdom. We must discover it ourselves after experiences which no one else can have for us and from which no one else can spare us. – Marcel Proust

Wisdom we know is the knowledge of good and evil, not the strength to choose between the two. – John Cheever

There is nothing in which real wisdom cannot be displayed. – Leo Tolstoy

Though wisdom cannot be gotten for gold, still less can it be gotten without it. – Samuel Butler

A wise man does three things: first, he himself does those things which he advises others to do; second, he does not do anything against truth; and third, he is patient with the weaknesses of those around him. – Leo Tolstoy

Hatred of the bourgeois is the beginning of wisdom. – Gustave Flaubert

Wisdom is the understanding of life's eternal truths. – Leo Tolstoy

We cannot bring ourselves to believe it possible that a foreigner should in any respect be wiser than ourselves. – Anthony Trollope

Now that I am sixty, I can see why the idea of elder wisdom has passed from currency. – John Updike

There is a wisdom that is woe; but there is a woe that is madness. – Herman Melville

China

The anger of the sages comes from true human fellow-feeling. Our anger comes from our own personal ideas. – Hong Yuan

Every person has a sage within his breast. It is just that people do not fully believe in this sage and bury it away. – Wang Yangming

People who are great do not lose their childlike minds. Children are true sages. – Zou Shouyi

A wise man looks for everything inside himself; a foolish man seeks it in others. – Confucius

Sages reduce desire and follow nature. – *Huainanzi*

Sages do not dress or behave ostentatiously. They wear what no one looks at, do what no one watches and say what no one disputes. – *Huainanzi*

It is a great misfortune for those engaged in learning to take the sayings of the sages as mere verbal exercises. – Xue Xuan

Religious Leaders and Writers

It is impossible for a man to attain wisdom unless first . . . he frees himself completely from the mist of ignorance and the dust of sin. – Maximus the Confessor

Wisdom is always good, true and beautiful. – Priest-monk Silouan

Wisdom is the discerning exercise of Knowledge. Neither deep learning nor profound knowledge is Wisdom. Judicious use of knowledge makes for Wisdom. – Zarathustra

He that thinks himself the wisest is generally the greatest fool. – Charles Caleb Colton

A scholar's wisdom comes of ample leisure; if a man is to be wise he must be relieved of other tasks. – Sirach

There are not many wisdoms but only one. – Augustine of Hippo

Desirelessness is wisdom. – Ramana Maharshi

The more a person analyses his inner self, the more insignificant he seems to himself. This is the first lesson of wisdom. – William Ellery Channing

To learn wisdom is to learn the virtues; to learn the virtues is to perform virtuous acts; and to perform virtuous acts is to perform acts which are according to right reason. – Johann Geiler von Kaisersberg

Wisdom is the knowledge of divine things. – Josse Clichtove

Wisdom is characterized by intellect and intelligence, the state which is opposite to wisdom by lack of intelligence and by sensation. – Maximus the Confessor

Dramatists and Humorists

The wise man thinks once before he speaks twice.
– Robert Benchley

It is not wise to be wiser than necessary.
– Philippe Quinault

A man should never be ashamed to own he has been in the wrong, which is but saying, in other words, that he is wiser today than he was yesterday.
– Alexander Pope

Who makes up the majority in any given country? Is it the wise men or the fools? I think we must agree that the fools are in a terrible overwhelming majority, all the wide world over. – Henrik Ibsen

Education. That which discloses to the wise and disguises from the foolish their lack of understanding.
– Ambrose Bierce

'Tis better to be fortunate than wise. – John Webster

Miscellaneous

The wisdom of silent men is beyond proof, though proverbial in every language. – Bergen Evans

It is the folly of the world, constantly, which confounds its wisdom. – Oliver Wendell Holmes

Love is the wisdom of the fool and the folly of the wise.
– Samuel Johnson

JUDGE: I have read your case, Mr Smith, and I am no wiser now than I was when I started.
F. E. SMITH: Possibly not, My Lord, but far better informed.

Faith without wisdom is a dangerous thing.
– Steven Runciman

I am not able to make use of the wisdom of the sociologists because I do not speak their language.
– Freeman J. Dyson

An optimist is a person who sees a green light everywhere, while the pessimist sees only the red stop-light. The truly wise person is colour-blind. – Albert Schweitzer

Wisdom directs the course of lands and cities and ships. – Pseudo-Phocylides

Men who work the soil cannot dream, and wisdom comes to us in dreams. – Wovoka

Which of these is the wisest and happiest – he who labours without ceasing and only obtains, with great trouble, enough to live on, or he who rests in comfort and finds all that he needs in the pleasure of hunting and fishing? – Micmac chief

No one is wise at all times. – Pliny the Elder

A man is wise with the wisdom of his time only, and ignorant with its ignorance. – Henry David Thoreau

Wisdom is never a superior knowledge but is, instead, the indomitably personal experience of a complete living. – Marc Edmund Jones

REFERENCES

Introduction

1 Aristotle, *Metaphysics*, 981b–982b.
2 Cicero, *Tusculan Disputations*, 3.5.
3 Augustine of Hippo, *Enchiridion*, 2.
4 Bendt Alster, *The Instructions of Suruppak: A Sumerian Proverb Collection* (Copenhagen, 1974).
5 Joseph Campbell, *The Hero with a Thousand Faces* (Cleveland, OH, 1956), p. 121.
6 Plato, *Republic*, 514–17.

1 Wisdom, Gods and Goddesses

1 Richard H. Wilkinson, *The Complete Gods and Goddesses of Ancient Egypt* (London, 2003), p. 216.
2 A. C. Bouquet, *Sacred Books of the World* (Harmondsworth, 1954), p. 113.
3 The translation is that of the Revised Standard Version.
4 John Ray, *The Wisdom of God Manifested in the Works of the Creation* (Glasgow, 1750), p. 35.

2 Wisdom, Myth and Legend

1 Bendt Alster, *The Instructions of Suruppak: A Sumerian Proverb Collection* (Copenhagen, 1974).
2 Anne Paludan, *Chronicle of the Chinese Emperors* (London, 2008), p. 8.
3 Geoffrey Ashe, *The Ancient Wisdom* (London, 1977).
4 J. M. Cook, *The Persians* (London, 1983), p. 228.
5 Alison Jones, *Larousse Dictionary of World Folklore* (Edinburgh, 1995), p. 429.
6 Joel Chandler Harris, *Uncle Remus: His Songs and his Sayings* (New York, 1982).
7 Jones, *Larousse Dictionary of World Folklore*, p. 429.
8 Trevor Curnow, *Wisdom, Intuition and Ethics* (Aldershot, 1999), chap. 4.
9 Eusebius, *Preparation for the Gospel*, trans. Edwin Hamilton Gifford (Eugene, OR, 2002), vol. I, p. 451.

10 Most of the relevant texts about Enoch can be found in *The Old Testament Pseudepigrapha*, ed. James H. Charlesworth, vol. 1 (London, 1983).
11 David Rohl, *The Lords of Avaris* (London, 2008), p. 528.

3 Wisdom in History

1 Edward Conze, *Buddhism: Its Essence and Development* (New York, 1959), p. 34.
2 The translation is from the Revised Standard Version.
3 The translation is from the Revised Standard Version.
4 D. T. Suzuki, *What is Zen?* (New York, 1972), pp. 63–4.
5 Surahs 27 and 34.
6 Josephus, *Antiquities of the Jews*, 8.6.4.
7 Patricia O'Grady, *Thales of Miletus* (Aldershot, 2002), pp. 273–5.
8 Plato, *Protagoras and Meno*, trans. W.K.C. Guthrie (Harmondsworth, 1956), p. 77.
9 Anne Paludan, *Chronicle of the Chinese Emperors* (London, 1998), p. 69.
10 Ibid.
11 Ingrid Fischer-Schreiber, *The Shambhala Dictionary of Taoism*, trans. Werner Wünsche (Boston, MA, 1996), p. 32.
12 John Blofeld, *Taoism: The Road to Immortality* (Boulder, CO, 1978), p. 23.
13 John Julius Norwich, *Byzantium: The Apogee* (London, 1991), p. 104.
14 Friedrich Heer, *The Holy Roman Empire*, trans. Janet Sondheimer (London, 1968), p. 81.
15 William Coxe, *History of the House of Austria* (London, 1847), vol. I, p. 117.
16 Miguel Leon-Portilla and Earl Shorris, *In the Language of Kings* (New York, 2001), pp. 141–2.
17 Ian P. McGreal, ed., *Great Thinkers of the Eastern World* (New York, 1995), p. 435.
18 Ibn Al'Arabi, *The Bezels of Wisdom*, ed. and trans. R.W.J. Austin (London, 1980), p. 71.
19 Raymond Van Over, ed., *Eastern Mysticism* (New York, 1977), vol. I, p. 421.
20 Reimund Kvideland and Henning K. Sehmsdorf, eds, *Scandinavian Folk Belief and Legend* (Minneapolis, MN, 1988), p. 286.
21 J. N. Farquhar, *Modern Religious Movements in India* (Delhi, 1967), p. 44.
22 T.M.P. Mahadevan, *Ramana Maharshi: The Sage of Arunacala* (London, 1977), p. 17.
23 Jonathan Lyons, *The House of Wisdom: How the Arabs Transformed Western Civilization* (London, 2009), p. 63.

4 Wisdom and Literature

1 Fritjof Capra, *The Tao of Physics* (New York, 1977), p. 17.
2 S. Radhakrishnan, *The Principal Upanisads* (London, 1953), p. 22.
3 Ibid., pp. 672–3.
4 Ibid., p. 280.
5 Patrick Olivelle, *Upanisads* (Oxford, 1996), p. 276.

6 Bill Porter, *Zen Baggage* (Berkeley, CA, 2009), p. 8.
7 Edward Conze, *Buddhist Wisdom: The Diamond Sutra and The Heart Sutra* (New York, 2001), p. 5.
8 Edward Conze, ed., *Buddhist Texts through the Ages* (New York, 1964), p. 146.
9 Porter, *Zen Baggage*, p. 8.
10 Jay L. Garfield, ed. and trans., *The Fundamental Wisdom of the Middle Way: Nagarjuna's 'Mulamadhyamakakarika'* (New York, 1995), p. 49.
11 Joseph Kaster, ed., *The Literature and Mythology of Ancient Egypt* (London, 1970), p. 166. I have taken the liberty of amending the translation slightly.
12 Ibid., p. 169.
13 Ibid., p. 179.
14 Ibid.
15 Ibid., p. 185.
16 Miriam Lichtheim, *Late Egyptian Literature in the International Context: A Study of Demotic Inscriptions* (Freiburg, 1983), p. 81.
17 Ibid.
18 Ibid., p. 73
19 James H. Charlesworth, ed., *The Old Testament Pseudepigrapha*, vol. II (London, 1985), p. 500.
20 Ibid., p. 501
21 Charles Allen and Sharada Dwivedi, *Lives of the Indian Princes* (London, 1986), p. 19.
22 Ibid., p. 120
23 Ibid., p. 90.
24 Sakya Pandita, *Ordinary Wisdom: Sakya Pandita's Treasury of Good Advice*, trans. John J. Davenport (Boston, MA, 2000), p. 214.
25 Ibid., p. 142.
26 Hung Ying-ming, *The Roots of Wisdom: Saikontan*, trans. William Scott Wilson (Tokyo, 1985), p. 9.
27 Ibid., p. 79.
28 Ibid., p. 99.
29 Ibid., p. 110.
30 Miguel Leon-Portilla and Earl Shorris, *In the Language of Kings* (New York, 2001), p. 245.
31 Miguel Leon-Portilla, *Aztec Thought and Culture*, trans. Jack Emory Davis (Norman, OK, 1963), p. 147.
32 Ibid., p. 149.
33 Lichtheim, *Late Egyptian Literature*, p. 205.
34 Aesop, *Aesop's Fables*, trans. S. A. Handford (Harmondsworth, 1954), p. 113.
35 Ibid., p. 156.
36 Ibid., p. 69.
37 Charles Speroni, *Wit and Wisdom of the Italian Renaissance* (Berkeley, CA, 1964), p. 58.
38 Jacob Grimm and Wilhelm Grimm, *The Complete Fairy Tales of the Brothers Grimm*, trans. Jack Zipes (London, 2007), p. 426.
39 Ibid.

40 Eugene Watson Burlingame, *Buddhist Parables* (Delhi, 1991), p. 275.
41 John Holloway, *The Victorian Sage* (London, 1953), p. 1.

5 Wisdom and Divination

1 Cheiro, *Cheiro's Language of the Hand* (London, 1968), p. 33.
2 Trevor Curnow, *Wisdom in the Ancient World* (London, 2010).
3 Jim Tester, *A History of Western Astrology* (Woodbridge, Suffolk, 1987), p. 11.
4 Miguel Leon-Portilla, *Aztec Thought and Culture*, trans. Jack Emory Davis (Norman, OK, 1963), p. 118.
5 Georg Luck, *Arcana Mundi* (Baltimore, MD, 1985), p. 342.
6 James B. Pritchard, ed., *The Ancient Near East*, vol. II (Princeton, NJ, 1975), p. 169. I have simplified the presentation of the text a little.
7 Herodotus, *The Histories*, trans. Aubrey de Selincourt (Harmondsworth, 1965), p. 30.
8 H. W. Parke, *The Oracles of Zeus* (Oxford, 1967), p. 262.
9 Ibid., p. 268.
10 Ibid., p. 267.
11 Ibid., p. 273.
12 George E. Bean, *Turkey's Southern Shore* (London, 1989), p. 99.
13 Trevor Curnow, *The Oracles of the Ancient World* (London, 2004), p. 142.
14 John Hemming, *The Conquest of the Incas* (London, 1972), p. 56.
15 Alden Almquist, 'Divination and the Hunt in Pagibeti Ideology', in *African Divination Systems: Ways of Knowing*, ed. Philip M. Peek (Bloomington, IN, 1991), p. 104.
16 John Turpin and Judith Gleason, '*Ifa*: A Yoruba System of Oracular Worship', in *The World Atlas of Divination*, ed. John Matthews (London, 1992), p. 106.
17 Richard Wilhelm, ed. and trans., *I Ching; or, Book of Changes* (London, 1989), p. 240.
18 Ibid., p. xxi.
19 Ralph D. Sawyer and Mei-Chun Lee Sawyer, *Ling Ch'i Ching: A Classic Chinese Oracle* (Boston, MA, 1995), p. 127.
20 Ibid., p. 128.
21 Artemidorus, *The Interpretation of Dreams*, trans. Robert J. White (Park Ridge, NJ, 1975), p. 176.
22 Ibid., p. 188
23 Leo A. Oppenheim, *The Interpretation of Dreams in the Ancient Near East* (Philadelphia, PA, 1956), p. 258.
24 Ibid., pp. 270, 279.
25 Sigmund Freud, *The Interpretation of Dreams*, trans. James Strachey (Harmondsworth, 1976), pp. 274–5.
26 Joseph Kaster, ed. and trans., *The Literature and Mythology of Ancient Egypt* (London, 1970), p. 155.
27 Iona Opie and Moira Tatem, eds, *A Dictionary of Superstitions* (Oxford, 1992), p. 60.
28 Oppenheim, *Interpretation of Dreams*, p. 300.

29 Cicero, *De Senectute, De Amicitia, De Divinatione*, trans. William Armistead Falconer (Cambridge, MA, 1992), p. 259.
30 John Temple, 'Consulting the Oracles', in *The World Atlas of Divination*, p. 66.
31 Eva Shaw, *The Wordsworth Book of Divining the Future* (Ware, 1997), p. 51.
32 Nevill Drury, *The Elements of Shamanism* (Shaftesbury, 1989), p. 10.
33 Aldous Huxley, *'The Doors of Perception' and 'Heaven and Hell'* (London, 1977), pp. 27–8.
34 William Blake, *A Selection of Poems and Letters* (Harmondsworth, 1958), p. 101.
35 Joseph Campbell, *The Hero with a Thousand Faces* (Cleveland, OH, 1956), part 1.
36 David Freidel, Linda Schele and Joy Parker, *Maya Cosmos: Three Thousand Years on the Shaman's Path* (New York, 1993), p. 227.
37 Ibid.
38 Piet Meyer, 'Divination among the Lobi of Burkina Faso', in *African Divination Systems: Ways of Knowing*, p. 98.
39 William B. Sherden, *The Fortune Sellers: The Big Business of Buying and Selling Predictions* (New York, 1998), pp. 2, 5.

6 Wisdom and Philosophy

1 Cicero, *Tusculan Disputations*, trans. J. E. King (Cambridge, MA, 1996), p. 433.
2 Ibid., p. 435.
3 Dimitri Gutas, *Greek Wisdom Literature in Arabic Translation* (New Haven, CT, 1975), p. 63.
4 G. S. Kirk and J. E. Raven, *The Presocratic Philosophers* (Cambridge, 1971), p. 226.
5 Thomas Cleary, *Living a Good Life* (Boston, MA, 1997), p. 10.
6 Kirk and Raven, *Presocratic Philosophers*, p. 189.
7 Jonathan Barnes, *Early Greek Philosophy* (London, 1987), p. 119.
8 Ibid., p. 105.
9 Ibid., p. 119.
10 Richard D. McKirahan, *Philosophy before Socrates* (Indianapolis, IN, 1994), p. 119.
11 E. R. Dodds, *The Greeks and the Irrational* (Berkeley, CA, 1951), p. 146.
12 Barnes, *Early Greek Philosophy*, p. 192.
13 S. Marc Cohen, Patricia Curd and C.D.C. Reeve, eds, *Readings in Ancient Greek Philosophy* (Indianapolis, IN, 1995), p. 588. The quotation comes from Aristotle's *Metaphysics*.
14 Ibid.
15 Luis E. Navia, *Antisthenes of Athens* (Westport, CT, 2001), p. ix.
16 Epictetus, *The Discourses, The Handbook, The Fragments*, ed. Christopher Gill, trans. Robin Hard (London, 1995), p. 212.
17 Jason L. Saunders, ed., *Greek and Roman Philosophy after Aristotle* (New York, 1966), p. 130.
18 Epictetus, *The Discourses*, p. 286.

19 Benedict de Spinoza, *The Chief Works of Benedict de Spinoza*, trans. R.H.M. Elwes, vol. II (New York, 1955), p. 197.
20 Brad Inwood and L. P. Gerson, eds and trans., *The Epicurus Reader* (Indianapolis, IN, 1994), p. 29.
21 Ludwig Wittgenstein, *Tractatus Logico-Philosophicus*, trans. D. F. Pears and B. F. McGuinness (London, 1961), p. 72.
22 M. Saeed Sheikh, 'Al-Ghazali: Metaphysics', in *A History of Muslim Philosophy*, ed. M. M. Sharif, vol. I (Wiesbaden, 1963), p. 597.
23 Majid Fakhry, *A History of Islamic Philosophy* (New York, 2004), p. 316.
24 Ibid., p. 317.
25 Ibid.
26 Wing-tsit Chan, ed. and trans., *A Source Book in Chinese Philosophy* (Princeton, NJ, 1963), p. 30.
27 Shu-hsien Liu, *Understanding Confucian Philosophy: Classical and Sung-Ming* (Westport, CT, 1998), p. 18.
28 Chan, *A Source Book*, p. 65.
29 Ibid., p. 664.
30 Ibid., p. 668.
31 Ibid., p. 219.
32 Ibid., p. 148.
33 Martin Palmer, trans., *The Book of Chuang Tzu* (London, 1996), p. 69.
34 Thomas Cleary, ed. and trans., *The Tao of Politics* (Boston, MA, 1990), p. 94.
35 Ibid., p. 97.
36 Ibid., p. 98.
37 Mohini M. Chatterji, trans., *Viveka-Cudamani* (Adyar, 1947), p. 8.
38 Giovanni Pico della Mirandola, 'Oration on the Dignity of Man', in *The Renaissance Philosophy of Man*, ed. Ernst Cassirer, Paul Oskar Kristeller and John Herman Randall (Chicago, IL, 1948), p. 244.
39 Ibid., p. 250.
40 Ibid., p. 248.
41 Ibid.
42 Eugene F. Rice, *The Renaissance Idea of Wisdom* (Cambridge, MA, 1958), p. 107.
43 Ibid., p. 112.
44 Ibid., p. 117.
45 Ibid., p. 116.

7 Wisdom, Mysticism and Magic

1 Geraldine Pinch, *Magic in Ancient Egypt* (London, 2006), p. 105.
2 R. B. Parkinson, ed. and trans., *The Tale of Sinuhe and Other Ancient Egyptian Poems, 1940–1640 BC* (Oxford, 1997), p. 226.
3 R. O. Faulkner, *The Ancient Egyptian Book of the Dead* (London, 1985), p. 58.
4 Lucian, *Satirical Sketches*, trans. Paul Turner (Harmondsworth, 1961), p. 216.
5 Walter Scott, ed. and trans., *Hermetica: The Writings Attributed to Hermes Trismegistus* (Shaftesbury, 1992), p. 144.

6 Daniel Ogden, *Magic, Witchcraft and Ghosts in the Greek and Roman Worlds: A Sourcebook* (Oxford, 2002), p. 12.

7 David R. Cartlidge and David L. Dungan, *Documents for the Study of the Gospels* (Cleveland, OH, 1980), p. 205.

8 Lucian, *Satirical Sketches*, p. 222.

9 E. J. Holmyard, *Alchemy* (Harmondsworth, 1957), p. 98.

10 Peter Marshall, *The Philosopher's Stone* (London, 2002), p. 250.

11 Cherry Gilchrist, *The Elements of Alchemy* (Shaftesbury, 1991), p. 91.

12 'alchemy', *Encyclopaedia Britannica* from Encyclopaedia Britannica 2006 Ultimate Reference Suite DVD; accessed 22 May 2014.

13 Julian F. Pas, *Historical Dictionary of Taoism* (Lanham, MD, 1998), p. 182.

14 Ingrid Fischer-Schreiber, *The Shambhala Dictionary of Taoism*, trans. Werner Wünsche (Boston, MA, 1996), p. 197.

15 John Lash, *The Seeker's Handbook* (New York, 1990), p. 52.

16 Alain Daniélou, *Yoga: The Method of Re-integration* (London, 1973), p. 88.

17 Israel Gutwirth, *The Kabbalah and Jewish Mysticism* (New York, 1987), p. 17.

18 Gershom Scholem, *On the Kabbalah and its Symbolism*, trans. Ralph Manheim (New York, 1969), p. 100.

19 J.N.D. Kelly, *Early Christian Doctrines* (London, 1997), p. 23.

20 Richard Valantasis, ed., *The Beliefnet Guide to Gnosticism and Other Vanished Christianities* (New York, 2006), p. 19.

21 Julian Baldick, *Mystical Islam* (London, 1989), p. 91.

22 Ibid., p. 3.

8 Wisdom and Proverbs

1 G. L. Apperson, *The Wordsworth Dictionary of Proverbs* (Ware, 1993), p. vii.

2 Alan Dundes, 'On the Structure of the Proverb', in *The Wisdom of Many*, ed. Wolfgang Mieder and Alan Dundes (Madison, WI, 1994), p. 60.

3 Alexander Pope, *Collected Poems* (London, 1993), p. 65.

4 Bendt Alster, *Proverbs of Ancient Sumer: The World's Earliest Proverb Collections* (Bethesda, MD, 1997), vol. I, p. xxiii.

5 Linda Flavell and Roger Flavell, *Dictionary of Proverbs and their Origins* (London, 1993), p. 5.

6 Ibid., p. 14.

7 Alster, *Proverbs of Ancient Sumer*, pp. 12, 100, 277.

8 Ruth Finnegan, 'Proverbs in Africa', in *The Wisdom of Many*, p. 33.

9 Wisdom and the Present Day

1 Paul Heelas, *The New Age Movement* (Oxford, 1996), p. 1.

2 Aldous Huxley, *The Perennial Philosophy* (New York, 1970), p. viii.

3 Frithjof Schuon, *The Transcendent Unity of Religions* (Wheaton, IL, 1984), p. 149.

4 Heelas, *New Age Movement*, p. 19.

5 Bhagwan Shree Rajneesh, *Meditation: The Art of Ecstasy* (New York, 1978), p. 3.

6 Andrew Rawlinson, *The Book of Enlightened Masters* (Chicago, IL, 1997), p. 615.
7 H. P. Blavatsky, *The Key to Theosophy* (Pasadena, CA, 1987), p. 39.
8 John Gregory, ed. and trans., *The Neoplatonists* (London, 1991), p. 28.
9 Paul M. Allen, *Vladimir Soloviev: Russian Mystic* (Blauvelt, NY, 1978), p. 90.
10 Frederick Copleston, *A History of Philosophy*, vol. X: *Russian Philosophy* (London, 2003), pp. 224–5.
11 Ludmila Voronkova, 'Pavel Florensky', in *A History of Russian Philosophy*, ed. Valery A. Kuvakin (Buffalo, NY, 1994), vol. II, p. 649.
12 Sergius Bulgakov, *The Bride of the Lamb*, trans. Boris Jakim (Grand Rapids, MI, 2002), p. 39.
13 H. Odera Oruka, ed., *Sage Philosophy: Indigenous Thinkers and Modern Debate on African Philosophy* (Leiden, 1990), p. 208.
14 Paul Baltes and Ursula Staudinger, 'Wisdom: A Metaheuristic (Pragmatic) to Orchestrate Mind and Virtue toward Excellence', *American Psychologist*, LV/1 (2000), p. 135.
15 Monika Ardelt, 'Wisdom as Expert Knowledge System: A Critical Review of a Contemporary Operationalization of an Ancient Concept', *Human Development*, XLVII (2004), p. 276.
16 Carolyn M. Aldwin, 'Gender and Wisdom: A Brief Overview', *Research in Human Development*, VI/1 (2009), p. 3.
17 Trevor Curnow, *Wisdom, Intuition and Ethics* (Aldershot, 1999), chap. 3.
18 Ibid.

Conclusion

1 Ludwig Wittgenstein, *Philosophical Investigations*, trans. G.E.M. Anscombe (Oxford, 1972), p. 32e.
2 Miguel Leon-Portilla and Earl Shorris, *In the Language of Kings* (New York, 2001), p. 564.
3 Trevor Curnow, *Wisdom, Intuition and Ethics* (Aldershot, 1999).

FURTHER READING

The Bibliography that follows this section lists all of the works cited in this book and others that have been used in writing it. Many more could have been added and it is by no means intended to be an exhaustive bibliography of the subject. For those who are new to the study of wisdom and of the different aspects of it explored here, it may be helpful to have some more specific recommendations as to where to go next. The suggestions for further reading below are intended to provide some useful starting points.

Introduction

For a different kind of introduction to wisdom from this one, Stephen S. Hall's *Wisdom: From Philosophy to Neuroscience* (New York, 2010) can be recommended.

1 Wisdom, Gods and Goddesses

A good place to continue exploring the themes and materials of this chapter is with a solid work of reference such as the *New Larousse Encyclopedia of Mythology* (London, 1968). Although it is no longer particularly 'new', it contains a great deal of useful and relevant information and is well illustrated. It does not cover absolutely everything discussed here, but it is certainly an excellent start. More recent is *The Oxford Illustrated Companion to World Mythology* by David Leeming (New York, 2008), which is differently arranged but also has a wide coverage. *The Penguin Handbook of Ancient Religions*, edited by John R. Hinnells (London, 2007), can also be recommended.

2 Wisdom, Myth and Legend

The recommendations made at the end of the previous chapter are relevant again here. To them might be added a handful more. The *Penguin Dictionary of Classical Mythology* by Pierre Grimal (Harmondsworth, 1991) is useful, so is *Everyman's Dictionary of Non-Classical Mythology* by Egerton Sykes (London, 1952). Neither is particularly recent (the French original of Grimal's book appeared in 1951), but both are full of fascinating material. For folklore the *Larousse Dictionary of World Folklore* by Alison Jones (Edinburgh, 1995) is as good a starting point as any.

3 Wisdom in History

The references given in this chapter point towards useful areas for further reading on specific topics. In addition to those sources, I have also made considerable use of the *Encyclopaedia Britannica*, which is available in paper versions, online and on CD-ROM. *Encyclopaedia Britannica* has little to say on Nezahualcoyotl, and for more on him the reader may wish to look at *Flute of the Smoking Mirror* by Frances Gillmor (Salt Lake City, UT, 1983). I have already alluded to the disproportionate number of men in the materials that have been assembled here, so I should recommend Margaret Smith's book on *Rabi'a* (Oxford, 1994) because, as its subtitle indicates, it also contains materials on 'other women mystics in Islam'.

4 Wisdom and Literature

The *Upanishads* and *Prajnaparamita* writings are difficult and it is best to approach them in the company of a good guide. A start may be made with Edward Conze's *Buddhist Wisdom* (New York, 2001). This contains translations of and commentaries on 'The Diamond Sutra' and 'The Heart Sutra', two important texts. James Wood's *Wisdom Literature* (London, 1967) is primarily about the wisdom literature of the Bible, but by seeking to locate it in its wider context, Wood also has a good deal to say about the relevant literatures of Mesopotamia and Egypt. In order to explore further the idea of the novel as a form of wisdom literature, readers may begin with John Holloway's *The Victorian Sage* (London, 1953). It is not a particularly easy read, but Aesop's *Fables* (Harmondsworth, 1954) is. John Garrett Jones's *Tales and Teachings of the Buddha* (London, 1979) explores the *Jataka* in an illuminating way.

5 Wisdom and Divination

It has to be said that many books on divination offer little in the way of either wisdom or knowledge. Two useful introductions to the general area are Eve Shaw's *The Wordsworth Book of Divining the Future* (Ware, 1997), which manages to cram a lot into its 300 pages, and John Matthews's *The World Atlas of Divination* (London, 1992), which is less densely packed but better illustrated. *A Dictionary of Superstitions* by Iona Opie and Moira Tatem (Oxford, 1992) is fun to dip into. My own *The Oracles of the Ancient World* (London, 2004) gives lots of information about how the ancient oracles functioned and where their remains can be found.

6 Wisdom and Philosophy

Many books on ancient Western philosophy manage to say very little about wisdom. One that says more than most is Pierre Hadot's *What is Ancient Philosophy?*, trans. Michael Chase (Cambridge, MA, 2002). Jonathan Barnes's *Early Greek Philosophy* (London, 1987) contains useful material on Pythagoras, Heraclitus and Empedocles. My own *Ancient Philosophy and Everyday Life* (Newcastle, 2006) is a brief introduction to the Cynics, Stoics, Epicureans and Sceptics. Many of the writings of ancient philosophers are very readable. The works of Epictetus collected in *The Discourses, The Handbook, The Fragments* (London, 1995) are a personal favourite. It is easy to find translations of the works of Confucius, Laozi and Zhuangzi in popular editions. Islamic philosophy is not as well served. The materials available in the various versions and editions of *Encyclopaedia Britannica* probably contain enough for the general reader to start with. On the Renaissance, by far the best thing is Eugene F. Rice's *The Renaissance Idea of Wisdom* (Cambridge, MA, 1958).

7 Wisdom, Mysticism and Magic

It is not easy to find books on magic that are both readable and worth reading. Frances King's *Magic: The Western Tradition* (London, 1975) is an honourable exception. Geraldine Pinch's *Magic in Ancient Egypt* (London, 2006) is recommended, and Daniel Ogden's *Magic, Witchcraft and Ghosts in the Greek and Roman Worlds: A Sourcebook* (Oxford, 2002) brings together a lot of interesting material. On alchemy, Peter Marshall's *The Philosopher's Stone* (London, 2002) is both readable and informative. Marvin Meyer's *The Gnostic Discoveries* (New York, 2005) is excellent on the Nag Hammadi discoveries and contains plenty of excerpts from important texts. Gershom Scholem's *On the Kabbalah and its Symbolism* (New York, 1969) is getting on a bit now, but still worth reading. Julian Baldick's *Mystical Islam* (London, 1989) covers much interesting ground on Sufism.

8 Wisdom and Proverbs

The Wisdom of Many, edited by Wolfgang Mieder and Alan Dundes (Madison, WI, 1994), contains an interesting selection of essays about proverbs. Linda and Roger Flavell's *Dictionary of Proverbs and their Origins* (London, 1993) is a collection of proverbs interspersed with short essays and suggestions for further reading.

9 Wisdom and the Present Day

On the New Age movement, the best place to start is with Paul Heelas's *The New Age Movement* (Oxford, 1996). Very different in approach is Andrew Rawlinson's *The Book of Enlightened Masters* (Chicago, IL, 1997). Although it is not about the New Age movement as such, there is plenty of overlap. It is both encyclopaedic and entertaining. For sage philosophy, the article on 'African Sage Philosophy' to be found in the online *Stanford Encyclopedia of Philosophy* is a useful introduction with a substantial bibliography. A number of relatively recent writings by an impressive team of contributors can be found in *A Handbook of Wisdom: Psychological Perspectives*, edited by Robert J. Sternberg and Jennifer Jordan (New York, 2005).

BIBLIOGRAPHY

Aesop, *Aesop's Fables*, trans. S. A. Handford (Harmondsworth, 1954)

Aldwin, Carolyn M., 'Gender and Wisdom: A Brief Overview', *Research in Human Development*, VI/1 (2009), pp. 1–8.

Allen, Charles, and Dwivedi, Sharada, *Lives of the Indian Princes* (London, 1986)

Allen, Paul M., *Vladimir Soloviev: Russian Mystic* (Blauvelt, NY, 1978)

Alster, Bendt, *Proverbs of Ancient Sumer: The World's Earliest Proverb Collections*, vol. I (Bethesda, MD, 1997)

——, *The Instructions of Suruppak: A Sumerian Proverb Collection* (Copenhagen, 1974)

Apperson, G. L., *The Wordsworth Dictionary of Proverbs* (Ware, 1983)

Arberry, A. J., *Sufism: An Account of the Mystics of Islam* (London, 1979)

Ardelt, Monika, 'Wisdom as Expert Knowledge System: A Critical Review of a Contemporary Operationalization of an Ancient Concept', *Human Development*, XLVII (2004), pp. 257–85

Artemidorus, *The Interpretation of Dreams*, trans. Robert J. White (Park Ridge, NJ, 1975)

Ashe, Geoffrey, *The Ancient Wisdom* (London, 1977)

Baldick, Julian, *Mystical Islam* (London, 1989)

Baltes, Paul, and Ursula Staudinger, 'Wisdom: A Metaheuristic (Pragmatic) to Orchestrate Mind and Virtue toward Excellence', *American Psychologist*, LV/1 (2000), pp. 122–36

Barnes, Jonathan, *Early Greek Philosophy* (London, 1987)

Bean, George E., *Turkey's Southern Shore* (London, 1989)

Blavatsky, H. P., *The Key to Theosophy* (Pasadena, CA, 1987)

Blofeld, John, *Taoism: The Road to Immortality* (Boulder, CO, 1978)

Bouquet, A. C., *Sacred Books of the World* (Harmondsworth, 1954)

Boyce, Mary, *Zoroastrians: Their Religious Beliefs and Practices* (London, 1984)

Bulgakov, Sergius, *The Bride of the Lamb*, trans. Boris Jakim (Grand Rapids, MI, 2002)

Burlingame, Eugene Watson, *Buddhist Parables* (Delhi, 1991)

Campbell, Joseph, *The Hero with a Thousand Faces* (Cleveland, OH, 1956)

Capra, Fritjof, *The Tao of Physics* (New York, 1977)

Cartlidge, David R., and David L. Dungan, *Documents for the Study of the Gospels* (Cleveland, OH, 1980)
Cassirer, Ernst, Paul Oskar Kristeller and John Herman Randall, eds, *The Renaissance Philosophy of Man* (Chicago, IL, 1948)
Castaneda, Carlos, *The Teachings of Don Juan* (Berkeley, CA, 1968)
Chambers Dictionary of Quotations (Edinburgh, 2005)
Chan, Wing-tsi, ed. and trans., *A Source Book in Chinese Philosophy* (Princeton, NJ, 1963)
Charlesworth, James H., ed., *The Old Testament Pseudepigrapha*, 2 vols (London, 1983–5)
Chatterji, Mohini M., trans., *Viveka-Cudamani* (Adyar, 1947)
Cheiro, *Cheiro's Language of the Hand* (London, 1968)
Cleary, Thomas, *Living a Good Life* (Boston, MA, 1997).
——, ed. and trans., *The Tao of Politics* (Boston, MA, 1990)
Cohen, J. M., and M. J. Cohen, eds, *The Penguin Dictionary of Modern Quotations* (Harmondsworth, 1971)
Cohen, S. Marc, Patricia Curd and C.D.C. Reeve, eds, *Readings in Ancient Greek Philosophy* (Indianapolis, IN, 1995)
Conze, Edward, *Buddhism: Its Essence and Development* (New York, 1959)
——, ed., *Buddhist Texts through the Ages* (New York, 1964)
——, *Buddhist Wisdom: The Diamond Sutra and The Heart Sutra* (New York, 2001)
Cook, J. M., *The Persians* (London, 1983)
Copleston, Frederick, *A History of Philosophy*, vol. X: *Russian Philosophy* (London, 2003)
Corbin, Henri, *Histoire de la philosophie islamique* (Paris, 1964)
Coxe, William, *History of the House of Austria*, vol. I (London, 1847)
Curnow, Trevor, *The Oracles of the Ancient World* (London, 2004)
——, *Wisdom in the Ancient World* (London, 2010)
——, *Wisdom, Intuition and Ethics* (Aldershot, 1999)
Daniélou, Alain, *Yoga: The Method of Re-integration* (London, 1973)
Davidson, H. R. Ellis, *Gods and Myths of Northern Europe* (Harmondsworth, 1964)
The Discourse on the All-embracing Net of Values, trans. Bhikkhu Bodhi (Kandy, 1978)
Dodds, E. R., *The Greeks and the Irrational* (Berkeley, CA, 1951)
Dogen Zenji, *Shobogenzo*, vol. I, trans. Kosen Nishiyama and John Stevens (Tokyo, 1975)
Drury, Nevill, *The Elements of Shamanism* (Shaftesbury, 1989)
Eliade, Mircea, *Shamanism: Archaic Techniques of Ecstasy* (Princeton, NJ, 1972)
Encyclopaedia Britannica, Ultimate Reference Suite DVD, 2006
Epictetus, *The Discourses, The Handbook, The Fragments*, ed. Christopher Gill, trans. Robin Hard (London, 1995)
Fakhry, Majid, *A History of Islamic Philosophy* (New York, 2004)
Farquhar, J. N., *Modern Religious Movements in India* (Delhi, 1967)
Faulkner, R. O., *The Ancient Egyptian Book of the Dead* (London, 1985)
Ferguson, John, *The Religions of the Roman Empire* (London, 1970)
Fischer-Schreiber, Ingrid, *The Shambhala Dictionary of Taoism*, trans. Werner Wünsche (Boston, MA, 1996)

Flavell, Linda, and Roger Flavell, *Dictionary of Proverbs and their Origins* (London, 1993)
Freidel, David, Linda Schele and Joy Parker, *Maya Cosmos: Three Thousand Years on the Shaman's Path* (New York, 1993)
Freud, Sigmund, *The Interpretation of Dreams*, trans. James Strachey (Harmondsworth, 1976)
Garfield, Jay L., ed. and trans., *The Fundamental Wisdom of the Middle Way: Nagarjuna's 'Mulamadhyamakakarika'* (New York, 1995)
Gerritsen, Willem P., and Anthony G. van Melle, eds, *A Dictionary of Medieval Heroes*, trans. Tanis Guest (Woodbridge, 1998)
Gilchrist, Cherry, *The Elements of Alchemy* (Shaftesbury, 1991)
Gillmor, Frances, *Flute of the Smoking Mirror* (Salt Lake City, UT, 1993)
Green, Miranda J., *Dictionary of Celtic Myth and Legend* (London, 1992)
Gregory, John, ed. and trans., *The Neoplatonists* (London, 1991)
Grimal, Pierre, *Penguin Dictionary of Classical Mythology*, ed. Stephen Kershaw, trans. A. R. Maxwell-Hyslop (Harmondsworth, 1991)
Grimm, Jacob, and Wilhelm Grimm, *The Complete Fairy Tales of the Brothers Grimm*, trans. Jack Zipes (London, 2007)
Gutas, Dimitri, *Greek Wisdom Literature in Arabic Translation* (New Haven, CT, 1975)
Gutwirth, Israel, *The Kabbalah and Jewish Mysticism* (New York, 1987)
Hall, Stephen S., *Wisdom: From Philosophy to Neuroscience* (New York, 2010)
Harner, Michael, *The Way of the Shaman* (San Francisco, 1980)
Harris, Joel Chandler, *Uncle Remus: His Songs and his Sayings* (New York, 1982)
Heelas, Paul, *The New Age Movement* (Oxford, 1996)
Heer, Friedrich, *The Holy Roman Empire*, trans. Janet Sondheimer (London, 1968)
Hemming, John, *The Conquest of the Incas* (London, 1972)
Herodotus, *The Histories*, trans. Aubrey de Selincourt (Harmondsworth, 1965)
Hinnells, John, ed., *Penguin Handbook of Ancient Religions* (London, 2007)
Holloway, John, *The Victorian Sage* (London, 1953)
Holmyard, E. J., *Alchemy* (Harmondsworth, 1957)
Holy Bible, Revised Standard Version (Collins, 1973)
Hung Ying-Ming, *The Roots of Wisdom: Saikontan*, trans. William Scott Wilson (Tokyo, 1985)
Huxley, Aldous, *'The Doors of Perception' and 'Heaven and Hell'* (London, 1977)
——, *The Perennial Philosophy* (New York, 1970)
Ibn Al'Arabi, *The Bezels of Wisdom*, ed. and trans. R.W.J. Austin (London, 1980)
Inwood, Brad, and L. P. Gerson, ed. and trans., *The Epicurus Reader* (Indianapolis, IN, 1994)
Jones, Alison, *Larousse Dictionary of World Folklore* (Edinburgh, 1995)
Jones, John Garrett, *Tales and Teachings of the Buddha* (London, 1979)
Jones, Marc Edmond, *Occult Philosophy* (Washington, DC, 1977)
Kaster, Joseph, ed. and trans., *The Literature and Mythology of Ancient Egypt* (London, 1970)
Kelly, J.N.D., *Early Christian Doctrines* (London, 1977)
King, Francis, *Magic: The Western Tradition* (London, 1975)

Kirk, G. S., and Raven, J. E., *The Presocratic Philosophers* (Cambridge, 1971)
Klostermaier, Klaus K., *A Concise Encyclopaedia of Hinduism* (Oxford, 1998)
Knysh, Alexander, *Islamic Mysticism: A Short History* (Leiden, 2000)
Kuvakin, Valery A., ed., *A History of Russian Philosophy*, vol. II (Buffalo, NY, 1994)
Kvideland, Reimund, and Henning K. Sehmsdorf, eds, *Scandinavian Folk Belief and Legend* (Minneapolis, MN, 1988)
La Fontaine, Jean de, *Selected Fables*, trans. James Michie (London, 1982)
Lash, John, *The Seeker's Handbook* (New York, 1990)
Leach, Maria, ed., *Funk and Wagnall's Standard Dictionary of Folklore, Mythology and Legend* (London, 1972)
Leeming, David, *The Oxford Illustrated Companion to World Mythology* (New York, 2008)
Leon-Portilla, Miguel, *Aztec Thought and Culture*, trans. Jack Emory Davis (Norman, OK, 1963)
—, and Earl Shorris, *In the Language of Kings* (New York, 2001)
Lichtheim, Miriam, *Late Egyptian Literature in the International Context: A Study of Demotic Inscriptions* (Freiburg, 1983)
Liu, Shu-hsien, *Understanding Confucian Philosophy: Classical and Sung-Ming* (Westport, CT, 1998)
Lloyd, G.E.R., *The Revolutions of Wisdom* (Berkeley, CA, 1989)
Loewe, Michael, and Carmen Blacker, eds, *Divination and Oracles* (London, 1981)
Lucian, *Satirical Sketches*, trans. Paul Turner (Harmondsworth, 1961)
Luck, Georg, *Arcana Mundi* (Baltimore, MD, 1985)
Lyons, Jonathan, *The House of Wisdom: How the Arabs Transformed Western Civilization* (London, 2009)
MacCormack, Sabine, *Religion in the Andes: Vision and Imagination in Early Colonial Peru* (Princeton, NJ, 1991)
McGreal, Ian P., ed., *Great Thinkers of the Eastern World* (New York, 1995)
McKirahan, Richard D., *Philosophy before Socrates* (Indianapolis, IN, 1994)
Mahadevan, T.M.P., *Ramana Maharshi: The Sage of Arunacala* (London, 1977)
Marshall, Peter, *The Philosopher's Stone* (London, 2002)
Matt, Daniel Chanan, ed. and trans., *Zohar* (London, 1983)
Matthews, John, ed., *The World Atlas of Divination* (London, 1992)
Metzger, Bruce M., and Michael D. Coogan, eds, *The Oxford Companion to the Bible* (New York, 1993)
Mieder, Wolfgang, and Alan Dundes, eds, *The Wisdom of Many* (Madison, WI, 1994)
Narasimhan, Chakravarthi V., ed. and trans., *The Mahabharata* (New York, 1965)
Navia, Luis E., *Antisthenes of Athens* (Westport, CT, 2001)
Neihardt, John G., *Black Elk Speaks* (New York, 1972)
Nerburn, Kent, and Louise Mengekbach, eds, *Native American Wisdom* (Novato, CA, 1991)
New English Bible with the Apocrypha (Oxford and Cambridge, 1970)
Norwich, John Julius, *Byzantium: The Apogee* (London, 1991)
Oakes, Lorna, and Lucia Gahlin, *Ancient Egypt* (London, 2007)
Ogden, Daniel, *Greek and Roman Necromancy* (Princeton, NJ, 2001)
—, *Magic, Witchcraft and Ghosts in the Greek and Roman Worlds: A Sourcebook* (Oxford, 2002)

O'Grady, Patricia F., *Thales of Miletus* (Aldershot, 2002)
Olivelle, Patrick, *Upanisads* (Oxford, 1996)
Opie, Iona, and Moira Tatem, eds, *A Dictionary of Superstitions* (Oxford, 1992)
Oppenheim, A. Leo, *The Interpretation of Dreams in the Ancient Near East* (Philadelphia, PA, 1956)
Oruka, H. Odera, ed., *Sage Philosophy: Indigenous Thinkers and Modern Debate on African Philosophy* (Leiden, 1990)
Oxford Dictionary of Quotations (Oxford, 1966)
Palmer, Martin, trans., *The Book of Chuang Tzu* (London, 1996)
Paludan, Ann, *Chronicle of the Chinese Emperors* (London, 1998)
Parke, H. W., *The Oracles of Zeus* (Oxford, 1967)
Parkinson, R. B., ed. and trans., *The Tale of Sinuhe and other Ancient Egyptian Poems, 1940–1640 BC* (Oxford, 1997)
Partridge, Christopher, ed., *Encyclopaedia of New Religions* (Oxford, 2004)
Pas, Julian F., *Historical Dictionary of Taoism* (Lanham, MD, 1998)
Peek, Philip M., ed., *African Divination Systems: Ways of Knowing* (Bloomington, IN, 1991)
Petrocchi, Marco Curatola, and Mariusz S. Ziółkowski, eds, *Adivinación y oráculos en el mundo andino antiguo* (Lima, 2008)
Phillips, Charles, *An Illustrated Encyclopaedia of Aztec and Maya* (London, 2010)
Pinch, Geraldine, *Magic in Ancient Egypt* (London, 2006)
Plutarch, *The Rise and Fall of Athens*, trans. Ian Scott-Kilvert (Harmondsworth, 1960)
Porter, Bill, *Zen Baggage* (Berkeley, CA, 2009)
Pritchard, James B., ed., *The Ancient Near East*, 2 vols (Princeton, NJ, 1958–75)
Radhakrishnan, S., *Indian Philosophy*, vol. I (London, 1989)
——, *The Principal Upanisads* (London, 1953)
Rajneesh, Bhagwan Shree, *Meditation: The Art of Ecstasy* (New York, 1978)
Rawlinson, Andrew, *The Book of Enlightened Masters* (Chicago, IL, 1997)
Ray, John, *The Wisdom of God Manifested in the Works of the Creation* (Glasgow, 1750)
Rice, Eugene F., *The Renaissance Idea of Wisdom* (Cambridge, MA, 1958)
Rohl, David, *The Lords of Avaris* (London, 2008)
Sakya Pandita, *Ordinary Wisdom: Sakya Pandita's Treasury of Good Advice*, trans. John J. Davenport (Boston, MA, 2000)
Saunders, Jason L., ed., *Greek and Roman Philosophy after Aristotle* (New York, 1966)
Sawyer, Ralph D., and Mei-Chun Lee Sawyer, *Ling Ch'i Ching: A Classic Chinese Oracle* (Boston, MA, 1995)
Scholem, Gershom, *On the Kabbalah and its Symbolism*, trans. Ralph Manheim (New York, 1969)
Schuon, Frithjof, *The Transcendent Unity of Religions* (Wheaton, IL, 1984)
Scott, Walter, ed. and trans., *Hermetica: The Writings Attributed to Hermes Trismegistus* (Shaftesbury, 1993)
Seal, Graham, *Encyclopaedia of Folk Heroes* (Santa Barbara, CA, 2001)
Sharif, M. M., ed, *A History of Muslim Philosophy*, vol. I (Wiesbaden, 1963)
Shaw, Eva, *The Wordsworth Book of Divining the Future* (Ware, 1997)
Sherden, William B., *The Fortune Sellers: The Big Business of Buying and Selling Predictions* (New York, 1998)

Shushud, Hasan Lufti, *Masters of Wisdom of Central Asia*, trans. Muhtar Holland (Moorcote, North Yorkshire, 1983)

Smith, Margaret, *Rabi'a: The Life and Work of Rabi'a and Other Women Mystics in Islam* (Oxford, 1994)

Speroni, Charles, *Wit and Wisdom of the Italian Renaissance* (Berkeley, CA, 1964)

Spinoza, Benedict de, *The Chief Works of Benedict de Spinoza*, trans. R.H.M. Elwes, vol. II (New York, 1955)

Sternberg, Robert J., ed., *Wisdom: Its Nature, Origins and Development* (New York, 1990)

——, and Jennifer Jordan, eds, *A Handbook of Wisdom: Psychological Perspectives* (New York, 2005)

Stone, Michael E., and Theodore A. Bergren, eds, *Biblical Figures outside the Bible* (Harrisburg, PA, 1998)

Suzuki, D. T., *What is Zen?* (New York, 1972)

Sykes, Egerton, *Everyman's Dictionary of Non-Classical Mythology* (London, 1952)

Tester, Jim, *A History of Western Astrology* (Woodbridge, Suffolk, 1987)

Tolstoy, Leo, *A Calendar of Wisdom*, trans. Peter Serkin (London, 1997)

Townsend, Richard F., *The Aztecs* (London, 2000)

Trimingham, J. Spencer, *The Sufi Orders in Islam* (Oxford, 1971)

Valantasis, Richard, ed., *Religions of Late Antiquity in Practice* (Princeton, NJ, 2000).

——, *The Beliefnet Guide to Gnosticism and Other Vanished Christianities* (New York, 2006)

Van Over, Raymond, ed., *Eastern Mysticism*, vol. I (New York, 1977)

Weeks, Thomas W., and Dilip V. Jeste, 'Neurobiology of Wisdom: A Literature Overview', *Archive of General Psychiatry*, LXVI/4 (2009), pp. 355–65

Wilhelm, Richard, ed. and trans., *I Ching; or, Book of Changes* (London, 1989)

Wilkins, Eliza G., *'Know Thyself' in Greek and Latin Literature* (New York, 1979)

Wilkinson, Richard H., *The Complete Gods and Goddesses of Ancient Egypt* (London, 2003)

Williams, Paul, *Mahayana Buddhism: The Doctrinal Foundations* (London, 1989)

Wilson, Robert R., *Genealogy and History in the Biblical World* (New Haven, CT, 1977)

Wittgenstein, Ludwig, *Philosophical Investigations*, trans. G.E.M. Anscombe (Oxford, 1972)

——, *Tractatus Logico-Philosophicus*, trans. D. F Pears and B. F. McGuinness (London, 1961)

Wood, James, *Wisdom Literature* (London, 1967)

Yetts, W. Perceval, 'The Eight Immortals', *Journal of the Royal Asiatic Society of Great Britain and Ireland*, XLVIII (1916), pp. 772–806

Zaehner, R. C., *Hindu and Religious Mysticism* (New York, 1969)

ACKNOWLEDGEMENTS

The idea for a book along these lines has been going around inside my head for several years. The nudge needed to convert it from an idea into a reality came in the form of an approach from Ben Hayes of Reaktion Books. I am grateful to Ben both for that initial impetus and for his continuing support while the book was being written. During the writing process I have benefited from the financial support of the University of Cumbria, which made funds available for two visits to the British Library. Finally, I have to thank Nicky Meer for providing her usual combination of encouragement and constructive criticism.

Photo Acknowledgements

The author and publishers wish to express their thanks to the following sources of illustrative material and/or permission to reproduce it:

Images © Trustees of the British Museum, London: pp. 6, 12, 28, 46, 68, 124, 152, 178; © Victoria & Albert Museum, London: p. 92.

INDEX